NEVER TOO OLD TO TEACH

How Middle-Aged Wisdom Can Transform Young Minds in the Classroom

Neil M. Goldman

Rowman & Littlefield Education
Lanham • New York • Toronto • Plymouth, UK

This book was placed by the Educational Design Services LLC literary agency

Published in the United States of America
by Rowman & Littlefield Education
A Division of Rowman & Littlefield Publishers, Inc.
A wholly owned subsidiary of The Rowman & Littlefield Publishing Group, Inc.
4501 Forbes Boulevard, Suite 200, Lanham, Maryland 20706
www.rowmaneducation.com

Estover Road
Plymouth PL6 7PY
United Kingdom

British Library Cataloguing in Publication Information Available

Library of Congress Cataloging-in-Publication Data

Goldman, Neil M., 1964–
  Never too old to teach : how middle-aged wisdom can transform young
minds in the classroom / Neil M. Goldman.
     p. cm.
  ISBN-13: 978-1-57886-974-9 (cloth : alk. paper)
  ISBN-10: 1-57886-974-9 (cloth : alk. paper)
  ISBN-13: 978-1-57886-975-6 (pbk. : alk. paper)
  ISBN-10: 1-57886-975-7 (pbk. : alk. paper)
  ISBN-13: 978-1-57886-976-3 (electronic)
  ISBN-10: 1-57886-976-5   (electronic)
  1. Special education. 2. Effective teaching. 3. First year teachers. I. Title.
  LC3969.G65 2009
  371.102–dc22   2008034224

∞™ The paper used in this publication meets the minimum requirements of
American National Standard for Information Sciences—Permanence of
Paper for Printed Library Materials, ANSI/NISO Z39.48-1992.
Manufactured in the United States of America.

CONTENTS

CONTENTS

CONTENTS

ACKNOWLEDGMENTS

My sincere and heartfelt thanks go out to the following wonderful people:

To Mary Bay of the University of Illinois, Chicago, for the time and effort you spent in reading my first draft, for the invaluable feedback you provided that helped me immensely, and for teaching me how to be the best teacher I can be.

To Michael Elfand, whose candid advice from the perspective of a professional outside the education field, made this a better book.

To Tom Koerner and Bert Linder, for believing in my project and for your patient guidance.

To my colleagues and administrators, for your tireless patience, guidance, and support from the first minute of my first day. If it weren't for all of you, I don't know what I would have done. Thank you for hiring me and giving me your trust.

And, to my students: Thank you for your patience, thank you for teaching me, and thank you for being who you are that makes me want to go to work every day.

Please note that all names in this book have been changed. The fictitious name I used for a previous student might be the same as a student I have now, or will have in the future. If this happens, it is entirely a coincidence and is not intentional.

1

INTRODUCTION

He stood there, threatening me, six feet one, and he wasn't smiling. He just said something about giving him money. A tough, streetwise seventeen-year-old who's seen the inside of a jail cell, talking to a sinewy nonviolent middle-class English teacher with no martial arts experience.

I had only been a teacher for a few months. They didn't teach me about this in graduate school.

There was only a minute or so before the bell would ring to begin class, and I was busy near the front of the class talking with a few students and trying to get some handouts ready. Six feet one, seventeen-year-old, seen-the-inside-of-a-jail-cell David, one of my students, pulled me aside and said, "Okay, now Mr. Goldman, tomorrow morning before school right outside here (he pointed to the classroom doorway), I want you to bring me twenty bucks."

David was not smiling.

I looked at him dryly in the eyes, poker-faced. He looked back at me. The second hand on the clock clicked a few times.

David was a student, like many others, who often displayed challenging classroom behavior, but, ironically, it's this type of student whom you sometimes find yourself most looking forward to seeing every day. David is sort of like the hot peppers in the salsa; the peppers sting a little, but they certainly make the meal more interesting.

He continued, "I'll be here tomorrow about five minutes before school begins, and be sure you have the twenty bucks." I said, "Sure, no problem, you'll have your twenty bucks tomorrow morning." Then, I walked away. He sat down, eyeing me incredulously.

The next morning, sure enough, David was there, joined by several of his entourage who heard that I was going to give him twenty bucks. I handed him an envelope filled with paper. The look on his face was unforgettable; a mixture of surprise and delight. His friends, some of whom I had as students, were equally amazed. He opened the envelope hurriedly and took out its contents. His friends started laughing loudly, but David only had a wry smile on his face. He looked at me and said, "Very funny." He walked down the hallway.

Inside the envelope were twenty little squares of paper, each of which had a picture of a male deer on it. David got his twenty bucks.

Some of you will have read the previous true story and will think to yourselves how dangerous it is to be a teacher. David's words would probably appear menacing to an outsider, but to somebody who knows him, his comments were amusing and typical and were actually a sign of affection from him.

You might think how unpleasant and dangerous it is to work all day long in the same room with such difficult, challenging kids. You might say to yourself, how could anybody want to do this sort of work? In actuality, these questions reveal a mental image of my classroom that is nearly the opposite of what it is actually like.

My job is not dangerous, the kids are fascinating, it is a joy to uncover and learn about the complex nature of their personalities, and the relationships I have established with them have been some of the most rewarding of my life.

Thank goodness I made a decision to become a teacher, and thank goodness that I removed myself from my meaningless job in a cubicle. This is the story of the first year of the most difficult job I've ever had—teaching English to high school students with learning disabilities. This is also the story of taking the steps needed to transition from being a tiny tooth on an immense corporate gear to being a significant influence on the way that young minds are shaped and developed.

A corporate job in a cubicle, no matter what the salary, would never be able to convince me to walk away from my students. It's not a job for everyone—if you think that *your* supervisor is tough, and won't take any nonsense from you, and demands your best every day, and can be highly critical, wait until you have to teach Poe to a roomful of seventeen-year-old people. If you don't have the right personality, you won't make it through your first month, let alone your first year.

You have to be real; you have to be self-confident. If you lie to your students; if you try to be someone you're not; if you believe you can rule others by being aggressive, authoritative, and domineering; if you don't know what you're talking about, you're doomed. But, on the other hand, if you love watching young minds grow, have a generous amount of self-confidence, and enjoy the subject matter you're teaching, this job is probably right for you.

The rewards in this profession are intangible yet significant. In short, when you're a teacher, you realize that you matter. You make a difference. You really got through to the kid. Because of what you said and how you behaved, your student will know a little more, act a little more wisely, and think about more things before signing a contract on the dotted line.

Knowing that you were the cause of this improvement can give you the greatest feeling of fulfillment in your life.

This book will tell you what it's really like to be a high school special ed teacher. You should know about the triumphs and setbacks, the joys and disappointments, and the hidden things that went through my mind that I chose not to share with my students. Some of you will read these thoughts and think how shamefully naïve and amusingly inexperienced I am; on the other hand, some of you might get a few new ideas about how to handle a situation.

This whole career is very new to me, and I admit that I'm quite green. This isn't a book of advice; this isn't a book where I say that my way is the right way. It's just a book about what it was like for me, and I hope that each person gets something a little different out of it.

Another significant reason for writing this book is to let you know that Special Ed isn't what you might think it is. If you think that there are only a few special ed classes here and there, containing wheelchair-bound children that need help to read a stop sign, you're in for a surprise.

Our department is the largest one at our big suburban school. On average, from 10 percent to 25 percent of high school students in the United States receive some sort of special education services, and our school is no exception. Out of a student body of 3,800, over 400 students are in one or more special ed classes, and most of them are in classes like the one I teach.

Most special education students are normal-looking, intelligent, witty, moral, honest people who will most likely graduate from high school and either go to college, trade school, or into the world of work and become independent adults with jobs and cars and families of their own. They want to see themselves as competent adults and will work hard to both achieve their own goals and earn my respect as their teacher. They do have difficulty with some academic tasks, but we work together so they can overcome the obstacles that face them.

Their behavior can be maddeningly challenging and warmly endearing. Teaching them is the most intellectually and emotionally difficult thing I have ever done. I wouldn't trade it for anything.

Read on and discover what it was like during my first year. Read about the lessons that went well, the ideas that crashed and burned, the bewildering myriad of situations that suddenly arose, and the things I thought to myself to help me get through it with my sanity mostly intact. A friend of mine who is a teacher said, "Whatever you do, don't quit the first year." My goodness, do I understand why he said that.

Some days were wonderful and actually went smoothly, although they were the exception. Nearly all days were intellectually and emotionally draining and presented me with situations where I literally did not know what to do next.

But, within those days, there was much joy and satisfaction. The kids brought me through these situations with their kindness and patience. I guess they knew that I respected and liked them, and they cut me some big breaks. For that, I thank them. Also, I could not have survived the year without the support and advice of my colleagues and administrators; and to them, also, I send my heartfelt thanks.

So, here's what it was like to make this mind-boggling change in my life. Here's how I went from wanting to be a doctor, to working in the computer field for fourteen years, and then becoming a teacher. This last career change was one of the best decisions I have made in my life.

2

FROM A CORPORATE CUBICLE TO THE SPECIAL ED CLASSROOM

I never thought I was going to be a teacher when I was a child. I always thought that I was going to become a doctor because *The Hummin Bow-dee* was my favorite book when I was a child. "Bow-dee" is pronounced "bow," the thing that you put on top of a birthday present, and "dee," like the word "see," but with a "d."

The Hummin Bow-dee, *The Hummin Bow-dee,* ooh, how I loved the pictures in that book. It showed bones, the heart, fingers, toes, the eyes, every part of your body; there was red, green, blue, every color, and I could feel my arm and understand which bones were which. Something about it interested me very much, long before I knew how to correctly pronounce its title, *The Human Body.*

So, from a very young age, I declared that I was going to become a doctor. It was a logical progression from a child interested in the workings of the hummin bowdee.

My mother was thrilled with my interest, partly because she was Jewish (and nothing gives a Jewish mother more pride than to talk about her son, the doctor), and partly because of her thrilling fantasies of being sent on exotic worldwide cruises thanks to the 11 zillion dollars I would be making every year as an internationally renowned cardiac surgeon, or orthopedist, or whatever, as long as I wore a white coat and owned a single-family home in the suburbs near my uncle Melvin who wasn't a doctor but was a "successful businessman," the second-highest compliment (after "doctor") that came out of my mother's mouth.

Needless to say, my grandmother, who received her black belt in Jewish Grandmothering shortly after my birth, also supported my decision to the extreme. Of course, the contract she signed upon receiving her black belt forbade her from giving me more than one compliment every three months; the remainder of her comments had to be either a) criticisms of current or past behavior, b) pleas to consume more food, c) suggestions for improving my life, or d) detailed stories of things that happened to her in her life that illustrate The Right Way To Live And Think.

So, my hearing supportive words from her regarding my career decision was a very pleasant surprise and furthered my self-view as a Future Healer.

I told all my friends and teachers that I was going to become a doctor; this was usually met by smiles and congratulations. When you're young, and you announce a career choice, there isn't a better one than Doctor. Everybody supports you. Uncles and aunts buy you toy stethoscopes. Mothers and fathers buy you books filled with tantalizing pictures. You feel accepted and respected, and you look at the tantalizing pictures with a flashlight after Mommy kisses you good night.

Nobody mentions to the child the four years of college, four years of medical school, and two years of residency that are required before your career really begins to take off. Nobody mentions the immense cost of medical school, the long hours, the sleepless nights spent memorizing the bones of the foot, the malpractice lawsuits, and the surprise of earning a much lower income than expected. It's interesting that becoming a doctor is a universally admired career choice, yet it's a career that is only suitable to a small percentage of the population.

Yet, I pressed on. I took biology, chemistry, and physics in high school. I told people that I was going to be "pre-med" in college, even though I didn't realize at the time that such a term was meaningless and that there was no such major as "pre-med."

I was primed, I was pumped, I was going to college, and I was going to become a doctor.

I admit that part of the reason why I wanted to become a doctor was because I wanted to make a lot of money. When I went to the public library to look up career choices, doctors consistently were at the top of the list of income level, and I became enamored of the prestige and ability to obtain the exquisite material goods that went along with such high income. I'm not ashamed of this; it's typical of our materialistic culture.

Men are often judged by their income, especially young men. When a twenty-three-year-old male buys an expensive car, his buddies are going to tell him how nice it is and what beautiful lines it has. They will whistle at it, touch it, will want to drive it and go for rides in it, and will watch girls smile warmly at them when they're driving around in it. His friends will be jealous, they will compare themselves to him, they will do Internet searches to determine the amount he likely paid for it, they will think of his car when they get in their ordinary four-year-old car, and they will remember the smiling girls. They will think and remember all of these things when they look through the help wanted ads in the newspaper, when they choose their major in college, and when they think about what they want to do with their life.

I'm a man. At the time, I wanted money, respect, and power. (As I have gotten older, I'm less interested in the money and power part.) Being a doctor gives you those things, plain and simple. So I enrolled at Temple University and took biology, chemistry, calculus, and philosophy. I signed up for all the courses I was supposed to in order to increase the likelihood that I would be admitted to medical school. Becoming a teacher was the furthest thing from my mind.

College started. I went to classes—biology, chemistry, calculus, philosophy, and history; some interesting, some not so interesting, but all pieces of the machine that, when put together, would catapult me into prestige, money, and a white lab coat. I assumed that I would enjoy the courses I would be taking. I assumed that my interest in the courses would result in my performing very well academically. I knew that it would be work, but I assumed that I would be able to do it without a problem.

I was wrong.

The courses became harder and harder as the semesters continued. I had a difficult time understanding calculus, especially when taught by somebody who struggled to form a lucid English sentence. I realized that I found biology to be only a little bit interesting. I didn't get excited about the difference between a nucleus and a nucleolus. Adenine, guanine, cytosine, and uracil. Interphase, prophase, metaphase, anaphase, and telophase. Obturator foramen.

I had a hard time motivating myself to learn all of these words. Something, I slowly realized, was going very, very wrong.

I discovered the difference between casually reading a general public book about the human body and the memorization of hundreds of terms that was required of a person who was eventually going to cut open living human beings, remove parts of them, and sew them back up so they could attend their nephew's birthday party in two weeks.

I memorized the terms dutifully and spit them back on tests, earning Bs and Cs. Organic chemistry was another fresh hell. Do you know what a dihydrohalogenation reaction is? Neither did I, even after the lecture on it. I was taught at Temple University by a gentleman named Dr. Davis. He may have been a brilliant chemist, and a hell of a nice guy at parties, but after listening closely to many of his lectures, I still had little idea about the true nature of a benzene ring.

He was another example of universities hiring brilliant clinicians, renowned in their field, accomplished in their research, but who don't have the ability to teach a blindfolded man how to fall off a log. He made everything so difficult that it demoralized nearly the entire class. I remember that I studied hard for an exam, did the best I could, and got a 19 percent. He curved this score to a C. Can you believe that? A 19 percent, and you got a C.

All the students had done so poorly in this exam that a 19 percent represented a passing score. Think about what that does to you. You don't even get one out of five questions right, and you're still passing the class. You would think that my professor, a person who had the mental adroitness to toy with organic chemistry with ease, would be able to engage in some honest reflection about the quality of his instruction when he sees that most of his students don't understand most of what he's teaching.

But I digress.

My grades started slipping. I was under an intellectual strain and found the coursework I had undertaken to be tedious and uninteresting. I was used to getting good grades in high school—As and Bs. Here, in college, in preparation for my chosen profession, I was getting Bs and Cs. This was not good. Bs and C's do not get you into medical school, ladies and gentlemen. Plus, I was upset at a more fundamental level: why did I find these courses uninteresting? If I was going to be a doctor, I would certainly have to be titillated at the thought of an oxidation-reduction reaction or a discussion about alleles. But I was not.

Down went my morale, down went my grades, and I seriously thought about dropping out of college. Can you imagine what my grandmother would say?

But I couldn't drop out of college; that would have been profoundly stressful because I would have thought of myself as a quitter. So, what to do? I realized that the only course I truly found interesting was psychology; I had taken two of these courses so far, gotten very good grades, and found myself wanting to take more. I spoke to my counselor at college, and we decided that it would be the best thing for me to abandon the idea of being a doctor and take the courses that I really liked. I told her that I was hesitant to do so; that I felt that if I would change my major there would be a hundred voices in my head saying that I was wrong, that I was a quitter.

The career counselor, bless her heart, looked at me in the eyes and said, "Who are all of these voices you're talking about?" I looked at her, smiled, and said, "The voices are everybody but me." It was one of the most significant moments of my life, and I still remember it vividly, even after twenty-five years.

I changed my major to psychology and found myself enjoying college again. I started to get the high grades that I was accustomed to. I made the dean's list several times. Then, I graduated from college, went to graduate school, and got a master's degree in education.

My ultimate career goal was to open a private psychology practice. But, I discovered something new about myself in school; I enjoyed tutoring my classmates. I heard a number of times that when I explained something, it made sense to them. So, I figured that maybe I would become a college professor in case the private practice didn't work out.

My first job fresh out of graduate school as a psychological counselor didn't work out because my supervisor asked me to falsify patient charts or be fired.

What's that trite expression, "Welcome to the real world"?

He was concerned that the number of no-show patients was becoming excessive and that the clinic was in danger of losing federal funding because of the reduced enrollment in the community outreach programs. I told him that I had no control over the no-show rate. This irritated him. He told me, a little more slowly and a little more quietly, that I needed to fill out the paperwork to get the numbers to be where he wanted them to be. He was making me an offer that I couldn't refuse, to quote Mario Puzo's famous screenplay.

I quit the next day.

Eventually he was demoted, and the entire clinic was closed down as a result of a federal sting targeting falsified paperwork and misappropriation of federal funds at the clinic. Fortunately, I had quit before any of this came to light.

All through college and graduate school, one of my hobbies was computers, and I am not ashamed to say that I was a little bit of a nerd, although in my defense I didn't own black glasses, and I find pocket protectors completely unfashionable. While I was looking for another job, a family member who had recently been hired at a medium-sized national retail chain asked me for a little bit of help in my spare time with getting the computer aspect of his office off and running.

The prospect of some cash inflow was welcome. Quitting your first job on moral grounds is a laudable decision, but it has the perplexing side effect of leaving you with nothing but lint in your pockets.

I took the job.

To make a long story short, a temporary spare time job turned into a fourteen-year IT career at a growing national retail chain. Why did I take the job offer as a computer programmer after six years at college to be a psychologist? It does seem strange, given that the two careers are on nearly opposite ends of the spectrum. Why did I do it? Money.

I was offered an obscenely high salary, a job twenty minutes from my home, and health benefits. So I did it. I became Dilbert in a cu-bicle, increasingly marginalized, my work less and less meaningful, and after fourteen years on the treadmill, I decided I had had enough. A particularly grueling and meaningless project that was shelved almost as soon as it was completed was the impetus for me to start a new chapter in my life. I had decided to do one of the things I was pretty sure I wanted to do: become a teacher.

Interestingly, my fourteen-year career at the retail headquarters building strengthened my belief that being a teacher was a good ca-reer choice for me. During my time there, one of the favorite parts of my job was training people how to use computers. I enjoyed do-ing the presentations, I enjoyed my job in technical support where I helped people with problems, and I thoroughly enjoyed creating user manuals and colorful literature to help people use the software programs I wrote.

Partially because of this self-confidence, I applied (and was ac-cepted) to the University of Illinois at Chicago in their special edu-cation program.

Why Special Education? That's a good question. As I've said, I al-ways enjoyed psychology; I enjoy learning about psychopathology, developmental psychology, developmental disabilities, different theories of personality, and so on. As I was looking through the cat-alogs to decide what subject I wanted to teach, I had two choices based on my Bachelor's and Master's degree: psychology or Special Education.

When I started reading about the different sorts of students that special education teachers teach, I realized that Special Education was for me. When you teach Special Ed, you are part teacher, part psychologist, and part father. You have to know about adolescent emotional and cognitive developmental stages, the nature of reading disabilities and how to teach students to improve their reading despite their disabilities, the ways that expressive language deficits manifest themselves, effective cognitive and behavioral ways to control misbehavior, and much other knowledge from the domain of psychology, in addition to having thorough knowledge of the subject matter you teach.

It was learning about these requirements of a special education teacher that ignited the desire within me to choose that as my new career. When I went to school, I knew my decision was right because I found the coursework to be extremely interesting. What a contrast from struggling so pathetically twenty years ago in Dr. Davis's class! I was relieved to receive good grades in my graduate classes because it told me that I was getting the "big picture."

Within a few months of graduation, I was standing in a high school classroom, hand over my heart, reciting the Pledge of Allegiance, with fifteen high school seniors in the room with me.

I felt proud of myself for what I had done. Standing in the classroom, I felt lucky to be at the excellent school I work at now. I felt honored to be trusted by the administration to be responsible for the education of my students. Every day, I always try to do my best; sometimes it turns out well, and sometimes the lesson doesn't go the way I expect.

But, the kids have good hearts. They know that I'm in their corner and that I care about them, and as a result, for the most part, they care about me, too, notwithstanding the occasional razor-sharp invective hurled at me. The first year went by at different speeds. Some days went very slowly, some went a little faster, and the year was over before I knew it. After the last final of the first year, I remember standing in the hallway and thinking, "Is it over? Did a year go by that fast?"

It was the hardest job I've ever had, and there were many moments where I felt like a feather in a tornado. Somebody wrote somewhere that a teacher makes three thousand decisions a day, and I believe it.

"Mr. Goldman, I know we have to work in the library today, but I'm banned from the library because I cursed out a librarian last semester." Figure that one out, folks, and do it now because three other students are complaining that they can't get into the computer and two other students forgot their work packet and are begging you for an extension for a previous assignment due today.

Through it all, you must have confidence in yourself. That's probably the most important bit of advice I can give any new teacher. Trust yourself. Do what you think is right, and you'll be OK.

Being older helps, too. One of the advantages to being older is a certain level of self-confidence and mental stability that I don't think it's possible to have when you're twenty-two. Through all the difficult times, I always had self-confidence; not necessarily in my ability as a teacher but as a worthwhile, intelligent, moral human being who would be able to figure out how to do this. It seems to have worked because the administration asked me back for a second year.

3

THE UNFAIR SPECIAL
EDUCATION STIGMA

Special Education isn't what many people think it is. Here's what Special Ed really means in an actual high school.

But first, I want to ask you a question.

Are you normal?

Most people would say that they are, and that they hope that other people perceive them to be normal. Do you want to start a fight in a bar? Walk up to a guy and say: "You know what, buddy? You don't look normal. That's right, you heard me. You ain't normal. And from the looks of you, it looks like your mother ain't normal, either. I'll bet you got a sister. Tell me, pal, is she abnormal just like you and your mama?"

Watch what happens next. You'd better be able to run fast, and/or be wearing a bulletproof vest, and/or have upper arms the same diameter as a telephone pole, or else you'll probably be visiting your dentist, and possibly a plastic surgeon, in the very near future.

What's interesting about the whole scene just described is that there is a 50 percent chance that you were giving the other man quite a compliment, and that his reaction, although predictable, was entirely inappropriate. He was offended by being told that he and

Table 3.1. **Persons with significant abnormalities**

Person with abnormality	Abnormality
Bill Gates	Personal net worth
Allan Iverson	Number of points scored per basketball game
Kurt Cobain	Age at death
Liliane Bettencourt	Personal net worth
Jack Nicholson	Number of Academy Award nominations
Lucille Ball	Number of stars on the Hollywood Walk of Fame
Robert Wadlow	Height at age eighteen
Natalie McCaughey	Number of siblings with the same age
Bjorn Daehlie	Number of Olympic gold medals won

his family were not normal, but this is not a logical conclusion. For example, here are some people who are extremely abnormal in one form or another:

So, the next time somebody calls you abnormal, take a 50-50 chance and say, effusively, "Thank you very much!"

Of course, the term "abnormal" can go the other way and signify things that are perceived as negative in most cultures, such as poverty, incompetence, and unattractiveness. So it is understandable when people don't immediately display a wide smile upon being told that they're "not normal," but on the other hand there should not be an immediate and visceral negative reaction to being given this news; the words "normal" and "abnormal" merely describe a score. More information is needed before a conclusion can be made about the desirability or lack thereof in the term.

When you measure something about a group of people, such as height, wealth, jumping ability, and so on, the scores will tend to clump together in the middle. Generally speaking, if your score is within the center clump of scores, your score is normal. If you are out of the center clump of scores, your score is not normal.

This abnormality can be a good thing—it can mean you are a spectacularly attractive billionaire.

However, as you can imagine, the words "not normal" carry a powerful punch when they hit the ears of a child because most people assume that these words mean something bad. So, nearly all psychologists and educators withhold the use of the word "normal" and replace it with another word—"average," which statistically means the same thing: that most of the other people that were given the same assessment had scores that were close to your score. Plus, it's easier to hear that you are "below average" than to hear that you are "abnormal."

But, "average" doesn't have the greatest smell to it, either, although it suffers the same ambiguous fate as the word "normal"; it can mean something good or bad. Let's say that you play football. How would you feel if your coach told you that your running speed on the field is "average"? You'd probably be unhappy and would try to improve your running speed, although this may not be necessary; the coach may have been complimenting you when using the word "average" because the entire team comprises fast runners.

Many people replace in their mind the word "average" with the word "not very good": "She was an average piano player," "The meal you cooked for me was average," and so on.

Can you imagine a woman saying to her fiancé, "Please buy me an average wedding ring, and let's have an average wedding"? Probably not, and this illustrates the problem with the word *average*: people equate the word "average" with "blah, boring, run-of-the-mill." But, as I said, "average" means the same as "normal," statistically speaking: that your (insert whatever you want here) is about the same as other people's.

Most wedding rings are beautiful, and most weddings are elaborate, beautiful events. If you bought your fiancée a beautiful wedding ring and had a gorgeous wedding reception with delicious food, your (now) wife has an average ring on her finger, and you had an average wedding. It still doesn't sound very good, does it?

This illustrates one of the more significant issues in the field of Special Education: the problem of the powerful stigma of words.

Because of this stigma, many words that were once innocuous, clinical terms in the field of education and psychology have been retired long ago. Did you know that the words "idiot," "imbecile," and "moron" were bona fide, stigma-free terms to describe different levels of mental retardation in the first half of the twentieth century?

Then, once Moe, Larry, and Curly of the Three Stooges started calling each other these words, they became taboo.

People want to laugh *at* the Three Stooges—they don't want to be thought of as one of them.

So, the mental health field came up with the words "mentally retarded." "Retarded" is another example of a word that originally was free of stigma. The word "retarded" is simply a synonym for the word "delayed." But, after a few decades, this term also acquired a strong stigma.

Therefore, many educators and psychologists, and those in similar fields, are now using the term "cognitive delay" to describe students whose overall mental function, social and communication skills, and ability to do everyday things effectively are significantly behind their peers.

I wonder how long it will take for the kinder, gentler term of "cognitive delay" to acquire its own festering case of stigma, necessitating its retirement and the invention of different words to describe the same pattern of development.

Although this inevitable process of taking words out of usage does seem wasteful, it is necessary; people who are extremely capable yet limited by the stigma of a word or phrase, such as "handicapped person," deserve to see such phrases banished by social taboo. Imagine if you were born with only one leg. As a result, you would see and hear this word with maddening frequency:

handicapped handicapped handicapped handicapped handicapped
handicapped handicapped handicapped handicapped handicapped
handicapped handicapped handicapped handicapped handicapped
handicapped handicapped handicapped handicapped handicapped

How long would it take for the word to become part of you? How long would it take for this word to cause yourself and others to focus attention on your limitations and the things you *can't* do rather than your skills and expertise and the things you *can* do?

If people would stop using that word, they would likely stop seeing you as a pathetic, wretched cripple and start seeing you as a person who can do almost anything.

As a result of the stigma of words, some might call for the banishment of any adjectives that limit people. Some might say, "Why use the terms 'handicapped,' or 'different,' or 'cognitively delayed' at all? Why bring a person's differences to light and risk making that person seem less competent in the eyes of others? Let's just stop using all of these sorts of terms!"

This desire is well-intentioned, but such a change will never happen, and for an ironic reason: people who are different from the majority of others in a significant way often need a label stamped on their forehead in order to get what they need to flourish.

The reason why there are ramps cut into curbs at nearly all the intersections in major U.S. cities, and why there are electrically operated doors at nearly all the entrances to most public buildings, and why there are braille menus at McDonald's—features that cost extra money—is that people who have physical differences demand that the general public recognize their differences and remove barriers which prevent them from doing what typically developed people can do.

Ironically, they need to clearly advertise their differences so that the effect of these differences are minimized.

So, we will always need to use terms that distinguish students whose academic performance is not typical, or normal, or average. We need to give certain students a little extra help and teach them in a somewhat different way so that they can utilize their strengths to leap over the obstacles in the path of their academic progress.

For now, the term "Special Education" describes the process and product of modifying standard teaching methods and standard curricula to help all students learn as much as they can. It's a very broad term that includes everything from a teacher giving directions verbally and writing them on the board instead of just one or the other, to reading a mathematics word problem to a student with severe dyslexia, to helping a student come up with a plan to increase the amount of time that he can focus on the lesson, to providing a student with cerebral palsy the particular kind of wheelchair she needs to learn.

But, just like how the term "abnormal" came to mean only something negative in the popular consciousness, the term "Special Education" has come to mean something that is most likely very different from what it actually is.

When most people think of a special education classroom, they imagine a pathetic scene of sweet, tragically disabled children, in specialized wheelchairs, clutching a heart-shaped construction paper cutout that has written on it "I LOVE YOU" in silver glue glitter, smiling, staring vacantly into the air, uttering incomprehensible, laughterlike sounds through perpetually open, drooling mouths, attended to by buxom, steel-nerved women wearing white uniforms and sensible, no-slip shoes, and taught by young, enthusiastic, somewhat attractive, reasonably intelligent, dedicated, patient, unflappable twentysomething women straight out of teaching school.

The scene is simultaneously heartrending and heartwarming. You think to yourself something like "Oh, those poor kids, God bless them" or "Oh, I don't know how that teacher does it, she has a heart of gold." You shake your head in awe, fear, and pity.

If you imagine the above scene when you think of Special Education, you're probably wrong.

Children with a significant cognitive delay (sometimes called mental retardation) and children with significant physical disabilities comprise only a small percentage of all students who receive special education services in public schools. Of all students who receive special education services, the largest category—about 70 percent—comprises students who look "normal," act "normal," interact "normally" with others—because they *are* "normal." These students have a *specific learning disability*.

This term is used to describe a pattern of academic achievement that is more common than many people realize. This pattern includes the unexpected underachievement of a typical student in one or two specific areas. A student with a specific learning disability has difficulty when it comes to certain specific academic tasks, such as remembering a series of written directions, composing a well-written essay, or understanding the concept of fractions, which causes their performance in that specific area to fall significantly behind their peers. Other than this characteristic, these students are completely "normal."

Unfortunately, in the minds of the students of the school where I teach, "Special Ed" does NOT mean "normal." It means "abnormal"; it means "retarded"; it means "someone to laugh at"; it means "I don't have to work hard"; it means "don't expect me to pay attention"; it means "I can't do this"; it means "don't expect excellence."

What a great pity that all of these statements are both utterly false and extremely demoralizing to a competent young person. It's ironic that these harmful statements frequently originate within the minds of the very students that they harm.

One day, I was walking in the hall and overheard the following exchange between two friends; the first student was teasing the second student. ("SPEDdie" means someone in Special Ed; our department is abbreviated SPED in some of the school's course information literature.)

> *First Student*: "Ha, ha! I can't believe you did that! Are you a SPED-die or what?"

> *Second Student*: [irritated] "Shut up! I'm not retarded!"

If I overheard this conversation, my students have, too. Who knows how many times they have indirectly been told, "You're different, and not in a good way." SPED has a stigma which profoundly affects the attitude of the students who fall under its heading. But there's not much we can do about it. If I were to put some of my students in a regular ed classroom, their disability would quickly result in their becoming depressed and probably hostile in the face of the extraordinarily challenging work.

Will, one of my students who has a difficult time reading, said to me once, "What are you giving us all this work for? This is a special ed class!" (How many times have I heard that in the past year!) I said to him, "Will, I have some news for you. Special Ed doesn't mean that you can't do work or that you won't have to do work; it means that you can do it with just a little bit of help, which is why I'm here. I'll stop by in a few minutes to go over the assignment again. In the meantime, try to read through the instructions the best way you can and get started."

He stared at me blankly and looked down at the paper. He moved his face closer to the words and furrowed his eyebrows. Yes, Will started reading; he reads slowly, but he can read. Will has become an expert at avoiding the task by pulling out the special ed card, but I don't accept that card in my classroom. He ended up completing the assignment and turning in some of his best work.

The harmful effects of the SPED stigma manifest themselves on a daily basis; students attempting to talk inappropriately in class, attempting to sleep, turning in minimal work, not completing assignments, and so on. I say "attempting" because I don't allow inappropriate talk, or sleeping, or any of the other disruptive and maladaptive behavior that frequently surfaces in my students.

I once overheard Victor, one of my students, say to a friend in a vexed tone of voice, "This is the only class I get written up in, the only one. I have NEVER been written up in any of my other classes." He didn't realize that I was listening when he said this, so he wasn't doing it to antagonize me. Also, he wasn't proud when he made his statement; he seemed genuinely puzzled and slightly exasperated. (Up until that point, Victor had been written up a total of three times in class, each time for shouting out obscenities.)

It made me feel good to hear what he said because it told me that he was thinking about his behavior. He didn't say what some might expect him to say: "Mr. Goldman, that fucking asshole, keeps writing me up"; he used the words, ". . . I get written up for . . ." He seemed to recognize that there was a connection between his behavior and the consequences, which there certainly was.

I wondered after I heard his statement why he wasn't written up in other classes. I realized quickly that it couldn't be that Victor's other teachers permitted his cursing and refusal to follow instructions. It must be that he doesn't curse and refuse to follow instructions in the other classes as much as he did in my class. What did that say about me and everything about my classroom? When I started thinking about this, I started feeling insecure.

Was there something wrong with the way I was teaching?

Maybe the way I was treating him was irritating him to such an extent that it caused him to lose control. Maybe I was giving him work that was too difficult; maybe I was taking my philosophy of not accepting the SPED card too far, and I was giving him work of such difficulty that he was rebelling because his inability to complete the task made him feel stupid and incompetent.

You'd be amazed at how the insecurity of being a first-year teacher can cause your brain to go into high gear and make you start analyzing, reanalyzing, and overanalyzing every aspect of what you teach and how you teach. The fact is that teaching is a stupendously complex task, and it is impossible to effectively analyze anything more than very specific variables, and even that task is difficult because of your inability to control significant external factors, such as the student's mood, blood sugar level, amount of sleep, the weather, the phase of the moon, and whether the Cubs won last night or not.

I have had the exact same lesson, presented in the exact same way, go over very well in third period and fall apart in ninth period, and vice versa.

As I realized the difficulty of trying to discover exactly what was going wrong with Victor, I thought again about the SPED stigma. Were his obscene outbursts occurring because my response to them was to write him up and therefore to allow him to leave the room and escape the task? The detention he would receive as a punishment might be viewed by him as a worthwhile exchange for the reward of getting out of class. So, some of my professors at graduate school would say that his behavior (cursing) was being rewarded by escaping the task.

But let's look at this more closely: why was escaping the task rewarding? A friend of mine said, after I described the situation to her, "Maybe he's just lazy, and he doesn't want to do the work." That's possible, but if he was lazy, he would certainly not engage in behavior that he knows will result in his having to wake up early on a Saturday morning for two weekends in a row to serve a detention. Plus, Victor would put forth diligent effort from time to time and produce good work. People who are lazy are usually consistently lazy.

I became more and more certain that something that I was doing was triggering frustration on his part, and his outbursts were simply an involuntary reaction to this frustration.

As I thought back about when his disruptive behavior occurred, I realized it was usually in response to the class beginning to engage in some form of academic work, which could range from taking notes from a lecture I gave, or beginning to do some research from written materials, or having to write an opinion paper on a short video that was recently shown.

The question remained: why was Victor uncomfortable when asked to do academic work?

Maybe he was uncomfortable because he believed that he could not do the work. So, he invoked a tactic that is common in students with learning disabilities: "It's better to be bad than to be stupid." He was a skilled behavior researcher and quickly discovered the rule violations that would result in ejection from the classroom. This was puzzling, because he would occasionally engage his brain and produce quality work.

Frankly, I was hoping to reach him, hoping to show him that despite the things that he may have heard, he had a good brain and is capable of doing good, solid work. They told me in graduate school to give specific reasons for praise; don't just say "good job," but say *why* it was a good job. Good teachers should always try to put this into use when giving feedback to their students, including Victor. Teachers should say things like, "Well thought out logic," "Your grammar has improved significantly," "There were very few grammatical errors in what you wrote," or "good job of writing out 'a lot' instead of 'alot.'"

It's always exciting to get a good paper from a student like Victor because it gives the teacher an opportunity to give him the praise that he so desperately needs. However, this minor excitement was always met with disappointment on my part because of the completely flat response I got out of him when giving him back these papers. Victor would not make eye contact with me and would toss the paper aside lightly as if I was handing out fliers to the local senior citizens' celebration of Barry Manilow's birthday. His receiving back a good grade would have no observable effect on reducing the likelihood that he would engage in disruptive behavior later that day.

I so much wanted him to look at me, smile even slightly, and say, "Thank you," and see in that smile the beginning of a realization of, "Oh my God, I can actually do this!"

No such luck. Victor's academic performance continued to be inconsistent, and his behavior continued to be highly disruptive and disrespectful. But, a good teacher doesn't give up. I was going to be as patient and as persistent as I needed to be to try to get this little man to wake up and grow up.

In the classroom, sometimes change happens very slowly, and sometimes change happens so slowly that the teacher, who is right in the thick of things every single day, sees no change when in fact there is movement in the right direction.

Months passed, and I remember thinking one day, "Hmm, I haven't had to write Victor up in . . ." and I couldn't remember how long it had been; maybe three weeks, maybe a month? I looked over at him as he read quietly and thought to myself, "Oh my God, he's sitting and reading quietly." The first thought in my mind when I saw—no, not saw—*beheld*—this sight, was, "Thank goodness, he seems to have calmed down a little bit lately."

Marie, my supervisor, would later say to me when I told her about this, "Well, Neil, did you ever think that maybe it had something to do with you? Maybe the change in his behavior has something to do with your influence?" I said, "probably a little."

She responded, "PROBABLY A LITTLE?"

I remember that moment very well. It was the first time all year that an experienced educator—Marie had eighteen years in the classroom—validated my teaching and told me that what I did had an observable and positive influence on a student. I knew in my mind that I was teaching, but that was the first time that someone said to me that a student is a better person because of what I did. It made me feel so good to hear this, and that good feeling validated again to me the fact that I made the right choice to become a teacher.

The question remains: why was Victor being written up in my class but not any other one? I'll be honest with you: I don't know. I should have met with his other teachers, I should have spent time researching his disciplinary history to try to find some sort of pattern, or I should have sat down with him with a behavior checklist.

But, I didn't do any of those things.

This first year of teaching has been the most difficult job I've ever had in my life, and I didn't have the time to do all the things that I wanted to do or even was supposed to do. But, don't judge me too harshly. There was another event which interfered with my ability to further refine my behavioral intervention strategy with Victor.

Suddenly, in the beginning of the spring semester, he dropped out of school. Boom, just like that. No good-bye, no reason. I never saw him again. Even as I write this, I wonder how he is doing. I heard from another student that he started working for his family business. When he dropped out, he was failing almost all of his classes. Was it a mistake for him to drop out? How much did the special ed stigma contribute to his decision to drop out? Did he feel he was "retarded," and there was no use in trying? Did he look in the mirror every morning and say, "I'm too stupid to finish school"?

Would any teacher have the true answer to these questions?

4

THE THOUGHT

As I stood there in the front of the classroom, taking attendance, The Thought occurred again. It caused me to stop what I was doing, look at my students, and smile.

Interestingly, The Thought didn't make me smile because it was funny. It made me smile because it tantalized me somehow with my inability to categorize it. The Thought was part excitement, part nervousness, part amusement, part pride; but there was more to it that I couldn't understand. I think another part of it was the utter novelty of the situation. When you're hired as a teacher, you are, in many ways, hired as a parent to seventy-five students at once.

The Thought was, "I can't believe I'm their teacher."

I have a feeling that veteran teachers and the general public may read that and think, "What? What is he talking about?" But, I'm pretty sure that most new teachers will have thought The Thought themselves.

5

THE INTERVIEW

Her matronly face relaxed me somehow. She was the receptionist in the personnel department of the school district. A bowl of candy looked at me invitingly from the edge of her neat, clean desk.

But, you never know.

You never know whether a bowl like that is there on a desk belonging to a person because it represents a truly giving spirit who wishes to share her chocolaty love with her fellow employees, or whether that bowl is there because it's her bowl and Mrs. Mom would get just a little bit ticked off by an arrogant tie-wearing forty-two-year-old who tried to swipe one of her Bit-O-Honeys.

So, in the interest of obtaining gainful employment, I leave my fingerprints off of her candy wrappers.

A pox on her house for leaving Hershey's Kisses out like that, gleaming delicately in a reflected sunbeam. She looks innocent enough with her conservative hairdo, but disregard the smile, people. She knows what she is doing, oh yes. She relentlessly teases, tantalizes, and tortures those around her with the Crock o' Confections. Evil woman! Either put the bowl in a clearly public place, where people can find guilt-free means to pull the fillings out of their molars, or put the bowl out of sight in your neat little desk. I think of grabbing a few pieces of compressed corn syrup just to spite her when I'm interrupted by a friendly looking man.

"Mr. Goldman?" he asks. "Yes," I say. "I'm Darren," he says. "Hello, Darren, it's very nice to meet you," I say, as we shake hands heartily. Darren. His name is Darren. He has a nice tie on, and he seems very likable. I want to ask, "Darren, buddy, how are the wife and kids? Oh, and by the way, who are you?" He interrupts my thoughts with, "I'm the principal. It's very nice to meet you, too. Have a seat, and we'll be ready for you in a few minutes." He gives me a movie-star smile and hurries off down the hallway.

I sit down and think that he seems like a pretty nice guy. It was interesting to me—no, surprising—that he referred to himself by his first name. I liked the informality of it, but I also was slightly disarmed by it.

Before I had a chance to think any more about it, Miss Matronly-Sweet-Smile-I-Count-My-Precious-Little-Chocolates-Every-Morning-So-You'd-Better-Watch-Out tells me it's okay to go in, so in I go.

Did you ever have one of those moments when your brain goes into a suspended state for a second or two, and all it says is, "uh-oh"? This was one of those moments.

No matronly smiles here.

The room I walked into was a large, beautifully decorated boardroom, complete with a dozen leather chairs, long mahogany desks, original paintings on the walls, and nine—yes, nine—very well-dressed, very intelligent looking people staring at me. My ol' buddy Darren said, "Have a seat," and I did.

Picture this, folks. This is the first interview you've had to become a teacher. This is the first time you have been (or want to be) a teacher, after a long career of doing nonteacherly things such as replacing LAN cards and writing Select Case statements. You feel disoriented. You feel unprepared. You feel as though your lack of experience in the field will make you look like an impostor. Sure, you've had decades of business experience, and sure, you have graduated successfully from a reputable teacher education program at a local university, but you still feel like the lone lamb at a hungry wolves' convention.

The next hour was one of the most emotionally intense experiences of my life. These people asked me detailed questions and watched my reactions carefully.

They wanted to know why I wanted to become a teacher, why I wanted to work with special education students, what life experiences I've had that could prepare me to be a successful teacher, why I received a couple of low grades in college twenty years earlier, what books I was reading now, what books I read in the past, what I thought made a good teacher, and what I thought made a bad teacher.

They told me their own personal stories and watched my reaction.

I told them some anecdotal stories about what happened to me when I was student teaching in a rough high school in a large urban environment. Fortunately, they liked these stories. They asked me more questions. Some of these questions were intellectually demanding, requiring reflection and careful composition of an answer, and other questions were simpler, more personal, designed to help me reveal my personality.

These people were good at what they did. They were good in assessing a person's intellectual capability, moral sense, sense of humor, fears, values, favorite sports team, ability to reflect upon complex problems that never have and probably never will have solutions, knowledge of educational theory, ability to put theory into practical use in the classroom, ability to deal with maddeningly intractable child behavior, ability to be a politician with families and colleagues, and a long list of others.

After the interview, there were the usual smiles, handshakes, and "We'll give you a call." I went home and continued going through the process of sending out résumés.

About half an hour later, the phone rang. I don't know, maybe it was my tie, but they made the decision to hire me.

I'm glad I kept my hands out of the candy dish.

6

KNOT IN MY STOMACH

The drive to work takes about twenty-five to thirty minutes, depending on traffic. When I first started driving to work, my stomach would begin to knot up about five to ten minutes into the drive.

It wouldn't knot up for any particular reason; it was just a generalized feeling of anxiety. I wasn't used to this; during my previous job, I worked for the same company for almost fourteen years. Because I was so familiar with the job and the people who worked there, I never felt any anxiety on my way to work, even during periods where work itself was stressful. This anxiety thing was a whole different experience for me.

Anxiety is a nasty little tentacle-waving cockroach of a neurosis.

It crawls deep into the crevices of your mind and eats the glue that's holding together those precious brain cells that remember your favorite brand of barbecued potato chips and the phone number of your ex. While we're using cockroaches as a metaphor, let's examine them in more depth. If you've ever had cockroaches, you'll be on the lookout for them in every place you live for the rest of your life, even if you spray enough exterminating chemicals to kill a stadium full of rhinoceroses.

If you've ever imagined that cockroaches have a magical ability to sense your loathing of them, and you transform this loathing into seventy-seven more cockroaches, you've basically got the idea of how anxiety works.

Anxiety is difficult to eradicate, resistant to intervention, and feeds on itself. For example, people who have anxiety about sleeplessness usually find that the source of their sleeplessness is anxiety over their sleeplessness. Others worry that they're not going to be a good enough partner to hold on to the charming and beautiful person they have just begun dating, and so they protect themselves from the predicted future pain of breaking up by withdrawing and reducing their vulnerability, making themselves emotionally distant and uncommunicative, thereby dooming the success of the relationship. The ultimate failure of the relationship justifies in their own mind their fears of their not being an adequate partner.

The neurotic circle is complete.

These anxiety patterns are so true, so true—and so common. Oh, there's more, folks. Some people are even more skilled in the art of raising their own blood pressure. Some people transcend the aforementioned level of anxiety-propagating anxiety that they arrive at a level wherein merely the appearance of anxiety triggers self-uncertainty and more anxiety.

It's meta-anxiety: anxiety about anxiety.

The appearance of anxiety on the horizon of their awareness results in their questioning the truth of their self-knowledge, which if you know anything about psychology, is a very, very big thing, like finding wide cracks in the steel beams in the basement of your condo building. I am very proud to tell you that I successfully reached that level, thank you very much.

I was not used to questioning my self-image. Many things in my life have come and gone, including love, money, and good radio stations, but my favorable self-image has been my constant friendly companion for several decades. You could say that I was, and still am, a little arrogant on the inside, but you must forgive this arrogance based on its origins.

When I was in junior high school, I had what the family psychologist called an "inferiority complex," which is psychologist talk for "your son is experiencing the normal stressors of adolescence, including self doubt and a desperate desire to be accepted by his peers. He's also a skinny dweeb."

I don't know whether or not it was divine intervention or some complex mental self-protection mechanism that would have made Freud smile in his grave, but sometime during junior high school I said to myself, "I am [censored] sick and tired of worrying about what other [censored] people think." It was as if a weight had been lifted off my shoulders. I stopped worrying so much about what other people thought and allowed my own personality to develop. It was a beautiful period in my life.

Ever since then, I've always been a little cocky. But, you have to remember that this cockiness was put there as a way to replace terrible feelings of depression and self-doubt. My arrogance was my solace, like an adult emotional version of a warm, fuzzy teddy bear.

So there I was, driving to work, feeling so much anxiety and tension that I found myself questioning the wisdom of my decision to become a teacher.

As we've covered, the anxiety I was feeling was in and of itself causing anxiety because of my old nemesis, self-doubt. I was very disoriented by these feelings of anxiety. My teddy bear was gone. I didn't know what to think to make myself feel better, to make myself feel more confident about what I was about to do.

As is so often the case, my emotions read the facts carefully, weighed them with circumspection, and then tore up the sheet and did as they damned well pleased. Why was I feeling so nervous? Nine intelligent, well-dressed people selected me to join their faculty out of hundreds of other applicants. I graduated with a 4.0 average from an outstanding graduate teacher preparation program. See? The cockiness is coming out again right here in what you're reading.

I continued driving to school. You know when you're in a night-club and the music is loud—and you think that it can't get any louder—and then all of a sudden it gets much louder than you ever thought possible? That was how the volume of my anxiety level turned up when I turned around the corner and the image of the school building fell on my retinas.

Oh my God, look at all the students walking into the building. Oh my God, there are hundreds of them, thousands of them. Many of them are bigger than me. I felt the blood pumping in my neck.

In less than thirty minutes, fifteen of them will be staring at me as their teacher; in other words, the expert, the authority figure, the pedagogue, the imparter of wisdom, the disciplinarian, the father figure, the comedian, the motivator, the coach, the moral guide, the adviser, the coordinator, the forgiver, the encourager, the guy who gives them their grades.

Or, just as likely, the schmuck, the impostor, the guy who's out of touch, who's a nerd, who's weird, who's a loser, who's boring, who's pathetically unfunny, who's unprepared, incompetent, unknowledgeable, inconsistent, unlikable, unmotivating, and unlikely to last the whole year?

That's me.

7

CHOCOLATE
BROWNIES

Teachers often find that the most emotionally significant moments don't occur inside a classroom. A big moment for me occurred as I held a plate of chocolate brownies in a hallway.

During the last period of the day, a group of teachers, including me, had a meeting in the program coordinator's office. Laurie, one of the teachers I work with, brought an assortment of baked goods, which she had baked herself, God bless her soul. One of these creations was a plate of chocolate brownies—good chocolate brownies with toasted walnuts. No, no, not "good"; you have to understand—these brownies were far beyond good; they were actually the subject of gossip. Ladies and gentlemen, never were flour, sugar, and the powdered beans from the cacao tree blended together in a more sublime combination.

Laurie put the plate on the table; the meeting was not quite the same afterwards.

Mark, the program coordinator, shares my view of brownies, cookies, cakes, and all other such yumminess that exists on the planet. We would eat each and all of these morsels with rapture at every possible opportunity were it not for the fact that such activity has a nasty way of making belts tight in the morning. Nevertheless, each of us began going through the Phases Of Eating Fattening Foods, or PEFF:

Table 7.1. Phases of Eating Fattening Foods (PEFF)

Phase Name	Characterized by
Denial	Subconsciously ignoring the existence of the plate of creamy, warm, gooey, sinfully rich brownies, which has just been placed on the table three feet in front of your face. You glance at it and look away immediately.
Initial conflict	You hear the person who baked them say, "Please, everyone, have a brownie." Warring factions of brain cells immediately dig in their heels and began firing at each other.
Bandwagon reinforcement	You're grateful when you hear several of your peers say, "Oh, they look so good, but I'm going to pass, I need to lose some of this," as they slap their stomachs. Your desire for the brownies begins to wane.
Surprise hunger	Everything is going fine when you suddenly feel slightly hungry. You glance at the brownie plate. You then glance at your own stomach and take a drink of delicious, filling water. You look away from the brownie plate. You realize that you have not heard the last two sentences that have been spoken in the room. This is unfortunate, as you're responsible for taking the notes for the meeting. You vow to be more disciplined.
Aroma volley	After a few moments, you make the mistake of breathing in through your nose. The air you breathe in is contaminated with millions of evil brownie scent molecules. At this point, the primitive areas of your brain work their magic. The space under your tongue fills with saliva. You look at the brownie plate. Another sentence missed.
Ephemeral source hostility	Briefly, you feel irritation at the person who brought in the brownies. Doesn't she REALIZE that there are people present who are not as THIN AS A STICK? Evil wench.
	Guilt, guilt, guilt, now you feel guilt for that last thought. Great, a plate of guilt with a side of hunger at 7:15 in the morning.
Acquiescence preparation 1	You compare the size of the brownies to other brownies you have seen. You come to the conclusion that these brownies are, in fact, smaller than the average size brownie.
	-OR-

Table 7.2. (*Continued*)	
Phase Name	*Characterized by*
	You come to the conclusion that these brownies are, in fact, larger than the average size brownie, but you then realize that eating one slightly larger size brownie results in less Brownie Intake than eating two or three slightly smaller-size brownies.
Acquiescence preparation 2	You remember that you have not eaten breakfast. You realize that this omission has resulted in a calorie deficit that may justify eating one and only one brownie.
Acquiescence preparation 3	You also remember that the cafeteria serves salads for lunch. The omission of breakfast plus eating a salad for lunch will create a sufficiently large calorie deficit to justify eating one and only one brownie.
Acquiescence	You eat the brownie in one bite. Yowlm and it's down, just as pretty as you please.
Temporary relief	It's done. Finished. Eaten. It was worth it. Over with. Mmm, that was a good brownie.
The unholy persistence of hunger	Guess what, smarty-pants? It ain't over yet. Shockingly, without your permission, your stomach has unplugged the connection to your conscience. Five more, please, and make it snappy.
Noble yet fruitless extinction delay gambit	You do what most human beings do: employ a strategy that sounds good but is utterly worthless, namely, to simply try to wait out the relentless wave of hunger pangs.
Carbohydrate hallucination	The brownies begin speaking to you.
Capitulation with justification options	You discover the similarities between eating brownies and childbirth: the second one is easier; the third one is still easier, and then everyone stops counting.
	Over the next seven minutes, nothing you say can be clearly understood. This is the natural consequence of requesting your tongue to form speech sounds AND scrape chocolate off the roof of your mouth at the same time.
	You say to yourself one of the following:
	1) It doesn't matter if I've eaten 4, 7, or 8, does it? Who cares how many I've eaten, they're really good. I'm sick and tired of worrying about what I eat all the time.
	2) I'll work it off at the gym tonight.

(continued)

Table 7.1. *(Continued)*	
Phase Name	*Characterized by*
	3) They were small, anyway.
	4) It's not so bad; I never treat myself.
	5) I'll probably burn it off with this stressful job.
	6) I'll eat salads this week.
	7) I'll switch to light beer.
	8) I'll drink less beer.
	9) Cross off number eight.
	10) What brownies?

But I digress.

The upshot of this is that there were too many brownies even for both Mark and me to eat. At the end of the meeting, shortly after the final school bell rang, Mark begged me, pleaded with me, to take the plate of brownies out of his office and far, far away.

I was carrying the plate, walking down the hallway, wondering what I'm going to do with a plateful of brownies. Just at that moment a group of about eight students was walking toward me from the other end of the hallway. I thought to myself, "Oh, how convenient. I'll unload the brownies on these students." As the students approached, I stopped them and said, "Would you guys like some brownies?" I learned that few things make seventeen-year-old people happier than the offer of sugar, carbs, and fat—all at no charge. They surrounded me, googly-eyed, smiles on their faces, and grabbed them all. They had obviously mastered the skill of saying, "thank you" while simultaneously chewing.

Anyway, this was the moment I am talking about. It was this moment, where I watched them all smile and eat the brownies I had given them, that was, for an unknown reason, extraordinarily significant for me emotionally.

At that moment, I felt like their father.

It was a visceral, paternal pleasure—feeding kids.

At that moment, I wanted to thank the administration for hiring me and entrusting with me the duty of taking great care of these students.

At that moment, I was moved by the sacred power of the quasi-parental, quasi-mentor relationship that exists between a student and a teacher.

At that moment, I felt a sense of satisfaction that was more tangible than I believe I have ever felt in my professional career.

As you look back on your life, certain moments are written in your memory with bolder, darker ink than others. It's sometimes difficult or impossible to gain a great enough self-understanding so that you understand why certain moments are so significant. But, this was one of those moments. Maybe it has to do with my need to help others. Maybe there is something in it about being accepted by others. Maybe it's because I enjoy being in a position where I can positively change and influence young minds because I've treated them in a way such that they are receptive to my input.

Or maybe it's simply because I successfully got rid of the brownies and wouldn't have to go through another episode of PEFF later that night.

8

MASTERS OF BREVITY

Many times, people with disabilities devise clever ways to compensate for these disabilities.

Many years ago, I was friends with Craig, who had a moderate case of dyslexia. He said that ever since first grade, he found reading to be a time-consuming, difficult activity. Craig, however, was too intelligent, resourceful, and persistent to allow this disability to interfere with his success. He reflected upon his strengths and his weaknesses and realized that he enjoyed working with numbers. He said that his dyslexia didn't affect his ability to read and understand numbers as significantly as it affected his ability to read and understand large quantities of words.

So, after doing this analysis, he decided on the career he was going to take; he became a banker and soon rose through the ranks of a large metropolitan bank to become the senior vice president of international commerce.

He saw the obstacle, analyzed it, decided what to do to circumvent it, and then put his plan into successful action. Bravo to him for finding a way to get what he wanted.

Ideally, all people with learning disabilities will learn the same strategies; and these strategies, these ways of thinking, are some of the most important concepts we special educators teach students: how to compensate for and circumvent a disability so it is much less of a disability.

Many of us, even those of us without a learning disability, use these same compensatory strategies in our everyday lives.

A person who always loses his keys will benefit from putting a key hook in his closet and always putting his keys there when he comes in the door. A person who often forgets her briefcase for work will benefit from putting it in her car before she goes to bed. The development of miniaturized electronic devices have made these little reminders more accessible to more people.

Have you ever wondered why so many people are addicted to their Pocket PC, or PDA, or Smartphone, or some other similar organizational device? It stems from an innate desire within these people to be organized and an even deeper desire to overcome their organizational disability and view themselves as competent individuals. A chief criticism of the PDA is, "these people have poor memories; they use the device/calculator/reminder as a crutch. They should just slow down and think more; they should train their minds to work smarter."

People who make these sorts of comments feel that technology is an unnecessary, burdensome intrusion, or worse, the source of delayed mental development. But, they don't see the situation from the perspective of the possessors of thin, silvery, beeping, rechargeable, aluminum wafers with glowing plastic screens. The people who own these devices have done a competent job of analyzing their strengths and weaknesses and have devised a system to help compensate for their shortcomings.

A common issue that all teachers deal with is the avoidance and compensatory strategies their students have devised to overcome their extreme difficulty with reading and writing.

In response to this, should the teacher leave them be for the most part and simply teach them learning strategies (give them a PDA, so to speak), or should the teacher require them to read and write difficult things (take away their PDA and require them to practice remembering appointments), knowing it will be hard but believing they will benefit from the exercise?

Could it be that part of the reason why they are behind grade level in reading/writing/math/whatever is partially because of their disability and partially because they've avoided doing the schoolwork for years? Imagine what would happen if you went up to somebody who is highly dependent on their PDA and said to them, "I'm sorry, but you have to give this to me now so I can throw it in the trash. You should be able to remember all of your appointments without having to rely on this device. If this is hard for you, then work hard on improving your deficits by taking memory classes, doing memory exercises, etc."

It's likely that the person you're talking to would have a few words for you, and those words would not be "Happy Birthday."

One of the reasons why the person will likely be hopping mad with the prospect of losing their PDA is not because you're taking away technology but because they know in their heart that a loss of this device means a loss of their perception of themselves as competent. Do you have the right to take away their device? Do you have the right to tell them how their brain should work and how it should not work?

This conflict carries over into the classroom because of some of the remarkably brief writing samples I've received from my students over the past year. I asked my students to describe the plot of "The Wizard of Oz" after verifying that nearly all of them had seen the film. Many of the written responses looked like these:

- There's a tornado that blows across a Midwest farm and sends a little girl to a place she dreamed of. In the end, everything turned out okay.
- Little singing people dance down a yellow brick road with a girl, a dog, and a Tin Man to try to get the Tin Man a heart so he can get married.
- A story about a girl, a dog and a wizard. I thought the whole movie was stupid.

When I approach the students about the importance of including detail in what they write, I get the same response from many of them: "You asked me to describe the film, and I did. It was a film about a girl, a dog, and a wizard. What else do you need to know?" Then I say to them, what about the Wicked Witch of the West? What about Glenda the Good Witch? What about the scarecrow? What about "There's no place like home?"

The student responses to my questions are filled with justifications about how the omitted details are not important and therefore should never have been included.

These justifications are students' ways of avoiding their disabilities.

When faced with this resistance, I agonized over how much to push them. Would forcing them to face their disabilities head on, by insisting that they write in more detail, result in angry blow-ups and refusal to do work, or would it be just the thing they need to actually make measurable literacy gains?

Another example: an assignment in class one day was to correctly rewrite poorly written car and truck ads on eBay. One student named Cole—a likable, pierced, Goth wannabe—rewrote the ad but omitted 75 percent of the detail in the original ad. I sat down next to him to view his work and blinked a few times when I saw the few brief sentences on the paper. Here's how the conversation went.

"You're done?"

"Yeah."

"Okay, well, it seems like your ad is much shorter than the original ad."

"Yeah."

"You might have a difficult time selling the truck if this is your ad."

"Why?"

"Well, you omitted a lot of the detail of the original ad. For example, you didn't say anything about the color of the truck. I also don't see anything here about the condition of the interior."

"I don't need to write those things, there's three pictures in the ad. All these things are clearly visible in the picture. Why would I waste time writing down things that are clearly visible from one glance at the pictures?"

"Yeah, but Cole, I know that these things are visible, but the pictures aren't exactly the greatest quality in the world, you know. I mean, you can see that there is a tear in the front seat, but that's the only seat you can see in the picture."

"I know that! The pictures give you a good general idea of the interior of the truck. If you were the slightest bit interested in seeing the truck, you would then go and see the truck in person and see all the detail you needed. You're not going to make the decision to purchase the truck based on the writing in the ad or the pictures in the ad. They're only there to give you a general idea; if you're really serious about buying the truck, you're going to go see the truck in person."

"Cole, you're right, but part of the decision that a person has to make when viewing an ad is how likely is it that the owner of the vehicle is telling the truth about the condition of the vehicle. Most people, when they see an ad for a truck that's obviously not in the greatest condition, and they see that the ad has very little detail about the truck, might have opinions that the owner must be hiding something."

"Not necessarily. It's an old truck. Anybody who's looking for an old truck understands it's not going to be in perfect condition. Anybody who expects a truck that's fifteen years old to be in perfect condition is an idiot."

"Okay, that may be, and I admit that different people think differently. But the assignment is to rewrite the ad so it is more clear. When you rewrite something, you do want to trim down unnecessary things, but you don't want to omit important details like the color, the age, the condition of the seats, etc."

The conversation went like this for a little while longer until I realized what was going on.

Cole was doing everything he could, anything he could, to keep the focus of the conversation away from the fact that he has extreme difficulty with the process of locating details in text and recreating those details in grammatically correct sentences.

It was difficult for me to understand, and I still don't know as I reflect upon the situation, whether he really did believe all the things that he said about how to effectively rewrite the ad, or whether he was simply utilizing a well-rehearsed, effective technique for avoiding the writing process.

Most teachers struggle to decide what to do with such a vulnerable teenager. How much good or harm will it do to force a student to stare at his disability full on and make him extremely uncomfortable in the process? His steadfast claims that he does not *need* to write in a lot of detail is his PDA, so to speak. It's his technique for avoiding what he knows to be a deficiency and his method for preserving his self-image as an intelligent, competent young adult.

So what should teachers do about this?

On the one hand, we have the "He won't change" argument. This position would say this: Let's face facts. Cole is in the twelfth grade. He has been in special education English classes for many years. Ever since about the third grade, he has had extreme difficulty with writing cohesive and substantial sentences. There is nothing that any teacher is going to be able to do to magically change that fact. Cole is likable, is a good conversationalist, has solid career aspirations, and has a severe writing disability. His strengths coincide with his weaknesses.

The part of his brain that's responsible for organizing concepts into strings of English sentences is defective.

That's the word for it: defective. Not "different," not "trainable," but defective. That's a harsh word that I would never use with him or his family, but I'm using it with you so that you understand the reality of the situation. It's not that Cole hasn't been adequately or appropriately taught, it's not that he hasn't been given adequate chances, it's not that he hasn't been given the right educational materials, and it's not that he hasn't been put in the right classroom environment. It's because part of his brain is defective. Cole knows this. He's more aware of it than anybody else in the world, and the proof of this is the diverse techniques he has acquired to avoid writing, and the most effective one is to forcefully deny the need to write.

On the other hand, we have the "He needs more practice" argument alluded to earlier. This position would say that part of the reason why he is writing below grade level is the fact that he has had significantly less practice with, and exposure to, reading and writing than his peers in regular education classes. This position is supported by research, which shows that students who come from homes where there are few literacy activities and few chances to read and write will do significantly worse in English class than students who come from homes with a literacy-rich environment.

So what should you do as the teacher? Can you repair his brain? No. Can you teach him how to write like Poe? No. But, you can do two things: expose him to as much literacy as possible and teach him some strategies to help him compensate for his disability. Here's what I did in this particular instance; it was clear to me that Cole had difficulty with organizing his thoughts, and I believed that an outline might be just the scaffolding that he needed to hoist himself up to a higher level. I gave him a sheet of paper with a series of questions on it that needed to be answered in an effective ad:

- Make
- Model
- Year
- Mileage
- Color
- Condition of interior, overall
- Condition of dashboard
- Condition of front seats
- Condition of back seats
- Engine type
- Transmission type
- Body damage
- Does radio work?
- Does A/C work?
- 2 or 4 wheel drive?
- Been in any accidents?
- Rebuilt recently?

- Known existing problems?
- Why selling?
- Location of vehicle?
- Currently has a tag on it?
- Currently is being driven?
- Currently insured?

When I gave this sheet to Cole to use as a guide when reading the next poorly written eBay ad, the level of detail went up significantly.

He filled in almost all of these questions, and the ones that he didn't fill in were unanswered in the original ad. I then told him a simple technique for stringing together the above information into a paragraph. He did it. It was tedious, and he needed my help, but he did it.

The sheet with the questions on it was like his little Pocket PC. It gave him the structure he needed to accomplish a task that he would otherwise not be able to do. When he got the paper back the next day, it had an A on it. I looked at him and said, "Good job. The level of detail was much better than your previous work, and your sentence structure was almost perfect." He gave me a blank stare, looked at the paper, looked up at me, and smiled.

It was one of the greatest moments of my first year as a teacher.

My students can do it; it's just that they need more structure and more help than those without a disability.

Teachers should try to employ a hybrid approach to the two previous views of Cole's (and other students') poor literacy skills. They can benefit from as much practice as possible with reading and writing, and you should require your students to read and write many different things over a semester. You may hear questions like, "We're reading the WHOLE NOVEL?" or "HOW MANY pages do we have to write?" They will look astonished, but you will get through it together with some help from the teacher in the form of organizers and techniques to complete the assignment.

"Work hard and get it done with help" is a good way to summarize a lot of what happens in an effective special education classroom.

9

THE SHAMPOO BOTTLE

My students and I were doing a unit on English grammar, and the lesson of the day was on participles, which are "ing" verbs that can function as adjectives. For example, if you say "the crying baby," the word "crying" is a participle because even though "crying" is a verb, in that sentence it describes the baby and is therefore a participle. We got through the lesson okay, the students took the quiz, and I moved on to the next topic.

A few days later, Laurie, one of my students, came up to me and said, partially amused, partially surprised, "Mr. Goldman, you're not going to believe this! I was taking a shower this morning, and I happened to look at my bottle of shampoo. I saw that it said 'foaming bubbles,' and I thought to myself, 'Oooh, a participle! *Foaming* bubbles!' I cannot BELIEVE that I thought that . . . that this class was in my head in the shower, and I can't believe that I was reading my SHAMPOO BOTTLE and thought of participles. I just had to tell you that."

She was amused, but I had a huge smile on my face. I told her, "You see! Now you're the smartest shampooer on your block." She and I both laughed, but I laughed and smiled more.

CHAPTER 9

Do you know why?

Because she was listening in class, even though it looked like she wasn't.

She thought about what we learned outside of class, remembered the details of the lesson, and applied them correctly. This means that I was not the worst teacher in the world. Also, her coming to me with the story told me that she thought I was worth talking to.

Laurie, I want to thank you, thank you, thank you for telling me your story. It was one of the best moments of my whole first year.

10

SLEEPYHEAD

Kelly is skilled in the art of avoiding detection while sleeping in class.

Judging from the level of her skill, she has had many years of practice, and all this practice must have resulted in many years of successfully sleeping in class. I wonder if there is a connection with this successful sleeping and her poor academic performance in regular education classes?

Kelly was too adroit at the sleeping game to try something as amateurish as putting her head down on the desk (a tactic that several other students tried). That would result in immediate attention from the teacher, and so it would not do. She had more sophisticated body positioning techniques—here are a few of them.

Kelly's "Sleep and Get Away With It" Tactics:

Tactic one: when reading in class, put the book in your lap. Keep your back straight but tilt your head down slightly and roll your eyes down to look at the book. It looks like you're reading, but the position of your head, eyelids, and eyelashes are just low enough so that it's impossible to tell whether your eyes are actually open or closed.

This is known as the "pretend you're reading with good posture" position.

Probability of success: high. What gives you away: you never turn the page.

Tactic two: when completing a class assignment, place paper and pencil in front of you and hold a pencil to the paper as if you are actually writing. Put your left elbow on the table in front of you. Put your left thumb just under your left cheekbone; you will have to lean your head down slightly and to the left in order to accomplish this. Put the thumb-facing side of the end of your left index finger against the top of your forehead. It's the same sort of position you might take if, while reading, the sun suddenly shone into your eyes from the left. This is known as the "shield your eyes from the eyes of the teacher" position.

Probability of success: high. What gives you away: your pencil never moves.

Tactic three: Place your sweater, book bag, or any large object directly in front of you on the table. (There were tables in the classroom.) Put the current book we are reading in class flat on the table beyond the sweater or book bag so that the bottom edge of the book is touching the sweater or book bag. Extend your left hand out so that you can hold the book open. Put your right hand on top of the sweater or book bag, and then lean forward and lower your face until your chin is resting on the top of your right hand.

Then, for a little while, fake interest in the book and be sure the teacher sees that although you are leaning down and it looks as though you are resting your head on a pillow, you are in fact listening carefully and reading along with the rest of the class. After the teacher is confident that you are listening (this may take several minutes), he will move to a different part of the room for a little while, which gives you the opportunity to make up for the fact that you were talking on the phone until 3:30 in the morning.

Just close your eyes, close your eyes, close your eyes, ahhhhhh. This is known as the "book bag as pillow" position.

Probability of success: medium. What gives you away: it looks like you're sleeping and encourages the teacher to check on you often.

You will probably see many techniques that your students will try to use to sleep in class. When you ask your students, "What time did you get to bed last night," you'll get responses that will make you shake your head in disbelief. You'll hear "midnight," "two in the morning," "three in the morning," "I don't know," and "I don't remember."

One of my students told me that he didn't get to bed until 5:15 in the morning; he said he was just talking on the phone the previous night and lost track of what time it was. I asked him if he was tired during these long conversations. He said, simply, "yeah."

This brings to light one of the most significant obstacles in the path of the academic success of students: many of them are not getting nearly enough sleep.

How in the world can you ask a student to talk about the similarities and differences between two novels when she can't keep her eyes open? Some of my students drink several cans a day of Red Bull, Monster Energy Drink, coffee, cola, and other stimulants to help compensate for lack of sleep.

What my students don't realize is that there is no substitute for a good night's sleep, especially for a growing adolescent. All the stimulants in the world will not compensate for the lack of normal sleep cycles that happen when we give ourselves adequate time to sleep.

Sleep researchers have discovered long ago that dreaming is an essential process for the mind. It's true that sleep gives our body the ability to rest, but this is not the main reason why we need to shut our eyes for eight hours every day. We need to sleep because we need to dream, and the only way that we are able to dream enough is to give ourselves enough time to do it.

When seventeen-year-old students go to sleep at 1:30 in the morning and wake up for school five hours later, these students have been robbed of the ability to dream in REM (Rapid Eye Movement) sleep. REM sleep, which is when we dream, is a relatively small percentage of the total amount of time that we spend asleep, but it is essential that we get enough time for this crucial sleep stage. A lack of REM sleep results in a significant decrease in cognitive abilities, including the ability to focus, concentrate, and remember and process new information.

Drinking stimulants, such as energy drinks and coffee, makes the situation worse by interfering with normal sleep cycles. I've heard more than one of my students complain that they have a difficult time falling asleep, and I feel confident that part of the reason is high residual levels of caffeine in their bloodstream.

But, students don't think too much about the long-term effects of something that feels good now. So, psssst-glug-glug-glug. Down goes the syrupy-sweet stimulant cocktail. When does the resultant caffeine-fueled mania all come crashing down? About ten minutes into English class.

One of my students named Rudy was so sleepy during class that he literally could not keep his eyes open. I asked him to go get a drink of water, hoping that the physical movement would help get his blood going. When he came back into the classroom, his head hit the table within one minute. I asked him to please stand up, which he did. About a minute or two later there were giggles near where he was standing because Rudy's eyes were closed.

He was trying to sleep standing up.

How would Rudy's academic performance improve if he went to bed every night at 10 o'clock?

How much of the difficulty that he has with concentrating in class is attributable to a simple lack of sleep? Rudy's mother told me that he has five brothers and sisters at home, all teenagers, and it's difficult for her, a single mother, to keep track of when each of her kids gets to bed. She said that even if she wanted to get Rudy to go to bed, how would she get him to go to bed if he didn't want to go?

Who knows the answer to her question? I'm sure that all the nagging, pleading, promising, and threatening in the world couldn't compete with the teenage-boy allure for Rudy of being with friends, playing a video game, or talking to girls on his cell phone. It's an uphill battle for parents and teachers to fight.

We have a seventeen-year-old boy on our hands. He's a good kid, he wants to do right, but he's been captivated by the adult freedoms appearing on his life's horizon, and they are far more compelling than some nonsense about "getting enough sleep."

"What does that mean," he probably thinks; he's not even tired. So it's midnight? So what? And let's not forget about the fact that at this point in his life, testosterone makes up approximately 99.99 percent of his blood. It's 12:30 a.m., and he's talking on a cell phone at his friend's house, away from the ears of his mother, and on the other end of this cell phone is an eighteen-year-old girl with a body on her that makes him realize that there is, in fact, a God in heaven.

The girl he's talking to, also with blood viscous with hormones, finds Rudy particularly interesting and attractive and is making that clear to him by her tone and her words. Now how in the world is Mom going to get her son to hang up the phone (assuming he's in the house) and tell the bodacious beauty he's talking to that he has to go bwush his toofies now and go to bed? It's a difficult task. Difficult, but not impossible.

It takes the resolve of parents and educators to help us make sure that students get enough sleep. I believe that between 5 percent and 10 percent of my students would have a good chance of improving their academic performance enough to move up out of the special education classroom if they would only get enough sleep.

Teachers will hear excuses all the time that "I have ADD," or "I have a hard time concentrating." Oftentimes, these excuses are coming from the same students who cannot keep their eyes open. Parents, remember: your son may be six feet tall with a goatee and a surly attitude but don't be fooled—he's not an adult yet. He still needs to be told when to go to bed, especially if you hear from teachers that he can't keep awake in school.

11

DREW, THE HUMAN SPRING

Bounce, Drew, bounce. See Drew bounce.

Watch Drew sit down. Drew cannot sit down! No he can't. Drew must stand up again and go get a tissue.

Watch Drew sit down. Drew cannot sit down! No he can't. Drew must stand up again and ask if he can get a drink of water.

Watch Drew sit down and try to remain seated. He cannot do it! Watch Drew's foot tapping on the floor at the same time that Drew's pencil is tapping on the desk. When the bell rings, watch Drew walk down the hallway. Why, he has so much energy that he doesn't walk, he—what is he doing, boys and girls? Is he skipping? No, that wouldn't be very manly, would it, it's not quite a skip—it's sort of a hop. No, not a hop—sort of . . . well it doesn't really matter what we call it.

Drew is like a nine-volt battery that has been charged by a bolt of lightning. Guess what he eats for breakfast?

No, not a bowl of cereal and a banana. No, not oatmeal with some orange juice. No, not a few granola bars and a glass of milk. On his breakfast menu are two things: a giant chocolate chip cookie and a can of Coke.

Watch his foot shaking under the table like a jackhammer.

(Coke, like most drinks sold at convenience stores, contains mostly water and high fructose corn syrup. Look up "high fructose corn syrup" on the Internet. Every American consumes over 60 pounds of it each year, on average.)

His Breakfast Of Champions is eaten either just before first period or just after. Sometimes this is eaten in class. There is a school rule that prohibits students from eating or drinking in class, but I don't enforce the rule strictly.

I understand that there are mice in the school (I have seen several of them and gave them names like Ferocious Tiger and The Gaping Maw) and that the administration wants to cut down on subversive rodent activity in between the hallowed walls. But, ladies and gentlemen, I ask you this: a student looks at you with big saucer eyes and asks, plaintively, "Can I eat this granola bar? I'm really hungry." If you have a heart, of course you're going to tell him that he can eat it.

Something inside of me has a very soft spot for feeding people, as you know from the "Chocolate Brownies" story earlier. This probably came from my grandmother, who wasn't happy unless your jaw muscles were going to work on something she had recently baked. The decision I made to let students eat nonmessy food in the classroom also stems from my own physiology. If I'm hungry, I can't concentrate because my blood sugar drops.

When I start thinking of the granola bar in my briefcase, I have to eat it, and once I have, I feel better and more alert to whatever's going on around me. This fact about myself makes it difficult for me to deny a student eating a granola bar neatly in class.

Furthermore, my professors in college and graduate school never prohibited eating and drinking in class. In fact, several of them specifically said that we should feel free to eat and drink whatever we like. This was done in the interest of making a friendlier environment, and it worked. In the corporate environment, people bring coffee, bagels, Danish, and other goodies to meetings on a regular basis, and this is seen as completely acceptable.

I feel strongly that I should treat my students the way I know they are going to be treated when they enter the "real world." So, I don't think that it's appropriate for me to forbid all eating and drinking. The rule of the classroom, though, is to thoroughly clean up any crumbs or wrappers and put them in the trash, and nearly all of my students do it.

But I digress.

Let's return to Jackhammer Boy, a.k.a. Drew, who has just consumed 600 calories of sugar and fat on an empty stomach.

I'm not a doctor, but I believe that his blood sugar level is approximately 695 trillion, give or take a few Hershey's Kisses.

Now it's time for Drew to log onto the computer and do some Internet research to obtain some more facts which will improve the thoroughness of his upcoming presentation on the similarities between the life experiences of Elie Wiesel and Frederick Douglass.

Ha. What did we used to say in Philly? "Fuggeddaboudit." This is what will happen:

1. Drew will say that he can't find the papers that he used to write his previous research.
2. I will ask him where he put the paperwork that he was working with yesterday.
3. He will say, "I don't know, I think they're in my class folder." (Students are supposed to keep their work in a big folder in the classroom for convenience, so the work is not misplaced.)

   This annoys me, because we are currently in the library, and the class folders are two flights upstairs and down the hallway in the classroom. I'm particularly annoyed because the class originally met up in the classroom and he:
   • didn't pay attention when I announced to the class that we were continuing our research in the library downstairs. This fact was also written on a large schedule on the board for those people who are not auditory learners.
   • didn't pay attention when I announced to the class to make sure they had all the paperwork they needed to continue their library research.

- didn't remember where he put his paperwork even though I announced to the class, and also explained in writing within the description of the assignment, what to do with the paperwork at the end of every class.

4. I will remember that being a good teacher includes hiding your annoyance approximately fifty times throughout the day and being kind, patient, respectful, and helpful instead. In exchange for doing this, the teacher gets a big payoff: a better relationship with the student, and therefore a student who is more likely to try his or her best in your class. Since the room is being supervised by the library staff, I offer to sprint upstairs with Drew to get his folder.

5. Drew slightly beats me in the race up the stairs. It's not that I'm over twenty years older than him, you see. Don't forget about the Godzilla artery-clogging chocolate chip cookie in his system; it's hard to overtake a kid who only touches every fourth step.

6. We get to the classroom. He frantically looks through his folder and cannot find the paperwork. He looks at me warily, afraid of my reaction. See number four, above, and change "fifty times" to "fifty-one times." The contrite, bewildered look on his face makes my annoyance very short-lived.

7. I ask him if it's possible that the paperwork is in his book bag.

8. He says, "I don't think so."

9. I suggest we return to the library and look in his book bag. He agrees, and down the stairs we go. I almost win the race this time; his blood sugar is beginning to drop as his pancreas pumps out insulin.

10. Thank goodness that when I return to the library, the class is completely under control. We start to look through Drew's book bag. If Drew were alive in 1980, he would've been a valuable consultant to Oliver North regarding the fine art of losing paperwork.

I decide to call it not a book bag, but "The Unspeakable Thing." The Unspeakable Thing, or "The Thing" for short, is jammed with papers that are forwards, backwards, upside down, sideways, leftways, rightways, wrinkled, not wrinkled, folded, not folded, English, math, history, science, girls' phone numbers, urgent notices to his mother, blue papers, green papers, duplicates, originals, duplicate originals, Jimmy Hoffa, everything in the whole world was in The Thing.

When we opened it up, I was actually afraid of what Unspeakable Object might become visible from within the bowels of the Unspeakable Thing. But out on the table its contents went, and I would like to say at this time, thank goodness for the sturdy construction of library tables.

11. We took a divide and conquer approach and, miracle of miracles, within about thirty seconds I found the paperwork. A lottery-winning smile flashed on his face, and he was in front of a computer terminal in no time, working happily.

The point of this whole story is that Drew wasted about ten minutes looking for paperwork that he had in his possession the entire time. Why did this happen? Does it have something to do with the fact that he wasn't paying attention at the beginning of class?

Was it even possible for him to pay attention with his extremely high blood sugar levels?

This question comes to mind often throughout the day—is the lack of performance on the part of the student directly the student's fault, or is it due to factors that are beyond his or her control?

Was Drew told the importance of eating a balanced breakfast? If he was told, and chose to ignore it and eat junk food, were there any consequences at home? Did anyone ever do a blood sugar test on him? If he did eat a balanced breakfast, would that have a significant effect on his ability to concentrate?

He's eating the chocolate chip cookie and the soda pop because it makes him feel good. Why does it make him feel good? Does he innately know that the stimulation of the sugar in some way helps suppress the symptoms of an underlying learning disability? Or is the morning sugar shot the result of laziness on his part when he gets up in the morning? Does he have the opportunity in the morning to eat a nutritious breakfast? Is he trying to maximize the amount of time he can sleep in the morning because he went to bed way too late the night before?

Many teachers might, at this time, call his parents and ask them these questions. But don't be too hasty to do so. What if these questions offend them? What if they misinterpret your inquiries as a thinly veiled criticism of their parenting?

Anyway, what good would asking these questions do? Drew is in the twelfth grade. Will his father say to the teacher, "Oh my goodness! Thank you so much for calling! I had no idea about what my son is doing when he wakes up. I'll be sure to call my boss and tell him that I have to show up for work an hour late every day because I have to make sure that my eighteen-year-old son eats a nice, hot cinnamony bowl of oatmeal every morning before he gets off to school. Yes, Mr. Goldman, I'm sure that this simple thing will make a huge improvement in his grades, and I'm sure that he'll deeply appreciate the change in his morning routine and cooperate with my instructions fully. Even though we've known for many years that Drew has a documented learning disability, we never once thought about the Oatmeal Factor. Thank you so much for enlightening us."

So, instead of taking the parent route, teachers sometimes have to do a little mini-parenting in the classroom.

Don't be afraid to tell Drew that this super-sized chocolate chip cookie and can of caffeinated caramel-flavored high fructose corn syrup may be a big reason why he has a hard time concentrating. Suggest to him that he try switching to a couple of granola bars and a pint of low-fat milk and see how it goes.

For a long time after that, Drew did not eat in my class. He's an expert at avoiding conflict with others when it concerns the things that he likes to do. When I think about myself, I realize I'm exactly the same way.

Soon after Drew chugged his syrupy energy drink, his blood sugar began dropping. When you dump a lot of sugar into your system, your pancreas creates insulin that instructs your body to absorb the sugar. In some people, the body overabsorbs the sugar, creating a little bit of a low blood sugar condition. You've heard of it—it's called a "sugar crash."

Guess what happens to Drew during second and third period? He changes from "Jackhammer Boy" to "The Zombie From Planet Ambien." When first-period teachers talk to third-period teachers, sometimes they feel like they're talking about two different people. Surprise! Drew is having a hard time keeping awake.

You'll probably see your own first-period Jackhammer Boy with his head tilted significantly from the vertical when you walk past his third-period classroom. Lethargic students don't do well in tests, don't comprehend things well, and don't pay attention in general.

Another undesirable side effect of this roller coaster blood sugar ride is the distracting effect it has on the other students.

Every time the teacher has to tell Drew to stop talking, to sit down, to wake up, to get out a pencil, to stop drumming the pencil on the table, and so on, it distracts the other students, many of whom are easily distracted to begin with.

Hence, Drew's problem is really everybody's problem.

When one student displays distracting, immature, dysfunctional behavior, it interferes with every other student's education. When you're in the classroom facing such behavior, you must select within a second or two the body language, or comment, or request, or question, or facial expression, or hand gesture—or combination thereof— that will quickly get the distracting student back on track in a kind, respectful manner.

Most of the time it works, and sometimes it doesn't. But keep in mind that a student whose blood sugar is much too high or much too low doesn't respond to teacher interventions. If you ask a kid to focus, and this kid is tapping a pencil on the table at the same time that he's tapping his foot on the floor at the same time that he's looking around the room, he's not going to focus. If you ask a kid to pay attention and that kid looks depressed, is slumped in his chair, is having a hard time keeping his eyes open, he's not going to pay attention.

It has nothing to do with you as a teacher. You didn't select the wrong intervention, you didn't make the wrong comment, you didn't sit the kid in the wrong chair. You're faced with a difficult situation.

If the student is too hyperactive, the best thing to do is ask him to take a walk way down the hallway and back a few times. Remind him that you're asking him to do this because you're hoping that it will help him burn off some of the extra energy. This saves his reputation with his peers.

Reprimanding him is not the answer—it's only going to distract all the students, and it's not going to bring down his blood sugar. It's also going to make him feel hostile towards you because he *can't* calm down at that moment. He's not going to be paying attention in class, and by getting him out of the classroom for a few minutes you preserve the learning environment and help to work off his extra energy. When he comes back in ten minutes, it's likely that he'll be a little bit more under control, and a student under control is a good thing to have in a classroom.

If the problem doesn't go away shortly, you might think about contacting the family to try to get them to help out.

If the student is too lethargic, think about letting it go the first time because, again, you don't want to distract the other students from doing the work that they need to do. At the end of the class, talk to the student and ask them why they're having such a hard time staying awake.

Usually you'll get as a response, "I don't know." One tactic you might use is simply to have the student stand up upon being asked to wake up the second time in one class period. Then, remind him or her after class, or the next day, how important it is to stay awake and alert throughout the entire class. You can also try to tell the students that if they feel tired or sleepy, they can ask to go get a drink of water. Or, ask a student who's nodding off in class to run an errand down to the office.

There's always a risk that doing this will make a connection in a student's mind that "if I sleep in class, he'll send me down to the office and I can get out of here for five or ten minutes." If this sleepiness happens more than a few times, contact the family to engage their help.

It might be difficult to decide whether or not to contact the family regarding this issue, and in fact, most issues you will face with your students. There's no magic answer to the complex problems facing your students. Sometimes contacting the family is somewhat effective. Sometimes contacting the family results in a very pleasant, respectful response but absolutely no change in the student's behavior. You'll often find it difficult to get in touch with the head of the household, or the head of the household speaks a language other than English. (I wish that I was fluent in Spanish—it would help me out so much.) Once, contacting the family resulted in a very angry mother, which I'll tell you about in the next chapter.

Thank goodness they don't sell soda pop in public schools in this area. I think students should be prohibited from bringing outside food and drink into the school. If you would walk down the hallways during first and second periods and look in the classrooms, you will see a significant number of students trying to sleep or talking too much. You can almost guarantee that in that same classroom, either on the desks or in the trash, are mounds of cola cans and candy bar wrappers.

12

STOP HARASSING
MY SON

The school I teach in is a "good" school in a "good" suburban neighborhood.

The people in the neighborhood, the school board, the press, the students, and the administration would say (privately, of course, to each other—but never to anyone else who might mistake their comments as racist) that the types of students in my school are very different than the students found in the tough schools of inner-city America. I'm sure many parents who send their children to the school where I teach would never send their (sweet, innocent) child to a large inner-city school, and one of the main reasons for that is that they don't want their children exposed to drugs.

I'm sorry to tell everybody this and to taint the idyllic scene of a stately brick school surrounded by picturesque homes with chemically enhanced lawns, but many of the students who attend this school are illegal drug users.

Let's take a look at Jeff. He's friendly. He's cheerful. He's always at class on time. On the other hand, he's quiet and rarely contributes to class discussions, but the cheerful and cooperative nature of his personality results in his flying under the radar of most teachers. He completes his assignments on time, he asks limited questions if he's unsure of something, and he never complains if something is too difficult or too easy. I like Jeff; he's a pleasure to have in the classroom.

Jeff is an avid baseball player and a die-hard White Sox fan. He has a winning smile. He's accepted by his peers. He's a chronic marijuana smoker.

Previously in this book I've told you that a lot of my students don't get enough sleep. So, I never really paid much attention to the fact that Jeff's eyes were sometimes a little bloodshot. I never really paid attention to the fact that Jeff sometimes just stared down at the table for a few minutes, oblivious to the activity around him. I thought it was a lack of sleep, or lack of proper nutrition, both of which affect many of my students.

One day we were doing an activity where the students were calling out similarities and differences between two novels. I had put a Venn diagram up on the overhead and was using it as a visual way to help the students organize their thinking on this relatively complex task. I was sitting closest to Jeff as I was writing down in colored marker the facts that the students were calling out.

Jeff said a sentence or two as he sat next to me. His breath smelled like pot.

Now I'm going to tell you something that is the truth: I have never smoked marijuana in my life. However, I did go to college and believe it or not, many college students smoke marijuana. When you live in a college dorm, as I did, and your buddies are smoking weed down the hall, you can smell it everywhere. I have been to many parties where pot smoking took place. I have walked behind people on the street who were smoking pot, and my nose made it crystal clear to me what was happening. I have been friends for many years with a person who used to smoke an insane amount of weed. There's a place in Wisconsin called the Bong Recreation Area (look it up if you don't believe me), and we used to joke around with him that he should build a house there.

Because of all this, I know what marijuana smells like. It has an unmistakable, unique aroma. It does *not* smell like tobacco or clove cigarettes. It does not smell like burning wood, cooking, frying, roasting, or broiling anything. Pot smells like pot. It's sort of the same thing as a grapefruit. Nothing else tastes quite like a grapefruit except for another grapefruit. If I would sit you down and blindfold you and feed you a piece of grapefruit and then try to tell you that what I gave you is really a lemon wedge, or piece of watermelon, or piece of fried chicken, I'd be making a fool out of myself. You would never believe me, because you know darned well what a grapefruit tastes like. There's no way that I could convince you that the grapefruit you just ate was anything but a grapefruit.

The point of the above weed-grapefruit comparative essay is to illustrate how laughable it is when students deny that they've been smoking weed when there are practically clouds of smoke coming out of their mouth.

For the first time, I understood how a police officer must feel when a man who can barely stand up, who has just walked out of a bar, and who has breath that smells like bourbon, protests that he hasn't touched a drop of liquor all night, so help him God.

After I smelled the marijuana on Jeff's breath, I had to work to focus on the rest of the lesson. No wonder his eyes are sometimes bloodshot, I thought. No wonder I sometimes have to call his name a few times, upon which he suddenly looks up at me and says, "yeah?" with a dazed and vacant look on his face. At the end of the lesson, I asked him to stay for a minute; that I had to ask him a question. When all the students left, I nervously brought up the topic:

"Hey, Jeff, I want to ask you a question."

"Yeah? What's up?"

"What did you do before first period today?"

"Nothing." He looked at me intently.

"So you came straight to school from home?"

"Yeah."

"You weren't hanging out with anybody before school?"

"No." His face started to turn red.

"Nobody?"

"Well, I met up with a couple of guys and we walked to school to-gether." His face was getting redder, although he was maintaining his composure.

"Jeff, the reason I'm asking these questions is because I smell mari-juana on your breath." His eyes widened and his mouth opened, but he didn't say anything. His face turned a deep shade of red. "I'm a lit-tle concerned about it, actually. I'd like to take you down to the nurse to make sure that you're okay."

"I wasn't smoking marijuana," he said. His voice had a touch of panic in it, although he was speaking in a normal conversational tone.

"Jeff," I said. I looked at him in his eyes. He looked very frightened. I became upset because I feared that I had made a terrible mistake and had therefore, in a few moments, destroyed my relationship with him for the rest of the year. Yet, I continued, "I know what pot smells like, Jeff."

He started damage control. He said, "Well, the guys I was hanging out with were standing there on the street, and this car pulled up, and the guys in the car were smoking pot I think, and we couldn't hear what they were saying, so we stuck our heads in the car, and maybe when I did that it got the smell of the marijuana on my breath, but I didn't smoke any, I've never smoked marijuana! I just applied for a job, and they did drug tests on me, and the drug test came back negative!"

I realized at that moment that I had probably not made a mistake. If you stick your head in a car full of pot smoke for a minute or so, your breath won't smell like pot an hour later.

On the way to the nurse I felt two strong, dissimilar emotions. The first emotion I felt was fear. I was fearful that I was wrong. Even though the "I stuck my head in a car of pot smoke" excuse made me realize I was onto something, I thought to myself, what if he was telling the truth?

I was afraid, like I said before, that I had destroyed my relation-ship with him—and it's the relationship that I have with my students which is one of the most sacred things about my job.

STOP HARASSING MY SON

It's difficult for me to put into words the other emotion that I was feeling. I imagine the best way to describe it is to call it a strong paternal instinct.

I felt a strong impulse to shield Jeff from the people and substances who might do him harm. When I realized that Jeff might be doing drugs, I felt revulsion and was compelled to do something to stop it. This paternal instinct, this compulsion to protect him, made me feel that my actions were justified even if there was a chance that I was mistaken.

So down to the nurse we went.

On the way there, we said nothing to each other. He was clearly upset; his face was red, his eyes were wide open, and he was looking at the ground as he walked. I wanted to stop him and grab him by the shoulders and say, "Please forgive me for upsetting you, and I hope to God that I'm wrong. I'm sorry that I'm putting you through this—I'm only doing it because I care about you."

But then I thought to myself, what if I'm right? Then I would want to grab him by the shoulders and say, "What the hell are you doing, Jeff? What kind of people are you hanging out with? What's going to happen next, Jeff? Are you going to get locked up for drug possession, you dumbass? What happens when your good buddies ask you to try coke? Are you going to just snort it up your nose and say it's no big deal, and then two weeks later your mom finds you dead on your bedroom floor with a razor blade and a mirror by your body? I'm going to tell you what you're going to do, mister! You're going to go straight home from school and go straight to school from home every single day, and I'm going to call your family and make sure that happens!"

That's what I wanted to say, but I didn't say it.

Doing the right thing for a kid sometimes results in making that kid, whom you care for so much, hate your guts.

It's a tough thing to do. Being a teacher means simultaneously experiencing two, three, or four powerful, incompatible emotions and having to figure out which one to act on within three seconds. This happens dozens of times every day.

We got to the nurse's office, and I asked Jeff to sit down, which he did. I went over to the nurse and said quietly, "I'm bringing down this student because I smell mari . . ." The nurse interrupted me, started nodding her head up and down, and finished my sentence: ". . . marijuana on his breath, yeah, okay, I'll be right with him." It was as if the nurse knew what I was going to say. This was exceedingly strange to me; how could she possibly know what I was going to say, and why was she so matter-of-fact about it?

After thinking about it for a few minutes, I realized that there was only one answer to these questions. Jeff was not the first student today that had been brought down here for the same reason.

This was my prep period, so I told the nurse that I would wait to see how he was doing. She took him in to the inner office for a few minutes. The door opened, she came over to me and said quietly that his pulse was 162 and his blood pressure was "through the roof." I'm not a doctor, but I know that when somebody is sitting down in a chair his pulse should not be 162. When I run on the treadmill, my pulse is about 135 to 140. And what was going on with his blood pressure? Jeff is seventeen years old and in good shape. Something was definitely wrong, and I became glad that I followed my intuition and brought him down here.

The nurse said that she would contact the assistant principal and the family to come get him. I looked in through the open door and saw Jeff sitting there. He was so nervous that both of his legs were quivering, and his face was just as red as it was before. It was a strange feeling to realize that my actions over the past ten minutes were the direct cause of such extreme stress in a student. Others might say that if he had not been smoking drugs, he would have nothing to be nervous about.

I checked in later with Mr. Dunbar, the assistant principal. He said that he interviewed Jeff, and Jeff swore to him up and down that he did not smoke pot. He told Mr. Dunbar the same story that he told me—that he just had a job interview where he was given a drug test, and he passed the drug test. Mr. Dunbar told me that he did not notice the smell of marijuana on Jeff's breath or body.

This irritated me because I could smell the marijuana residue on Jeff's breath more clearly in the nurse's office, which was more confining than the large assistant principal's office. Mr. Dunbar told me that after talking with the family, he made the decision to keep Jeff in school for the rest of the day and have him continue to go to his classes.

This was an outcome I didn't expect, but I've learned since then that it's difficult and risky for a school administrator to contact a family and say with certainty that their son or daughter was under the influence of drugs, except for the most outrageous circumstances. Just because a student seems lethargic and that same student's eyes are bloodshot doesn't seem to be enough for the administration to make a decision one way or the other. The school does not give drug tests, so unless the child's behavior is so much under the influence that he or she cannot attend classes, little is done, and the student is allowed to continue on with the school day.

A few periods later, as I was coming back from lunch, I saw Jeff hanging out with some friends outside of my classroom door, which was usual for that time of day. I was relieved to see him, because I knew that he knew that I would show up at about that time. My reasoning went that if he was angry with me, he would avoid being near my classroom.

On the other hand, I was nervous because I wondered whether he was there to give me a piece of his mind for being treated unfairly. When we made eye contact, he said, "Hey." I said to him, "Are you okay?" He smiled at me and said, "Yeah." I smiled at him and said, "Good. I'll see you tomorrow morning." He said, "Okay." What a tremendous sense of relief I felt at that moment!

Students know, deep down, that the unpopular thing you're doing to them really stems from a feeling of affection and responsibility on your part. Even though it's written in their contract that they have to complain bitterly, underneath the complaining is an appreciation for you and for what you do, and all is forgiven and forgotten after a few hours pass by.

Around a week later, Jeff was not in his seat at the tardy bell, which was very unusual; his attendance and punctuality were always excellent. Oh well, I thought, he's probably sick. A few periods later,

I went to put in my attendance on the school's computer system, and I noticed that Jeff did not have an excused absence notation after his name. He was cutting class! It was early December and since the previous August he had never cut class—not once.

Something was wrong.

I wondered where Jeff was. I imagined him in a seedy basement somewhere, getting high, and became a little angry with myself at painting such a bleak scenario so quickly. By the end of the day, he still did not have an excused absence notation next to his name, so I called his family to see what was going on. His father answered the phone and explained to me that Jeff was sick that day in bed and that his wife was supposed to have called his absence in to the school. He apologized for not calling in the absence and said that he would call up the office right away and get it taken care of.

Jeff's father told me that he appreciated my calling. I said to him that it was the only thing that I could do. I told him that I know that he's interested in what's going on with his son and I'm sure he would want to know if Jeff didn't show up at school. He said that is exactly how he feels, and he again thanked me for the telephone call. The next day, Jeff showed up for class and was his normal cheerful self. I couldn't help noticing that his eyes were not bloodshot.

You think this story is over, don't you, esteemed reader? Well, hold onto your hat. If you're not wearing a hat, get one and hold onto it.

The next day I was walking past the counseling office, and Mr. Kendall, one of the counselors, asked me to come into his office for a few minutes. Mr. Kendall is an excellent counselor who takes a keen interest in the welfare of the students for whom he's responsible. After I sat down, he said, "Neil, we have a little problem, but I think I got it taken care of. Jeff's mother called me this morning, very upset. She said in a loud tone of voice that she wants me to pull Jeff out of your class because she feels that you are harassing her son."

I looked at him in stunned silence.

After a few moments, I regained my composure and said, "WHAT? Harassing her son? Why? Because I called the family because he cut class?" At about that moment, I could feel the adrenaline pumping through my bloodstream. I wasn't panicking, but I wasn't far from it.

I'm a first-year teacher. When you're a first-year teacher, they don't have to invite you back the next year, and if they choose not to invite you back, they don't have to give you any reason at all. I became angry with my supervisor right then and there because she was always saying to me to contact the family, contact the family, contact the family. She said on more than one occasion that it was the most effective method she had of improving academic performance and decreasing disruptive behavior. This was one of the first times I decided to actually take her advice and get involved with the family, and it was blowing up in my face.

And, I was thinking, what in the world is Jeff's crazy mother talking about? Harassing her son? I'm Jeff's teacher. I have a much greater responsibility to him than teaching him the difference between a gerund and a participle.

If a teacher has clear evidence that a student is using illegal drugs, especially in or near the school building, he or she is required to notify an administrator of the school. Not only that, but what would happen to a teacher if he or she knew that a student was using drugs and did nothing about it, and then the student was killed or injured? The result could be termination, a lawsuit, or both.

There is a word that's mentioned a lot in the school, and that is "enabler." We see a lot of enabler parents; they want to make things as easy and comfortable as possible for their children by removing as many rules and requirements as possible. This lack of structure and rigor is well-meaning but often results in a child whose academic performance, social interaction skills, and classroom behavior becomes worse rather than better.

I wondered if part of the reason for Jeff's drug use was his mother's inability or refusal to face facts. She wanted to remove her son from the influence of an adult who was making things a little difficult for him. This sort of thing gets me angry, and when I get angry, I think sarcastic things. I wanted to say to her, oh dear, dear, dear Mrs. "X." (I won't tell you her last name.) How horrible of me to harass your son like that. Okay, I'll leave your son alone so you can pick him up at the police station in six months after he's arrested for possession of a controlled substance.

Most of what I described in the previous paragraph went through my mind in only a few moments. I thought that my career was going to end only a few months after it started. Mr. Kendall said that Jeff has an anxiety problem (which I did not know about) and that he is nervous about coming to school and coming into my class, according to his mother. This statement was difficult for me to believe, because the day before, as I described earlier, Jeff was hanging around near my classroom and was all smiles when we spoke hours after he came out of the nurse's office.

I wondered what kind of strange interpersonal game was going on between Jeff and his mother. If Jeff was not extremely upset but was telling his mother that he was extremely upset, what was he getting out of this game? It's a question to which I still do not have an answer.

Thank goodness for Mr. Kendall's political skills. He reassured the mother that he thought that I was doing everything I was doing out of a genuine concern for her son's well-being and that I was absolutely not harassing him. He told her that he would tell me what was going on and asked me to have a brief conversation with Jeff where I reassured him that he was welcome in the classroom and that what happened in the past was in the past and forgotten.

This seemed to assuage the mother's anxiety. I thanked Mr. Kendall wholeheartedly for coming to my defense and helping the mother realize that my intentions were good and that of course I would never harass a student.

Later that day, I did see Jeff in the hall and pulled him aside. I said, "You know what happened last week, that's all in the past." He looked at me and said, "I know" in a friendly way. I said, "Jeff, I think you're an excellent student, and I always look forward to seeing you in the classroom. I wanted to make sure you knew that." He said, "Yeah!" and smiled again. I told him I'd see him tomorrow morning and kept walking down the hall.

As I write this, I continue to fervently hope that he got so frightened down in the nurse's office that it made him think more carefully about the types of people he chooses to spend time with before and after school.

13

THE DOMINO EFFECT

High school students have the extreme good fortune of being able to select from an enormous variety of courses. Some courses are required, such as mathematics, English, science, and physical education; other courses, called "electives," can be selected, cafeteria style, by the student. These diverse elective courses include such interesting studies as treble choir, culinary and pastry arts, stagecraft, constitutional law, flight training, Latin, Java programming, and dozens of others.

(If you would put the entire faculty of my high school together in a large room and stand before them, I believe you would have a difficult time asking a factual question that none of the faculty could answer.)

Many people don't stop to think that regardless of the course that a student selects, there are three skills that are necessary to complete the course successfully—reading, writing, and attending. By the way, when I use the word "attending," I mean it in both senses of the word—to pay attention to what's going on in the classroom and also to show up at school!

Even educators sometimes forget that examinations in most courses are just as much an assessment of the ability to read as they are an assessment of content area knowledge and the ability to apply that knowledge. A student who can't write well in history class might be misjudged as having a less than desirable understanding of the contributing factors of the First World War. A student who can't read well in math class might be misjudged as not understanding the mathematics concepts recently taught in class. Case in point: here's a typical math problem:

Julio, Vladimir, and Susan all live on the same long street that lies west to east and is 300 meters in total length. Julio lives at the western end of the block. Vladimir's house is 45 meters east of Julio's. Susan's house is 30 meters from the easternmost end of the block. If Vladimir walks from his house to Julio's, and Julio meets Vladimir, and they both walk to Susan's house, what total distance did Vladimir walk? Only count the distance that Vladimir walked along the sidewalk; disregard any distance walked up and down from the sidewalk to the front door, etc.

$$A. \quad 45+45+300-30-45$$
$$B. \quad 45+300-30-45$$
$$C. \quad 45+45+300-30$$
$$D. \quad 45+300-30$$

If a mathematics teacher believes that the above question is testing only mathematics knowledge, that teacher is mistaken.

The student first has to know how to read fluently, be able to gain meaning from what is read, remember the concepts recently learned in class, relate the meaning of the question to those remembered concepts, and be able to evaluate the four possible choices to find the one that is most likely correct.

If the student taking this test doesn't do well in English class, the student isn't going to do well on this kind of math test, either. Unfortunately, a student that falls into this category will often be held back in the mathematics curriculum even though his mathematics ability is at grade level. How frustrating that must be.

Another problem with multiple choice tests is the difficulty level of the answer choices. Interestingly, many educators overlook this. Here's an example of what I mean. It's a question that a student might find on a psychology test:

Carl Rogers developed "client-centered therapy" as a way to help clients partly by providing the client with unconditional positive regard. He believed that such a therapeutic environment would allow extremely shy or otherwise resistant clients to feel secure enough to openly explore their feelings about difficult life issues. Some criticized this approach as not providing enough feedback to the client and as preventing the psychologist from taking enough of an expert role in the counseling relationship.

Which of the following statements is least true about client-centered therapy?

A. Client-centered therapy can be effective with clients who are experiencing discordant reactions to life events.
B. Client-centered therapy is part of a larger group of psychotherapy models that utilize reductionism as a method of ameliorating the destructive impact of phobias.
C. Client-centered therapy focuses on unconditional positive regard.
D. Client-centered therapy gives the psychologist a subordinate position to that of the client.

Did you notice anything in particular about the above sample psychology test question? Focus your attention to the answer choices. If you noticed the high level of difficulty of the vocabulary within these answer choices, you're on the right track. Look at these difficult words: discordant, reductionism, ameliorating, subordinate.

Students taking the psychology test might have a clear understanding of client-centered therapy and may be able to competently explain it either orally or in writing, but if they have a vocabulary that is not at the level of this exam, they are going to do poorly on the test.

A common problem that arises with students is their not understanding the meaning of the answer choices. The problem is a lack of context for understanding the meetings of the words within these choices. Contextual clues are an important part of decoding word meaning.

When we are faced with a word we don't understand, we subconsciously do a contextual analysis of the sentence to discover the meaning of the unknown word. Here's an example:

> Rick was completely ensclophulated; for four hours, he had been moving heavy boxes outside in the searing July heat.

What does "ensclophulated" mean? You got a very good idea of what it means because you looked at the rest of the sentence and figured it out by the context. I'm sure nearly all people would agree that "ensclophulated" means either "exhausted," "extremely thirsty," or "overheated." In general, you figured out within a few seconds that "ensclophulated" did not mean "blond," "happy," "vegetarian," or "Catholic."

(By the way, I hope you haven't gone to the trouble of looking up the word "ensclophulated" because there is no such word. I made up a nonsense word to illustrate an example.)

Take another look at the answers to the above psychology test question. Response choice "D" talks about the subordinate position of the psychologist. This sentence does not contain any meaningful context clues that could enable a student to glean the meaning of the unknown word "subordinate" or any of the other difficult words contained within the answer choices. There's nothing in response choice "D" that gives any clue to what the word "subordinate" means. The only way to answer the question correctly, besides guessing of course, is to know what all of the words mean in all of the questions.

We are brought back to the same issue of the frustration of the student. Imagine a student who clearly understands what client-centered therapy is; it's possible the student may have undergone such therapy himself or herself.

But, because of difficulty with acquiring new vocabulary words, the student is unable to select the correct answer to the question even though he or she knows what the answer is and as a result will feel frustrated.

Frustration is the emotion we feel when a goal is blocked. Isn't it laudable that the student's goal is to do well in a test? Doesn't it show her underlying desire to be competent in the world and to become educated? These desires help define us fundamentally as people.

Imagine the far-reaching and detrimental effects on students when they are unable to achieve the result of these desires. The teacher thinks that some students don't understand the material, and the students know that the teacher thinks this, even though the students are aware that they understand the material.

This is fertile ground for academic frustration.

What would any normal person do when faced with a task that could not be accomplished, even after attempting this task over and over again? That person would likely begin avoiding the task; nobody likes to beat their head against a wall. When I see students who have documented learning disabilities avoid the task of reading and writing, I truly understand why they're doing what they're doing.

They remind me of how I felt at their age when it came to baseball. You may be wondering why I'm changing the subject to baseball, but it's a perfect illustration as to how well I understand why some of my students will do anything but sit down and read a book. Here's why.

Baseball is so American, so central to the American culture of maleness, that it made the cut into that inane automotive advertising slogan, "baseball, hot dogs, apple pie, and Chevrolet."

I was not good at baseball.

This fact made other Americans whisper that there was "something wrong with me." If you were an American kid, you played baseball. There was no discussion, there was no back talk, there was no complaining, there were no excuses.

This is what you did: you picked up the bat, you walked over to the plate, you waited for the perfect pitch, you swung with grace and power, you connected with the ball like a diagram from a high school physics textbook, you knocked the ball over the heads of the outfielders, you ran like a gazelle with a firecracker in its ass around the bases, you slid home, and you remained manly and calm amid the congratulatory cheers of your teammates.

If you were playing the outfield, you stood calmly and watched the action at the plate like a hawk. You had the quasi-supernatural ability to move to the optimum position just as the opposing team's batter cracked the ball up into the air. You possessed the ability to instantly calculate the ball's trajectory, move to the perfect location to catch the ball, which was now plummeting towards you at a hundred miles an hour, lift your glove up into the air, and listen to the ball thwack into it and stay there like the glove had been recently dipped in rubber cement. You did not drop the ball.

Then, in the twinkle of an eye, you transferred the ball to your right hand and rocketed it with perfect accuracy towards whichever baseman should receive it. The ball had been accelerated with such precision power by you that it made another loud thwack into the baseman's glove, who, of course, also caught it with aloof precision.

That's what you did if you were a normal kid. I didn't do any of that, which made me feel like I was not normal.

I didn't have the ability to connect the bat to the ball. Like I said, something was missing in my brain that allowed me to do that. You could have thrown ten pitches to me; I would've swung at all ten, even the ones that were so far outside that they almost hit the first baseman, and missed nine out of ten. The one pitch that I would've hit would have either flown up behind me or hopped pathetically on the ground like a wounded pigeon.

With catching, I was a little better, but still not good enough. I was afraid of getting my face smashed in when catching the ball, so I always reflexively looked away just before the ball was to hit my glove. Here's a news flash: when you're not looking at a ball, you can't catch the ball. My friends, or should I say, the boys I was playing ball with, used to yell out kind and patient phrases such as, "GOLDMAN, WOULD YOU STOP LOOKING AWAY FROM THE GODDAMNED BALL FOR CHRISSAKE" or some other such encouraging comments.

It's a tough thing to do, to see a heavy orb whistling towards your face at 60 miles an hour and not turn away from it. It was a natural inborn reflex within my brain to protect my eyes and my face from something that could shatter my zygomatic arch into a million little pieces.

I'll never forget the image of a boy at summer camp who was hit in the face with a baseball that had just been bat-whacked by one of the strongest kids in the camp. One of the counselors ran out to the pitching mound, scooped up the groaning, bloody, half-conscious boy, and literally ran him to the nurse's office with a look of panic and horror on his face. It took the boy a few weeks before he came back to camp, and he was forbidden to play baseball for the rest of the summer.

The upshot of all this was a guarantee of either being laughed at or vilified by my peers when attempting to play the most American of all games. No matter how hard I tried, I could not meet their quality standards. I was always picked last when the teams were being chosen, and it was a rare moment indeed when I heard any encouraging or positive words from anyone. The counselor in charge of the game, or maybe some boy who took pity on my lack of ability, would shout instructions to me as I approached the plate and attempted to hit the ball.

If I had a nickel for every time I heard, "KEEP YOUR EYE ON THE BALL—KEEP YOUR EYE ON THE BALL—DON'T SWING AT A BAD PITCH," I would have enough money to purchase the lives of all those who laughed at me and send them to a remote island far from America, bound in heavy, rusty chains.

Thank you very much, Joe DiMaggio, for telling me to keep my eye on the ball. My goodness, it's a good thing you gave me that suggestion, or otherwise I would've kept my eye on my thumb, or on my right foot, or maybe I would've closed my eyes and started thinking about mmmmm, how much I loved the smell of warm apple pie—but you got all of that nonsense out of my head, Babe Ruth, you gave me the divine directive to look at the ball that I was about to hit with the bat.

I wanted to go over there and shake his hand and say, "that last time that you said that—that last time that you told me to keep my eye on the ball—that last time—that's the one that helped me. All the times before that, you and a hundred others who have told me to keep my eye on the ball, all of those instructions were no good. But you, you sports genius, you baseball pedagogue, you were the one who persisted with that same instruction, and after the 473rd time, it finally sunk into my thick head to keep my eye on the ball. My life is different now—watch me crack bats in half and smash the windshields of cars parked behind the fields with the raw power and baseball ability that has suddenly surged into my body. Watch me! Watch me!"

Off with each of them to that remote island, bound in heavy, rusty chains.

Didn't they realize that I was the *only one* that had fifty different instructions screamed to me by ten different people? None of the other boys needed to be told these things; I hated the fact that the upcoming crystal clear display of my lack of ability became even more real, more painful, more undeniable by the trumpeting fanfare of their useless but well-intentioned instructions.

Didn't they realize the stigma and embarrassment that was attached to such simple instructions? When a good pitcher stepped up to the plate, everyone got quiet because everyone in the outfield was nervous about what would happen. Didn't they realize that their instructions to me were meaningless because my brain was not good at the gross motor coordination required to hit a baseball consistently? No matter how much you try to train a dog to distinguish between red and blue, you can't, because the dog's physiology does not permit the perception of color. Didn't they realize that I put more pressure on myself to do well than any other person?

This scene played itself out over and over again through the early days of my childhood. My friends laughed at me, I was called names, all of the cruel things you hear about how young children treat each other are true. A few times some people tried to pull me aside and help me practice my swing, or practice my throw, but it was too late.

I had begun to hate playing baseball, and I decided one day that I was never going to play it again.

This was something unheard of—a boy who doesn't play baseball? There must be something wrong with him. Yes, there was something wrong with me—I didn't have the skill to play well, and I was tired of the pressure, the humiliation, and all the other bad stuff that goes along with lacking an innate skill that your peers expect you to have.

But, when I decided that I wasn't going to play, a few more adjectives were added to the list—disobedient, defiant, difficult to manage, unwilling to play with other kids. In other words, weird.

The camp counselors were frustrated that I refused to play and tried a variety of techniques to get me to participate in the game, including threats, promises, ostracism, man-to-man talks, and a lot of other well-intentioned techniques, but none were effective. (Are you making connections between this story and students with learning disabilities?) My parents always characterized me as extremely stubborn, and they're right. When I made up my mind either to do something or not to do something, almost nothing in the world would be able to convince me otherwise, and baseball was most certainly no exception to this rule.

I was not going to play, and there was nothing they could do to make me. It's interesting that although the counselors wanted me to play, my peers really didn't care one way or the other, probably because I—oh, what's the word, sucked. One time, some of my friends got together and suggested that I be the manager of the team, which was actually extremely clever because it allowed me to participate in the game while at the same time not requiring me to touch a bat, a ball, or a glove, which thrilled me and all the others to no end.

I found this to be an act of kindness, and I took up their offer; after all, I did like the guys and did want to be part of the group. I wonder now as I write this if the manager idea actually came from them or whether it originated from one of their older siblings, parents, or adult acquaintances. So, during the next game, I was the manager, which worked out for a few minutes, but I soon realized that I had no idea what I was doing and began feeling ineffective and incompetent.

That was the last game where I took on a supervisory role. From then on, I just avoided the whole baseball thing, although deep down I wished to participate in it. This refusal to participate in baseball soon generalized to most other sports.

Now, years later, I have watched some baseball and softball games and I realize, wistfully, that I really wasn't that bad. I've seen some serious games recently where spectacular blunders were made. I probably should have ignored the complaints and the taunting and continued practicing. But, then again, we all need to remember how sensitive young people are to criticism. It was less painful for me to be excluded from the game than to be brutally insulted when I made a mistake.

Keeping this in mind, I need to introduce another concept to make my point. In the field of psychology, there's a term called stimulus generalization, which can be explained like this.

Say, for example, that a child ate a little piece of red bell pepper and did not like the taste of it. Later in the day, the child's father offers her a little piece of tomato. The child will likely say no because in the child's mind, all red foods taste terrible; the child's mind has not yet developed to the point where it can understand the concept that two foods, both of which are colored red, have very different flavors. The stimulus of the unpleasant taste of the first red food generalizes to all red foods.

I had a friend years ago who had a dog that did not like men, which illustrates stimulus generalization in the dog—if the dog sees a larger, heavier human being with a deeper voice, it puts this human male in the same category as all human males and fails to realize that it is possible that one human male may be extremely kind to him even though a different human male may very well have, in the past, been cruel.

Stimulus generalization is a good thing because it helps to keep us alive. If we ate a little piece of a certain kind of mushroom and got violently ill, we would likely try to avoid all mushrooms in the future. Even though this may deny us the pleasure of eating nonpoisonous mushrooms, it does an effective job of keeping us alive. Have you ever heard of someone who's afraid of snakes? This is another example of stimulus generalization—if it slithers and has no arms and legs, is to be screamed at and jumped away from, regardless of whether it's a little harmless garter snake or a big, poisonous rattlesnake.

Guess how stimulus generalization manifested itself in my mind? You got it—like I said, I avoided most sports almost entirely. I wouldn't play kickball, I wouldn't play hockey, I wouldn't play basketball, and I certainly wouldn't play football. If a bunch of guys got together on a flat surface to push each other, run around, and hurl a sphere at each other, you could guarantee that I was not there.

Similar to my performance in the sports arena, stimulus generalization manifests itself in my students; it's responsible for their pervasive dislike of most academic work. As soon as they walk into a classroom and see pencils, paper, and books, they retreat in their mind just as effectively as I retreated when I saw the bats and gloves come out of the storage shed. The title of this chapter is "The Domino Effect," which is really another way of saying stimulus generalization.

Once a student starts to do poorly in English, he will have a difficult time in math, and then he will have a difficult time in history, and consumer education, and so on. The stimulus generalizes—first it's English class, then it's the idea of opening a textbook, then it's the idea of writing, then it's homework assignments, then it's the more general stimulus of a classroom, and then we really begin to lose the student.

If you want to understand why students slip away from us academically and behaviorally, think back to my retelling of my experiences at home plate. The same feelings of frustration, humiliation, despondency, depression, and self-loathing that appear in the sports arena also appear in the academic environment.

Just as most field sports require good eye-hand coordination, physical strength, and the ability to run fast, almost all academic courses require three main things: the ability to read, write, and pay attention.

Most of my students have difficulty with one or more of these things. Can they be blamed for behaving the way they do?

Can they be blamed for beginning to act out within the first five minutes of the first day of the school year? They haven't planned this behavior—it's a reflex; they hear "open to page 33," and their stomach ties up in knots. It doesn't matter whether they're in English class or math class or history class—they know that they can't read well just as I knew that I couldn't hit the ball. They know that they can't write past the fifth grade level just as I knew that I was going to throw the ball straight to the first baseman, but it wouldn't reach him.

So, they do the minimum work necessary, or they start talking to the person next to them so they get thrown out of class, or they sleep, or they take out a blank piece of paper and start drawing sketches—anything to avoid doing the assignment.

This sets students into a relentless downward spiral of failure.

A student knows that he or she cannot write well, and so balks when asked to write, delays getting started, writes the minimum necessary, finishes early, and complains the entire time that the assignment is "stupid" and "boring." Because the student didn't make an earnest effort, the writing ability stays the same, which means it's getting worse relative to the other students who are progressing at a normal rate.

Academic ability is very much like income. Because prices are always increasing, income must constantly increase in order to maintain equivalent purchasing power over time. It's the same thing in an academic environment; because teacher expectations and the difficulty of the schoolwork is always increasing, writing, reading, and comprehension ability must constantly improve in order for the student to maintain the status quo of academic performance.

So, the student with a learning disability does not practice, and therefore the skills remain the same. Time moves on, and the student is found to be performing at below grade level within a short time. Students are made aware of their subpar performances, which further frustrates them and makes it less likely that they will genuinely try to improve and more likely that they will act out and get in trouble at school.

This cycle continues of not practicing, not getting better, watching a performance drop, getting more frustrated, becoming less likely to practice and more likely to continue to decrease in ability. It's a maddening downward spiral that sometimes cannot be stopped.

Further aggravating the situation and feeding the cycle of failure are well-meaning teachers who yell out their version of "KEEP YOUR EYE ON THE BALL!"

They say things such as, "SUZANNE, PAY ATTENTION," or "JAMES, PLEASE CONTINUE WRITING; YOU ONLY WROTE A FEW SENTENCES." These reminders have their place, but teachers shouldn't be repeating them hundreds of times. For heaven's sake, Jimmy *knows* that he has only written a few sentences. Suzanne is *not* going to suddenly and dramatically improve the percentage of time she pays attention just because you said "pay attention." These redirections are important and are part of good teaching, but when they're said over and over and over again, they become ineffective. They change from being somewhat helpful teacher vocalizations to unwelcome reminders of a disability.

I've found in my life that sometimes bad things happen for good reasons, or at least when bad things happen, some good can come out of them. Now that I'm a teacher, I see that my painful memories of attempting to play baseball have given me a greater understanding of the frustration my students feel when reading and writing.

Every time one of my students says something like, "Awww, I don't feel like reading this," I remember the frustration I felt every time I struck out, and I think before I react. My childhood baseball memories also help me understand why some of my students exhibit challenging behavior when faced with academic tasks that they know deep down they cannot accomplish as well as they would like.

The expression, "as well as they would like," brings up another interesting point. My students want to be able to read and write with fluency and to perform well academically in general, even though their statements and their behaviors might indicate otherwise.

I'll tell you something secret about my childhood baseball experiences: deep down, I desperately wanted to hit that ball.

When I approached the plate, I begged myself to please, please just hit it.

Pay attention, keep your eye on the ball, don't worry about what other people say. The other kids rolled their eyes up to the sky because I couldn't hit the ball consistently, and they probably thought that there was a big difference between them and me, but I was very much like them, really.

I wanted to hit the ball much more than they wanted me to.

I wanted to be buddies with them, I wanted to be accepted by them, I wanted to be viewed as competent, I wanted to be fought over when sides were chosen in the game. I stepped up to the plate many times and put a glove on my hand many times, with a desperate hope that somehow I would be better today, that I wouldn't strike out, that I would make the big catch, that when I threw the ball to the second baseman, it wouldn't fly over his head.

It's the same thing with my students. Once they get over their complaining about having to open the book and turn to page 133, it's fascinating to watch them begin in earnest to try, yet another time, to try to read just a little bit better, to understand just a little bit more, to write at least one complete sentence without any grammatical or spelling errors.

So, don't get irritated when they turn in incomplete work. Don't give them dirty looks when they summarize a long film in four sentences, leaving out major plot points. Remember what it was like to strike out partially because of nervousness and partially because of inability.

Always try to respond to substandard student work in a helpful, understanding way.

Keep in mind that your students may not be used to that. The first five or ten times that you come over to them to look at their work, they might eye you warily. They will probably worry that you will criticize and belittle them. Some students might refuse to let you see their work for a short while as they work up enough courage to face what they felt would be unavoidable teacher criticism and cruel snickering from their classmates.

But they will all learn, after a short while, that there will be no belittling in your classroom.

There will be no reason to feel shame, there will be no sneers, no snide comments, and no eyes rolled to the sky. Sit down next to them and help them. Tell them what they did that was good, and give them the guidance they need to improve. When the students relax, when they understand that they are in a safe environment, their performance improves somewhat because they feel secure enough to take academic risks, and risk-taking is a key component of academic progress. When they realize that you will only try to help them and not hurt them, they will be more receptive to your suggestions, which is also an important part of improving your skills, whatever they may be.

In this environment, more often than you expect, they do it. Some of them hit the ball over the fence from time to time. They explain the motivation of a character, and they're right. They author a short dramatic scene, and it's truly suspenseful. I'm so glad to be there with them to see the smiles on their faces when they hit that home run.

14

REACHING CARL

Carl was one of the quietest students in my class, and I could never seem to reach him.

He was pleasant, cooperative, always had his materials with him, and almost always completed his homework; he was a great student to have in class. The problem was his extreme resistance to contributing verbally, regardless of the activity in the classroom. During the entire first semester, he did not raise his hand to ask or answer a question or contribute to a discussion in any way. He always completed assignments and cooperated with everything I asked him to do; it was clear to me that he had learned years ago how to "fly under the radar" and not do anything to attract the attention of the teacher.

This is a common technique used by students with disabilities: avoid scrutiny by being a perfect angel.

But, don't let that work well with you; try to circulate through the classroom and keep an eye both on students that are misbehaving and students who are trying to avoid attention by remaining quiet and being cooperative. I would regularly go over to him and ask him how he was doing on the assignment, ask him to expand on some of the things he had written, and so on. The resulting conversation was pleasant, although it was always brief. Some speech therapists might say that Carl had an expressive language deficit because no matter what the question, even if I asked him about high interest things like what he did over the weekend, what he did on his family's farm over Thanksgiving break, and so on, he never said more than a few short sentences.

One day, I was able to encourage him enough to finally volunteer an answer, and I'm going to tell you how it happened. I don't want you to get the impression that I think I'm some kind of master teacher; his voluntarily calling out an answer to a question was one of the biggest surprises of the school year.

Good teachers give their students a well-rounded education. I had heard in graduate school, in my own personal life, and from the administration of the high school, that students are graduating from high school without a broad education.

Oh, they could calculate the cube root of 100, and tell you the events of the Second World War, and explain the difference between a solute and a solvent and a verb and an adjective, but they didn't know a lot of practical matters, such as what the fine print means on a credit card advertisement, why more RAM is better in a computer, and why it's not a good idea to be mean to people whom you might need as friends one day. Business owners, parents, and the community in general have been calling on educators to provide students with more than just what my father used to call "book smarts."

So, I try to incorporate a variety of activities, materials, and lectures in class to try to broaden my students' education. Prior to my being a teacher, I was a computer programmer and systems analyst for many years. When I casually mentioned to my students terms like "hard disk," "the computer doesn't have enough RAM," "if you make a website, make sure you get a good hosting company," and other such phrases, most of them returned blank stares to me.

Most of them didn't know what a hard disk was, they didn't know what RAM was, they didn't know how a website worked, they didn't know how e-mail worked, they didn't know to get a free e-mail account, they didn't know how to upload pictures and videos so other people all over the world could look at them for free, and they didn't know about message boards and the fascinating and extraordinary opportunity they provide for you to communicate with people all over the world about nearly any topic of interest. In fact, you could reverse the logical statement and say that what they did know about computers and how they operated could fit on a small piece of paper.

This lack of knowledge is not acceptable. Try to incorporate one or two units on computer technology into the English curriculum. Some might argue with you that this is an unorthodox step, but in fact the state of Illinois has over thirty educational objectives in the English language arts, and several of them include achieving fluency in the use of technology to prepare presentations in electronic media to communicate for a variety of purposes.

As your students learn about how computers work, they will have to read, do research, make comparisons, write summaries, interpret graphs and charts, evaluate what they have read from a variety of sources, listen to each other's opinions, and engage in other tasks and activities that involve higher order thinking processes and that help students achieve a surprisingly high number of educational objectives in the Illinois learning standards for high school English language arts. (Some of your students will resist this sort of thing; read more about this phenomenon in the chapter "Why are we learning this in English class?" later in this book.)

Any time you expose your students to a new concept and watch them furrow their eyebrows in thought, you should feel satisfied. This is exactly what happened when I required them to perform some simple calculations in binary math, the same kind of math that a computer processor does. I know that this is not related to the study of symbolism in Romeo and Juliet, but English class is more than just that, as I have said.

By requiring students to learn a new concept, and read instructions about how to make calculations using this new concept, and then actually having to make those calculations, and evaluating their answer based on specific criteria to assess the accuracy of the answer, teachers help students improve the same concentration and critical thinking skills that they will need when they read their first lease or write their first letter to an insurance company.

Plus, a trick to getting kids with literacy disabilities to engage in the lesson is to introduce them to new things. Novelty is like fresh air in the classroom. No, binary math isn't in the English curriculum, but reading directions, studying projector presentations, listening to instructions, and writing the results of an analysis are.

The task involved reading instructions in a PowerPoint presentation on the projector screen and using a series of cards with ones and zeros on them so they could simulate how a computer performs math. The activity only lasted for about twenty minutes and was something that the students had a lot of fun with. They enjoyed using the cards and engaging in a different sort of activity, and all the time the room was full of excitement as my students' brains kicked into high gear.

It came time for the students to call out the answers to some of the exercises. I went through each "test" question one by one on the projector, and students called out their answers. On the second question, Carl called out his answer before anyone else, and it was right. I had to quickly compose myself so as not to appear too shocked to the students and especially to Carl.

"Good job!" I said, and moved on to a more difficult question. Within a few seconds of the appearance of the more difficult question on the projector, Carl had figured out the answer and called out the correct number before anyone else in the class. I said, "Carl, you're really good at this, you know that? You ought to go into computer programming." He looked up at me with a faint smile on his face, and we locked eye contact. I had never seen him look at me like that with pride and pleasure showing clearly on his face. His smile broadened.

I had reached Carl.

I must be honest with you that I was questioning the relevance of the activity to English class; after all, they were largely doing arithmetic and logic in their head. What would happen when my students' parents asked them, "so what BOOK DID YOU READ in English class today?"

Of course, during your first year of teaching, second-guessing the wisdom of your lessons is a constant activity, like swatting mosquitoes. The enthusiasm my students were showing toward this activity helped reduce my feelings of self-doubt, but they persisted—until I heard Carl call out correct answers to questions again and again. I had stumbled onto an activity that Carl could sink his teeth into and excel at, and the resulting smile on his face was another high point of my first year of teaching.

Maybe I had helped him discover a strength he didn't know he had, and maybe this discovery could help give him direction when choosing a career once he graduated in four short months.

I learned that diversity is good in the classroom and that you can't predict how well a lesson will go on until you actually try it. Let's say you try a lesson that doesn't go well; maybe the kids found it boring, or you discovered that it was too difficult. You shouldn't view this as a failure on your part as a teacher; you should learn from the experience and move on.

And, when you're lucky enough to have stumbled onto something that the kids enjoy even though it's an activity that you yourself doubted (even though you designed it), it's a beautiful thing that you should cherish. But, don't make the mistake of thinking that just because a lesson you designed went well that you should win Teacher of the Year; believe me, other wonderful ideas you have will fall flat on their face.

But that day, Carl felt good; he felt competent; the other students looked at him with surprise and awe as he called out correct answer after correct answer. It doesn't get better than that.

15

MY MOTHER TORE
THAT SHIT UP

Years ago there was a TV movie called "Sybil," starring Sally Field, about an adult woman with multiple personality disorder who manifested sixteen distinct personalities. Sybil had one of the most extreme cases of this disorder ever recorded, and the range of personalities and behaviors she showed was astonishing and shocking. Joanne Woodward, who played Sybil's therapist, came upon Sybil one day as she was exhibiting one of her many personalities, the bizarre behavior of an emotionally damaged young child.

When the therapist saw what Sybil was doing (I can't remember exactly what it was), she shouted out a famous line that referred to Sybil's cruel parents: "My God! What the hell did they do to you!?"

I wanted to exclaim the same thing to Alice, one of my students.

Thank goodness that Alice didn't have multiple personality disorder because her one personality was more than I could handle. When I saw the unnerving and extremely distracting behaviors she showed in the classroom, I realized that this is a child who may have grown up with little structure in the home, and I thought to myself, just like Sybil's therapist, what the hell did her parents do to her?

Later I amended this question to be, what the hell did her parents do and *not* do to her? By "not do to her," I mean, not praise good behavior from her in a meaningful way, not set limits, not give consequences for unacceptable behavior, not instill a sense of self-respect.

Alice would not (or could not) stop talking to other people around her, would not follow classroom and school rules, and was foulmouthed and disrespectful to me.

She sometimes completed classroom assignments with near grade-level competence, but she did not respond in a meaningful way to the praise and encouragement I gave her when she did so. Nearly every day, Alice would exhibit one or more of the following challenging behaviors. These behaviors could be exhibited at any time; it didn't matter whether it was before class, during a time when I was actively teaching a concept, during the middle of a student presentation, during a film; nothing seemed to be effective at getting this student—a student with intellectual competence and great potential—to focus on the lesson.

- Eating food in a messy way
- Taking out her cell phone to text message someone
- Talking to the person next to her, the person three seats away from her, the person five seats away from her, or the person on the other side of the room
- Yawning in a loud, exaggerated manner
- Making faces and giggling at other students
- Complaining out loud about the lesson: "I can't believe we have to do this shit," "This bullshit is so lame," and so forth.
- Playing the Ignore-The-Teacher game, which involves an almost religious devotion to completely disregarding the existence of the teacher and what he says
- Playing the Explosive-Indignation game, which uses the Ignore-The-Teacher game. You play this game by first playing the Ignore-The-Teacher game for a short time, and then as the teacher repeats the request the third or fourth time, suddenly exclaiming, "GOD DAMN! WHAT DO YOU WANT?"
- Ignoring me when I say, "Good morning, Alice"

Now, you might think to yourself when reading this description of this student, "How in the world do you do it?" Many people have said to me, "I don't know how you can deal with these kids." A member of the security staff in the school where I teach said to me in the hallway once, "You do a great job of handling those brats you have in your classroom." In graduate school, I met many people who said, "High school Special Ed? Oh my goodness, I could never do that. I'd be afraid to! To be in that classroom all by yourself with a bunch of those big kids—whewwww! Not for me!"

For some unknown reason, that's not the reaction I have when faced with students like Alice. Sure, there are times when I get frustrated and angry, but these emotions don't come to the surface much. Rather, I become curious as to why she is behaving the way she is, and I view the situation sort of like a puzzle.

In graduate school, several professors who are experts in classroom behavior management implied, as did much of the scholarly reading assigned to us in those classes, that there is actually an answer to the problem of Alice's behavior. All I had to do was apply the perfect combination of the most appropriate teacher responses, and she would be transformed before my eyes into a model student.

As my grandmother used to say, "Feh!"

There is no magically effective response or combination of responses to a student who displays dysfunctional layer upon dysfunctional layer of inappropriate behavior.

A famous psychologist named Albert Ellis developed Rational Emotive Therapy in which, among other things, he examined what he called Ten Irrational Thoughts and the damage that they can cause. One of them is, and I paraphrase, "Every problem has a solution, and I should be able to find that solution. If I don't or can't, I'm stupid and incompetent." This irrational thought was haunting me for months. Nothing I tried was helping Alice reduce the number of times that she displayed dysfunctional, disruptive behavior in the classroom.

I tried speaking to her quietly and privately in the hallway before class. This did not work because she would walk away from me as I was speaking to her.

I tried addressing her behavior in class, by saying something like, "Alice, please stop speaking to Freddie and focus your attention up here on the board." This worked for literally seconds at a time. She would stop talking and face her body toward the board just long enough for me to divert my attention away from her and back to teaching.

Once she saw that I was back on track with teaching a lesson, she would quietly turn her body back to Freddie and continue gesticulating towards him, giggling, laughing, and distracting nearly everybody in the classroom. She was an expert at complying with teacher requests quickly so as to make it appear in the mind of the teacher that she was being compliant. In fact, this was simply an effective technique to deflect teacher attention away quickly. There was no intention, it seemed (or ability), on her part to change her classroom behavior in the long term to any significant degree.

One of the first things that I tried was a behavior point system with visual feedback, something that would, I'm sure, elicit smiles and supportive nods of the head from my graduate school professors. I had to explain the system to her at the beginning of class, in front of all the other students, because Alice would routinely walk away from me if I tried to talk to her privately outside in the hallway.

I explained that she was being given five opportunities to correct her disruptive behavior before being written up and sent down to the assistant principal's office. Each time her behavior was corrected, a dot was drawn on the board. I did this so Alice could have a visual representation of the adverse effects of her behavior on the board, which I hoped would help give her some tangible, immediate feedback. It was partially effective, but only when it reached the fourth dot.

Alice knew all about the fourth dot.

It was the only thing she really needed to pay attention to; a clear indication that it was time to change her behavior, which she was entirely capable of doing if she wanted to, I think, and I emphasize the words "if she wanted to." (In fact, most modern behavior research strongly encourages educators and parents to find something that a child *wants to do* and use that as a potential reward—a reinforcer—when the child exhibits a positive change in his or her behavior.)

Much to my relief, it appeared to work. For the first day or two, after about ten or fifteen minutes, Alice had three or four dots next to her name, and once she did, her behavior changed. She turned around, faced the activity that was going on in the classroom, and started acting much more mature. I started feeling so, so, so good about myself. Changing student behavior is a piece of cake, I thought, all you need to do is apply a little bit of behavior theory to these simple classroom problems and they'll disappear faster than snowflakes at Kilauea.

Just in time for me to begin feeling completely smug about the genius of my "dot on the board" system, it began to fail, and I had absolutely no idea why.

When you build a thing, regardless of whether it's a better mousetrap or a behavior management system, and that thing fails, it's unfortunate that it failed, but it's worse if it fails and you don't know why it failed. At least when a thing you build fails, and you know why it fails, you can look at the broken parts, replay the failure in your mind, pinpoint the feature or part which was incorrectly designed or executed, and rebuild the thing with a redesigned part or feature such that the likelihood of future failure is greatly reduced.

But when the thing you built fails utterly, destroying itself, smoking, steaming, hissing, squeaking, emitting an acrid smell, and dropping down on the ground in a pile of broken parts, and you have no idea why everything fell apart so fast, there's no way that you can learn about what to do better next time so you can rebuild the thing to operate the way you want it to.

Very quickly, I was looking at the broken, acrid-smelling, utterly failed attempt at a behavior management intervention.

After the second day or so, Alice, upon seeing dots go up next to her name on the board, suddenly changed her reaction to the dots. After I drew the fourth dot on the board, she loudly proclaimed to a friend of hers on the other side of the classroom (during class, it didn't matter if the person she was talking to was five inches or five feet away from her; she simply adjusted the volume accordingly), "I don't give a shit, let him write me up."

The fifth dot went up. I reminded Alice to please turn around and continue writing her assignment. She did not.

I wrote her up and sent her down to the assistant principal's office. As she left the classroom, she wore a defiant smile and mumbled a series of barely recognizable expletives. Interestingly, the other students became quiet and showed me, through their behavior, that they knew that Alice's behavior was clearly inappropriate; she did not receive any support from the other students when she was asked to leave the classroom. I was disoriented and somewhat upset at the sudden failure of my system, and I had no idea why it failed.

Most new teachers will then wonder what went wrong, what was the flaw in the dot system, what should have been done differently, and most of all, why did a system that worked so well for two days suddenly fail so miserably?

Don't engage in the irrational thinking described earlier; don't assume that there is a solution to this problem that was clear, yet hidden, and the fact that you have not uncovered it shows that you are an incompetent oaf.

You're not an incompetent oaf.

What I failed to realize at the time was that I was working with a live human being, and not only a human being, but an angst-filled, emotionally volatile teenager whose maddeningly unpredictable behavior gets its energy from two understandable conflicts: the desire to love and be loved that fights with the fear of being unloved and unlovable and the desire to assert independence which fights with the desire to conform and be accepted by peers. My goodness, Alice herself probably didn't understand why my behavior management idea worked one day and not the next, or maybe she did, but she didn't want to tell me.

This was only one month into the school year. The intervention of writing her up was clearly not working; she had already been written up two or three times for the same thing—excessive talking and disruptive behavior and refusal to comply with my requests to participate in the current classroom activity. As I said earlier, my supervisor strongly encouraged me to get in touch with the family, so I decided to try to do so. When I called the house, I only got an answering machine, so I decided to do the old-fashioned thing and write a letter.

Here's the letter I wrote to Alice's mother:

Dear Ms. X,

Please allow me to introduce myself; I am Alice's English teacher.

Lately, Alice's behavior in class has been more and more distracting. She has been sent to the assistant principal and written up at least five times over the past month for being disobedient and disruptive in class.

Alice will likely fail this course if she does not listen more and talk less in class.

I am writing this letter to you to invite you to school for a meeting with me. This meeting will help us come up with a plan to help Alice succeed in this class. I recommend that Alice be present at the meeting.

Date: (removed)
Place: (removed)

If you cannot make the meeting, please e-mail me at (removed) to arrange for an alternative time. Unfortunately, there is no phone in the classroom. Thank you very much for your help.

I sent it off in the mail and was nervously awaiting the meeting, which was in about a week and a half. I rehearsed in the car as I drove to and from school what I would say to Alice's mother at the meeting.

About three days later, as I was talking to students at the front of the class before the tardy bell, Alice walked in and started talking to some of her friends. She positioned herself and adjusted the volume of her voice to ensure that I clearly heard what it was that she was saying.

She said, "Do you believe that shit? He thinks he's so smart, sending my mother some stupid ass letter about some stupid ass meeting. My mother got that letter, and she tore that shit up. She tore that shit up and threw it right in the trash. [mumbling . . . mumbling] . . . sending my mother some stupid as letter about [imitating me] 'Oh, Alice isn't behaving in the classroom. I want her to be sure to pass the class.' My mother tore that stupid shit up."

I could feel my face burning with embarrassment and anger.

Alice got me—she did it—she pushed buttons I didn't realize that I had. I hate being in a situation where my emotions get away from me like a greased pig and run wild around my brain, smashing highly fragile illusions and dusty old archetypes into bits.

I wanted to say things to her that would have gotten me in trouble with the superintendent.

I wanted to tell her to sit down and shut her filthy mouth. I wanted to tell her that if her mother actually did tear up the letter, it was because her mother was heartsick and mind-numbingly frustrated over the disgraceful, outrageous, obnoxious, offensive, vulgar attitude and behavior that she showed.

I wanted to tell her that her mother tore up the letter because she couldn't take another reminder of the obstinate, insolent person her daughter had become, that she had no solutions to the problem, and that this was a pathetic situation indeed.

I wanted to say to Alice that I felt pity for her if I were wrong and her mother committed a worse act—tearing up the letter because of apathy toward the welfare of her child. I wanted to say to her that I understood now why she was the way she is—she got it from her mother.

What kind of a mother would receive a letter from her daughter's high school in which a teacher shows concern for her daughter's grade, clearly expresses the fact that her daughter's outrageous misbehavior is jeopardizing her ability to obtain a diploma, shows a willingness to spend time with the family after hours to work on a solution to the problem, and then takes that letter, tears it up in the trash in full view of her daughter, and continues doing what it was that she was doing?

All these thoughts and emotions flashed through me in a few seconds at the same time that I was trying to advise another student as to how to best complete an assignment that he had not yet turned in. If you're thinking of becoming a teacher and you have a hard time multitasking, take my friendly advice: choose another career.

Embarrassment was also a powerful emotion at that moment.

The students she was talking to also were minor players in the misbehavior game in this class; they were the ones she spoke to, they were the ones who laughed when she said something outrageous, they were the ones who were her defense attorneys (unpaid with money but paid with lesson-avoiding entertainment) when consequences were occurring as a result of her noncompliance with classroom rules. They taught me to get her away from those students as quickly as possible and get her to stop boasting loudly to the entire class that my attempt at behavior intervention had failed so laughably.

I thought that her words were making me look foolish, therefore making me ineffective at controlling her behavior and the behavior of the entire class. I could see doom in the future. I felt ineffective, unprepared, and disoriented. But, I chose to say nothing, mostly because I couldn't think of anything to say that wouldn't result in a curtly worded letter from the human resources department.

It turns out that this was an extremely good decision, although I didn't know it at the time. As I'm learning more and more as I get older and older, it's usually better to keep your mouth shut.

Further compounding the emotional roller coaster was sort of a simultaneous meta-analysis that was occurring. Why was I getting so angry? Could it be that I'm not going to be a good teacher? Could it be that I am going to feel like this frequently, and it's going to make it impossible for me to treat all students with the same amount of compassion and respect as I'm supposed to? The hostility I felt toward Alice troubled me.

I was supposed to be an unflappable rock of compassion and equanimity. All these things were going through my mind at the same time when the tardy bell rang. I was "on." One by one, the faces turned towards me in anticipation of my starting the class.

Some people may think that becoming a teacher at forty-two is sort of late, and that because of my "advanced age," I may not have the stamina to be successful. But I say to these doubters that there are distinct advantages to inserting yourself into this environment in the middle of your life, and one of the advantages became clear at this moment—I was old enough to know my strengths and my weaknesses, and I knew that one of my strengths is that I *know* that I have a good brain and a good heart, and that I know that I've been through many difficult situations in the past, and that I have been tough enough and resourceful enough to get through them just fine.

It was time for me to get a little bit of attitude myself. I was the damned adult in charge in *this* classroom.

As I said previously, I did not address her description of the letter-tearing event with her mother, and I continued on as usual. Much to my great relief, the class, including Alice, became quiet and cooperative, and the lesson proceeded without much further incident. Alice was relatively quiet after that, and her behavior was much improved from the usual "Would you sign my petition to be Juvenile Delinquent Of The Year award" routines.

In fact, Alice's mother did not appear for the meeting, and did not e-mail me. There were no messages from her in my mailbox; she did not call or make an attempt to contact me through the front office. I tried calling the home but simply got an answering machine, as usual.

I wonder, even to this day, about the truthfulness of Alice's story. I think that maybe she intercepted the letter, read it, and threw it out in a place where her mother would never be able to find it. Her behavior improved somewhat after that day. She was still a distraction, but she was more compliant with my requests and cursed me out with less vigor and with PG-rated words, rather than the NC-17 vocabulary with which she began the school year.

What was the purpose for her loud announcement at the beginning of class? People do things for reasons; even when somebody does a seemingly random act, perhaps this random act satisfies the person in some way because they planned to do a random act that day. What was the purpose of the loud talking down she had indirectly given me?

Nobody else had known about the letter, so she felt no public embarrassment about my sending it. By making the announcement she did to her peers, she revealed to them, either knowingly or un-knowingly, that her behavior was jeopardizing her grade and that it was so inappropriate that it prompted extraordinary action from the teacher.

Was this giving her more esteem in the eyes of her peers?

When she was making the announcement, they listened to her passively but offered no overt encouragement. I had a good rela-tionship with the other students, and I didn't hear any comments like, "Oh, he's an asshole anyway." They simply listened to her with-out much reaction.

Perhaps she was, deep down, upset at the message within the let-ter but didn't want to acknowledge its message, so she sought out her peers for encouragement and validation. This is something we all do as adults—when faced with an accusation of inappropriate be-havior on our part, we usually will call the friends who we know are most likely to defend our behavior and "forget" to call the people we know who might validate the outrageously unfair criticism we have received.

Or, maybe I was on target initially, and her mother had in fact torn up the letter into little pieces and thrown it in the trash in full view of Alice.

Imagine how that would make a seventeen-year-old girl feel!

Maybe it made her think that her mother didn't care or was too busy to deal with it. It certainly modeled inappropriate behavior—tearing up a letter on school letterhead without showing the com-mon courtesy of at least an attempt at a response to a letter that had a kind tone. I would not be surprised if this scenario did take place and that her mother exhibited a lack of interest in doing what needed to be done to ensure the success of her daughter as she grew to adulthood.

The tearing up of the letter might have been simply another un-kind act added to the thousands of previous unkind acts which col-lectively formed a two-pronged assault on Alice's well-being—one prong deflating her self-esteem because her mother's inaction demonstrated that she felt that Alice was not worth her time, and the other prong holding Alice's social and emotional development at bay by the withholding of appropriate guidance and consequences for her irritating behavior.

I think the letter was a good thing for me to have done, despite my moments of anger, despair, and embarrassment that Alice's victory speech produced. A few weeks later, she was working on a group project next to Freddie, one of her compatriots. Freddie began acting very immature, became off task, and started arguing with Alice about something totally unrelated to any academic activity. I walked over near them, but they didn't see me because I was behind them. I heard the following exchange:

> *Alice*: "Dag, Freddie, you're acting crazy. I mean, you want me to act crazy and shit, too, and I do, but you're just acting crazy, like a little kid or something."
>
> *Freddie*: (A hurt look on his face; these two are friends.) "Alice, you're changing on me. What do you mean, I'm acting like a little kid?! You're changing." (Alice looked straight ahead.)

What I heard this, I wanted to jump up and down and scream, "WOOOOOOHOOOOOOOOOOO! MY BABY'S GROWING UP!"

Alice was changing, and Freddie knew it.

This was the first time that I had ever, ever, ever heard Alice criticize Freddie's childish behavior. This little, seemingly insignificant verbal exchange between these two was one of the highlights of my first year as a teacher.

It was significant to me because they didn't know I was standing there; their exchange was a real exchange and allowed me a rare genuine look at what Alice was thinking. It was extremely rewarding for me to see, almost before my eyes, Alice's maturity lurch forward; it seemed like almost at that moment she gained insight into my perspective—that her behavior was immature and inappropriate. Maybe she realized that if she was old enough to have a baby, she was old enough to be able to control her behavior.

As the year continued, I tried other behavior interventions with Alice. I found that the most effective one was simply moving her to another area of the classroom where she was not facing, and not in proximity to, the other students who triggered her off-task behavior.

Her grades improved because she was able to focus her competent intellect onto the task at hand. She seemed uncomfortable when I praised her for her academic work, and her face was blank when I handed back her first A. She knew that I did not give her the A—I am a tough grader and require that my students earn their grades—she knew that she earned it and seemed unprepared emotionally for seeing the clarity of the connection between her effort and the good results that she was capable of producing.

Alice's attendance was excellent, which sometimes, I admit, used to frustrate me, and this frustration made me feel guilty. More than once I thought to myself, "My goodness, can't she cut class once in a while?" Then, I'd feel bad about thinking these things. Then, I realized that thinking these things didn't mean that I had to quit my job.

(One of the funniest things that happened to me when I was student teaching was when I was walking down the hallway to my classroom. Eddie, one of my students, saw me, rolled his eyes in an exaggerated way, and yelled out, "GOD—DAAAAMMMMMMMNNNN!!!! DON'T YOU EHHHHHVERRRR MISS . . . ONE . . . DAY!!!" I couldn't help myself—I cracked up, and he managed a smile, too. I sometimes thought about saying the exact same thing to Alice as she walked into the room, and this thinking made me have to stifle a giggle.)

Suddenly, Alice stopped showing up for class.

Day after day, her seat was empty. This was very unusual—something was wrong. I went down to the assistant principal's office, and one of the staff members told me that her family had transferred to Chicago and that she had withdrawn from this school.

The emotion that I felt at that moment clarifies the fact that sometimes it's the most challenging student that you grow the most attached to. I was disappointed. A little bit of me was relieved because she was frequently a disruption in the classroom despite my most inventive attempts at behavior interventions. But, I was also disappointed and sad. I was disappointed because I knew I would probably never see her again, and I wouldn't have the pleasure of seeing her academic performance and her self-esteem improve.

I was sad because I found out that she was moving into a neighborhood where there were known to be drug gangs and high crime rates. She was just on the cusp of making measurable improvement in the way that she thought and the way that she viewed herself, and now she was going to be transferred into a neighborhood and a school with far more opportunities to be pulled into delinquent behavior.

I am in no way criticizing the school Alice transferred to or the dedication and passion of its faculty and administration, all of whom, I am sure, share my love of students and my loathing of those who would lead them to harm.

She did not yet have the self-esteem or the maturity to resist the temptation of gang influence. I feared that the work I had done, and the work that my dedicated colleagues had done, would be undone quickly in her new environment. I never did see Alice again, but I hope that she stays alive, stays strong, and makes the right decisions that will allow her to realize her true potential.

Alice was also a participant in another failed attempt on my part to control classroom behavior; this is detailed in the chapter "The Crashing and Burning of a Group Contingency" later in this book.

16

THE WISE ENFORCER

It's very common for students to change their behavior—and the way they react to your behavior—from one day to the next, even from one hour to the next.

As a new teacher, it's easy to blame these mood swings on yourself, but you have to remember that there is a bigger picture that needs to be viewed before judgment can be passed on your teaching ability. Much of the time, the mood swings are the result of factors entirely out of the control of the teacher.

When I was student teaching, I had a student named Donna who was usually in a good mood and participated readily in class discussions. She had the slightly unacceptable habit of getting into fistfights with other girls from time to time, but I was always amused by the fact that she would often become belligerent and physically violent literally five feet from the door of the assistant principal's office.

This ensured that her fight was extremely short-lived, resulting in minimal risk of injury while preserving her tough reputation. One day Donna was in a very different mood—she was noncompliant with my requests, quiet, and reluctant to participate in class discussion. We had some minor unpleasant words, but I decided to let the issue go, give Donna some space, and let her be in a bad mood because I realized that something was wrong.

When you're a teacher, you don't need to be the top dog all the time; you sometimes need to put your ego aside and let an affront go. Doing so can sometimes result in a much better relationship with a student, and a more cooperative and understanding student, in the future.

Later, upon speaking to my mentor teacher, I discovered that something was indeed very wrong; Donna had been assaulted by her grandfather with a hammer earlier that morning.

She had escaped serious injury and decided to attend school, even though she had to wear long pants and long sleeves to hide the bruise marks on her arms and her legs. Donna's change in mood had nothing to do with my teaching or my classroom management skills. This illustrates how it's important, when teaching, to use your wisdom and listen to your heart when making spur-of-the-moment decisions about how to handle disruptive behavior.

If this entire incident had been videotaped, I'm sure that many teachers would have criticized the way I handled the situation; they might have said that inaction on my part would show to the students that I'm not in control of the classroom and would increase the likelihood that serious misbehavior would occur in the future.

I disagree.

Imagine how you would feel in the following situation: You are driving home after work, and you have just picked up your three-year-old son from day care. You are stopped by a police officer and given a ticket for traveling 36 miles an hour in a 35-mile-an-hour zone. The police officer has a stern demeanor and is not interested in listening to your side of the story.

You then drive to the supermarket to pick up a few groceries. You park in the parking lot, remove your son from the child seat, and start walking with him toward the store. Just then, another police officer walks over and, in a gruff and authoritative manner, gives you a ticket for littering. You begin to object that you have not littered, but he raises his voice and in a condescending, arrogant way, he says that your son dropped a small candy wrapper from his hand just as he exited your car. He hands you the ticket, tells you about your court date, and walks off.

Highly irritated, you go into the store, do some shopping, and return to your car, which has a ticket on the windshield. On the ticket it says that your front bumper is one half inch over the yellow dividing line between the parking spaces, which is a clear violation of section 11.3 subparagraph (b) of the vehicle code in the town where you live. Instructions for paying the fine are listed on the ticket.

Answer this question: at this moment, what's your attitude toward police officers?

Do you feel grateful to them? Do you feel that they're doing a good job, and their strict enforcement of every letter of every law is good for you, your child, and the community?

Do you believe that the three tickets you received in the past thirty minutes are going to make you more compliant, more cooperative, calmer, and safer? Are you going to say to yourself, "My goodness, I'd better watch how I park and drive, and I'd better watch Junior's hands to make sure he isn't littering in our beautiful supermarket parking lot! Thank goodness the police are conscientious around here and have stopped me before I've done more damage to myself and the community!"

Of course not.

You're going to be angry and resentful, you're going to feel that you've been unfairly singled out, and you're going to feel like taking off time from work and fighting all of these tickets in court. You plan on telling the judge that the police are overzealous in their enforcement of the law and there are much more important ways for them to be spending their taxpayer-paid hours than ticketing a young parent for a series of insignificant infractions of the law.

True, you did break the law, and in all three cases the police officers were entirely justified in giving you citations for these infractions. But, what would you do if you were the commander of the police officers who wrote these tickets? It's likely that you would say something like the following. "Yes, Officer Jones, these laws are on the books, and it is true that your job is to enforce the law in an authoritative manner. However, you must remember that the power you possess to enforce the law must be used judiciously. Law enforcement exists for several reasons: to protect the public, to enforce the law, and to help people whenever possible.

"Ultimately, though, police officers such as yourself have the larger and more important purposes of reducing the amount of crime in our community while at the same time improving the relationship between the police and the public. In order to accomplish these objectives, you must remember that the people you protect and serve are fallible people; they have emotions, fears, and desires, and nearly all of them wish to do good.

"Because of this fact, you must include compassion, circumspection, and wisdom when deciding how to act when witnessing minor infractions of the law.

"I cannot stop you from giving citations for things like speeding one mile an hour over the limit. However, I ask that you think about the effects that such actions on your part will have on the relationship the police have with the public. I believe that by giving the citations that you did to this person, you have damaged his relationship with all of us.

"Perhaps if you, upon witnessing his violations of the law, had educated him about the littering law, about the parking law, and about the speed limits, rather than giving him citations for these infractions, you would have been more effective at encouraging him to comply with the law in the future.

"Perhaps giving him tickets for all three citations within thirty minutes also was not an effective use of your power.

"Perhaps if you had chosen to not give a citation for the littering violation and the parking violation and only educated him about the speed limit, it would have been even more effective at helping him and other members of the public to see the police just as much as educators as enforcers. Perhaps this improved view of the police by the public would help them to work with us more closely, help us catch more serious criminals, and comply with the community laws more consistently.

"Officer Jones, remember to use your heart and your wisdom when making the decision to pull out your ticket book or your handcuffs."

The same speech could be made to teachers, especially teachers of students with disabilities that adversely affect classroom behavior. Students know the difference between acceptable and unacceptable behavior, and this goes both for the student who is acting out and the other students who are observing the situation.

There will be times when you choose to not immediately react to an act of misbehavior. This may result in a better relationship of the student and better behavior from him in the future. Your not acting on the minor misbehavior at that time—I don't mean ignoring it, I mean letting it go for the moment and addressing it later, privately—will probably not result in a loss of classroom control. The other students are perfectly aware that the misbehavior is inappropriate and will watch the situation quietly to see what you do.

Here's an example. One day, Alice (from the previous chapter) came into the room eating a bag of potato chips and began passing the chips out to some friends.

I said, "Alice, please put the potato chips away; we're going to begin class." She ignored me. I walked over to her and said, "Alice, what did I just ask you to do?" She indignantly said, "Damn, man, why don't you relax?" as she closed the bag, threw it down by her book bag, rolled her eyes, and sat down, muttering things under her breath, as usual. I said, "Thank you very much." The situation was over in ten seconds.

Many teachers would have said to her, "Don't you tell me to relax! Don't you tell me what to do; I tell you what to do! When I tell you to put the potato chip bag away, you do it immediately. Don't you give me a hard time or talk back to me when I ask you to do something, do you understand me, young lady?" But that would have only escalated the situation, given her the big payoff of irritating the teacher, and interfered with the educational environment.

Believe me, it was difficult for me not to say what was on my mind, but I'm glad I didn't.

17

LEAVE ME BE, I'M DOING FINE

At the high school where I teach, subjects are divided into a series of different "tracks," which group students of different ability levels. In the English department, there are four tracks: Special Education (or Level One), Prep, Accel, and Honors. Students are placed in these different tracks based on their academic performance, personality, and desire.

Deciding which of these tracks to be placed in can be a stressful experience for many students because being placed in a higher track is more prestigious, yet it's more difficult and therefore more likely to result in a poor or failing grade.

Naturally, student personalities vary widely; some students who are getting an A in one track are proud of their accomplishment and don't want to risk losing the A by moving up to a higher track, while others getting a lower grade, like a B or C, will still want to try to move up to a higher track because of the increased prestige associated with it.

Conversely, students must sometimes move down an academic track because of poor academic performance. This is usually a difficult decision but not always; some students are surprisingly mature regarding decisions to move down a track and are at peace with the process. Wisely, they would rather be in a classroom that will give them enough opportunities to learn and succeed and therefore improve their self-image than be engaged in the grueling, demoralizing battle of being in a class that's too difficult for them.

You have to put kids into the right academic environment so that they have the opportunity to succeed.

If you were put in a room with one hundred marbles all over the floor and a shoebox and told that you had to collect the marbles and put them in the box within ten seconds, you wouldn't even try because you would know you couldn't do it. The same thing will happen if you put a kid with an expressive language deficit in an Honors English classroom where the students have to give twenty-minute oral presentations.

This is a very sensitive area for the psyche of a turbulent young mind, and teachers must be compassionate and respectful when talking to students about either moving up or moving down a track.

As a special education teacher, a number of my students are ones that couldn't quite make it at the Prep level, and when they walk into my classroom, it's their first experience in Special Ed. Earlier in the book, you read about the unfair special education stigma; imagine what's going through the minds of these students when they realize that the only place they can succeed in the classroom is in the lowest academic level offered in the school—Special Education.

(It's interesting to note that the special education department has its own internal "tracks" because of the extremely wide range of ability within the approximately four hundred students we serve. Some students are academically competent and just need a little bit of extra support in the classroom, while other students may have a moderate cognitive delay, a severe physical disability, or other circumstance that makes it impossible for them to get an adequate education in my classroom. Students in special education that cannot benefit from my classroom can be placed in a variety of other academic and physical environments that will serve their needs and help them to get the best education they can.)

One of my goals as a special education teacher is to give my students enough skills and enough confidence so that they can move up from the special ed curriculum to more mainstream classes.

This may not be possible with most students, but there are a small number that possess the skills and ability to make the jump. There were two students in particular in my classes who showed an impressive improvement in their ability to write and to understand what they read. In particular, their grammar improved, their sentence structure improved, their behavior in class improved, everything about their performance indicated to me that they were ready to move up to Prep level. Both students were in eleventh grade and, I thought, would be excited about the idea of getting out of Special Ed for twelfth grade.

I was wrong, which surprised me very much.

First, let's talk about Bill. Bill is an amiable, friendly, generally well-behaved student who performs well academically but requires a lot of support from his teachers. This means that he frequently says one of the following things to me when he has to do independent work. I am not exaggerating—he has said each of these things to me, and many other statements similar to them, at least five to ten times throughout the year:

- "Can you help me with this?"
- "Does this look okay to you?"
- "Is this okay? Is it right?"
- "I'm not sure what I'm supposed to do with this."
- "Am I going to get a good grade on this assignment?"
- "Am I doing okay in this class?"
- "I don't know if I can do this."
- "Don't you think this is kind of difficult?"
- "Do you expect me to answer all these questions myself?"
- (In the middle of a test) "Did I get this question right?"
- (In the middle of a test) "Is this answer sort of what you're looking for?"
- (In the middle of a test) "Can you explain what you mean by this?"

When students ask you these questions, try to balance their desire for reassurance and support with their need for more confidence to work independently.

Depending on the individual situation, sometimes you will sit down next to him and work with him one-on-one for a significant amount of time; other times when you feel he's being whiny and overly dependent, you might require him to fly on his own and do his best work without support. All through this process, give him the confidence that he needs by praising his good work.

When you hand such a student back a B or an A, say to him something like, "Bill, you did a great job. You tried, and as a result, you handed in some of the best work I've seen from you. Good job." In Bill's case, the reaction was almost always extremely positive when being given back a good grade; this seems to be a powerful reward for his good work. You'll be relieved and gratified when students react well to being given a good grade because a number of my students don't seem to care one way or the other about what grade they get.

As the year went on, Bill's performance improved. During a two- to three-week period in the middle of the spring semester, he began handing in outstanding work on a consistent basis. I made copies of his written work to support the conversation I was about to have with him, which was about his moving up from Special Ed to Prep. It was time to have the conversation with him. I knew where I usually saw him in the hallway when I came in first thing in the morning. I decided that I would pull him aside discreetly in the hallway the following morning and talk to him.

Sure enough, there he was talking to his friends the next morning. He waved at me, as he usually did, but when he saw me walking toward him with a slight smile on my face, his face changed from a smiling one into one of mild apprehension and fear. Upon seeing this from him, I smiled even more because I wanted to communicate to him as quickly as possible that he should not worry, and that he wasn't in any trouble. Here's how the conversation went:

Me: "Good morning, Bill."

Bill: "Hey, what's up, good morning. What's wrong? Am I in trouble?"

Me: "No, you're not in trouble. I wanted to talk to you about the work you've been doing in English class lately."

Bill: (His face turned blank, and his eyes widened. The poor kid looked very nervous and unhappy within a split second. It was interesting to me that someone who had been turning in such good work and had improved his writing so significantly was seemingly unaware of this and assumed that he was about to be banished to the mythical School of the Dunces.) "What's the matter with it?"

Me: "There's nothing the matter with it, Bill, it's excellent."

Bill: (Now his eyes were wider, but at least he was smiling.) "It is? Really? You're not just saying that, are you?"

Me: "No, I'm not just saying that. Bill, your work lately has been really outstanding. Your grammar has improved a tremendous amount. You answer almost all the questions exactly right, you understand everything that's happening in class, and I'm very impressed and proud with how much you've improved your work. It really is excellent." Bill stood there, dumbfounded, smiling silently. I continued, "Bill, I want to ask you a question."

Bill: "Yeah?"

Me: "How would you like to move up to Prep level next year?"

Bill: "NO!" (Pause.) "Really?" (Pause.) "No."

(This was fascinating. His immediate, knee-jerk reaction was to say "NO!" He exclaimed his denial within the blink of an eye of my asking him about moving up to Prep level—it was said so quickly that it definitely represented his deep-seated emotional reaction to my question; there was not enough time for him to think about a plan, a tactic, motivation, or anything else. What he told me by the immediacy of his denial was that he was afraid of Prep; that he thought he couldn't do it. Where in the world did this come from, this utter lack of self-confidence; this self-image that said, "I can't do it, and I shouldn't try.")

Me: "No? Really?

Bill: "No, I don't want to go to Prep. I can't."

Me: "Why?"

Bill: "Because I get the help I need in your class. I can't make it in Prep without some additional help. Mr. Goldman, you sit by me and help me and you help me work through the problems and help me figure out the answers, and I'm not going to get anything like that in Prep class."

Me: "Bill, most of the time you figure everything out on your own, you know. I just give you a little bit of support, but I don't give you any of the answers. You're perfectly capable of doing the work all by yourself, and from what I've seen lately, you're ready to go up to Prep."

Bill: "No, Mr. Goldman, I don't want to go to Prep. I like your class; I like what we do, I'm happy there, and I want to stay there, is that okay?"

Me: "Of course it's okay. You can stay there if you want. I just wanted to tell you that I think that your work has been excellent lately, and I wanted to see how you felt about moving up to the next track. But if you want to stay in my class, that's okay.

Bill: "Okay, thanks."

I have Bill during ninth period. Later in the day, when he walked into the classroom, he looked at me, and a smile came over his face. He said nothing, sat in his usual seat, and we continued with class. About a week or so later, I walked up to him and asked him if he still felt the same way about his decision. He assured me that he wanted to stay in Special Ed next year.

From that point on, I did not put any pressure on him to change his mind.

Maybe I should have approached this differently; maybe I should've had a meeting about it, showed my colleagues his work, and gotten more people involved. But, after all, it all comes down to the individual student and what's best for him. He was doing a lot of thinking, reading, writing, and learning in my class. His grades were high, his self-confidence was good, and his behavior was usually acceptable with the exception of his wanting to sleep every once in awhile.

Just because a student is getting an A in a class doesn't automatically mean that he or she should be forced up to the next track if he or she is not ready, academically or emotionally.

On the other hand, sometimes I wonder if I really did do the best thing. What would have happened to Bill's self-image if he was more or less forced to go up to Prep, and he did do well? Even though it would've been a risky proposition, with the possibility of failure, shame, and frustration, it also held the promise of putting him in a more intensive academic environment, allowing him to look in the mirror and say to himself, "I'm just like all the other kids," which is such a significant statement for students who have been in special ed classes.

But, I didn't feel qualified or ready to make that decision, mostly because I was a first-year teacher. Another important reason why I didn't want to push him up and out if he wasn't ready was something that happened to me when I was a counselor at summer camp many years ago.

When I was a child, I went to summer camp every year for seven years in a row, and one of the activities I liked the most at camp was swimming in the pool.

The pool was the best, and the absolute best was when it was a "free swim," which meant you could play and splash and yell and try to dunk your friends and have breath-holding contests and lap races and tag games and generally burn up six million calories every three minutes until the bottoms of your toes started bleeding; and even that didn't really matter because when you limped away from the pool you were tired and happy and your middle ear was filled with chlorinated water.

I was always a relatively competent swimmer, and I could do most of the swimming strokes pretty well. When I became a junior counselor, I volunteered to work at the camp's pool. It was a lot of fun to help the kids learn how to swim, watching some of them be simultaneously terrified of and transfixed by the water. The pool was supervised by an authoritative nineteen-year-old girl named Aunt

Susie, who I imagine was some sort of failed Olympic hopeful, judging by the intensity with which she barked orders at everybody who worked and played within her dominion.

One conversation I had with another counselor about Aunt Susie always stuck in my mind. I said to the other counselor, "She commands respect, doesn't she?" The other counselor said, "No, she doesn't command respect, she DEMANDS respect." This was said by the other counselor without the slightest hint of affection; to paraphrase Arthur Miller, Aunt Susie "was liked, but she wasn't well-liked." Nevertheless, Aunt Susie and I got along mostly because I realized that if I wanted to work at the pool, I had to be servile, and I was. As I think back about Aunt Susie, I realize that now she's almost fifty; I hope that she lightened up and enjoyed the remainder of her youth.

One of the responsibilities of being a counselor at the pool was to certify children in different swimming skills; this involved going through a preprinted checklist, asking the child to perform different swimming strokes and techniques, and checking whether or not this child has done them adequately. When the child completes all the requirements of the checklist, he or she gets a certificate stating that a certain level of competence has been reached.

One day, I gave such an exam to a younger child that I had known for a year or two. I put him through all the paces, and he performed the swimming strokes adequately, as far as I knew. This went on for about twenty minutes, and I told him that he had completed all the requirements successfully and that he was now a "Junior Swimmer," I think the term was.

The child was elated at achieving this goal and went on his business frolicking in the pool, boasting to his other friends about his accomplishment.

Everything was just ducky until Aunt Susie came along.

She reviewed what I had done and told me that I was not qualified to give this exam. She asked me what formal swimming training I had received, and I said, "Well, only the training I got here at camp," which of course was not enough for her. She called over the younger child that I had just certified and asked him to repeat one or two of the strokes that were listed on the requirement sheet. The child did them, nervously, but Aunt Susie announced that the strokes were not being done correctly, that the certification that I had just produced was invalid, and that the student would have to take the exam again another day. She took the sheet of paper I filled out and placed it in the trash can.

Never have I seen the mood of another person change so quickly.

The younger boy I had just certified was devastated. His elation vanished and was replaced with a fury that frightened me and caused me to feel guilt and remorse for what I had done. He hoisted himself out of the pool as fast as he could and ran towards the changing area. I tried to apologize to him and tell him that I didn't realize that Aunt Suzie was going to be so strict and that I was sorry about the whole thing. I practically had to run next to him so that he could hear the apology I was giving.

He would have none of it. He refused to look at me, refused to talk to me, and began crying when I tried to make him feel better.

The whole thing was a disaster, and it was entirely my fault. I took it upon myself to assume that I was qualified to perform a task, and I hurt somebody deeply in the process. Of course, Aunt Susie could've handled it better; she could have shown some restraint, she could've seen the distraught expression on the kid's face and responded to it with kindness; she could've kept a healthy perspective on the entire situation—she was a counselor supervising an eight-year-old child at summer camp, not a world-class trainer being paid a million dollars to forge an Olympic superstar.

But, in the end, the blame lay at my feet, and I never forgot the experience. Many years after this happened, its memory remains fresh in my mind, and it helped guide my actions with Bill and his potential move up to Prep. The last thing I wanted to have happen was to push Bill up to Prep and then have his Prep teacher tell him, and me, that the work would be too difficult for him.

I was a first-year teacher, and I didn't have enough knowledge and experience about the written and unwritten rules at this school regarding moving students up or down a track. I didn't want to risk doing again what I had previously done: to push a child forward before he's ready and tell him that he's going to be fine when in fact I did not know this. So, I let Bill stay where he was, I let him be happy, I let him feel competent, and I let our relationship continue to thrive.

Did I do a disservice by not putting more pressure on him to move up to the next academic track? I don't know.

Bill clearly didn't want to move ahead, and, after all, he's almost eighteen years old; almost an adult, almost a man, and certainly old and intelligent enough to be able to make at least a few wise decisions mixed in with the unwise decisions that teenagers so frequently make.

Maybe he intuitively knows his ability level; maybe even if, deep down, he was capable of doing the work, he would not do well in Prep English because he wouldn't be in an environment where he felt supported. His being placed in a classroom which he perceived as too difficult and not supportive enough might result in his failure not because of an inability to perform the academic work, but because he *thought and felt* that he couldn't do it.

You can think about this sort of thing for a long time and still not come up with what you think is a good answer. So, when you see a student like Bill in your class, don't give him, or any of your other students, an easy time academically. Push him to do his best; encourage him to try to get an A. He'll probably do it, too.

Now we're going to turn our attention to a student in the same academic situation as Bill but with a very different personality. Theresa also had the ability to move up to the next level, and you'll read about that in a few pages, but first you need to know some background information about her.

I'm going to say something that teachers aren't supposed to ever say, at least not to the general public. Theresa holds the dubious distinction of being the first student whom I disliked from time to time.

I chose my words carefully in the previous sentence, because I don't want you to think that I disliked her all the time and daydreamed about her being strapped to a giant catapult and flung to the moon amid the trumpeting fanfare of the faculty at my school.

She was pleasant more often than unpleasant, she had real academic ability, and she was delightfully honest and open with me about events that happened in her life and her opinions about these events. But, it was one of these moments, where she told me how she felt about something, that made me dislike her—at least for that day.

Before class, Theresa came in and sat down with an unusual smile on her face, in contrast to her usual saturnine disposition. Here's the conversation that followed:

Theresa: "Mr. Goldman, you're not going to believe what happened, it is so funny."

Me: (Smiling.) "Oh, I'll probably believe it! What happened?"

Theresa: "I got into a fight—well, not a fight, an argument—with my dad yesterday or whatever. He was all yellin' at me and stuff, 'You gonna this' and 'You gonna that' and whatever. So anyway, when he was walking down the steps, he tripped and fell and broke his leg, ha ha ha, I was laughin' and laughin'."

Me: "He fell down and broke his leg?"

Theresa: "YEEAHH!" (Laughing and smiling.) "He fell down and broke his leg. He had to crawl over to the phone and call 911, and they took his ass to the emergency room. The whole thing was soooo funny."

Me: (Stunned.) "Didn't you call 911 for him? I mean, the guy just broke his leg! Wasn't he screaming out in pain or something?"

Theresa: "Hell no! I ain't going to call 911 for his sorry ass. He was the one who yelled at me, and he got just what he deserved; if he hadn't been yelling at me, he probably wouldn't have fallen and broken his leg. I was laughing the whole time; I thought it was the funniest thing I saw."

Me: "Theresa, didn't you say this is your father?"

Theresa: "Yeah, it's my father."

Me: "Wow." (That's all I could think to say at the moment, I was so dumbfounded.)

I thought to myself, Neil, keep your mouth shut and don't pass judgment.

You're her English teacher. You're her English teacher, and it's not your job to tell her what you think about what she did last night. So, I wisely took my own advice and kept my mouth shut, but I never quite felt the same way about Theresa after that. My goodness, her father fell and broke his leg right in front of her eyes. He was probably screaming in pain and begging for her help. Even if you're angry—furious—at your father, a scene as extreme as this is likely to move even the most hardhearted person to some act of compassion.

Or, if your relationship with your own father is so strained and consists of such abuse and acrimony that you would allow him to writhe in pain and do nothing to help him, at least you wouldn't come in the next morning and discuss how amused you were by the whole situation with your English teacher.

My goodness, what did she think I would say in response to her story? "Good for you, Theresa! It's a shame his sorry ass didn't break his other leg, too. Good job, sweetie! Be sure to write 'I am an asshole' on the back of his cast with indelible marker while he's asleep. That shit will REALLY be funny!"

As I got to know Theresa better, I saw that she was a person burdened by a combination of an emotional disturbance and a home environment lacking in moral guidance and academic support. This made my heart go out to her, in a way, and she responded to this well; despite the poor first impression, she and I entered into a relatively healthy teacher-student relationship which was marked by occasional arguments and rough spots when I demanded that she perform to her academic ability and act like a mature student.

Years ago, a friend of mine, during an argument, said something to me that has stuck in my head: "Neil, not everybody thinks the way you do." I have invented a corollary to this statement, which is, "Not everybody expresses their emotions the same way you do."

I remembered these quotes a number of times when working with Theresa; she expresses herself in a very different way than what I'm used to, and this has resulted in quite a bit of confusion and communication breakdowns during the time that I have known her. When I've thought she was angry at me, she has come up to me and said excitedly, "Mr. Goldman, Mr. Goldman! Guess what?" and proceeded to tell me about something that happened to her, or she has come up to me and asked me my opinion about something that's quite personal; these actions showed me that she trusted me and had a good regard for my opinion, which of course made me feel great.

I believe, after getting to know Theresa over the past year, that she misbehaved partly because she wanted to interact with me. The few times I've asked her to step out into the hall with me for a private conference, she has done so readily, although when she got out there, she argued with me about almost everything I said. The argument was the reward for her.

One day, unbeknownst to me, I was about to give her a huge pay-off by trying a tactic which I don't believe I'll ever try again.

During the last month or two of school, Theresa was slacking off academically, which was unlike her; even though her behavior was hit and miss, her academic performance was usually good. During this particular day, she decided that she was going to try to sleep during a writing assignment. I pulled her out into the hallway so as not to disturb the other students.

A common conversational pattern took place, during which I asked her why she wasn't doing the assignment and she responded with a series of not-completely-honest answers and excuses for her behavior.

In the past, Theresa had used profanity with me, and I wondered what would happen if I used mild profanity with her.

I never used strong language in my classroom because I believe that modeling good behavior is an important role of a teacher. But, I wanted to know if the extremely limited, private, judicious use of a colorful word or two would cut through her protective shell, shake up her world a little bit, and help her to put me in a different category than "that guy that talks at me, talks at me, talks at me, blah blah blah blah blah whatever."

So, I said to her the following, privately in the hallway: "Theresa, next year in twelfth grade it's going to be quite different in this room. The work is going to be more demanding, and the expectations of the students are going to be higher, and all of this 'sleeping in class' and 'talking back to me all the time' bullshit has to stop."

What a schmuck I was. I gave her the biggest payoff of the year. Do you know those bells and whistles and alarms and whoop-whoop sounds that slot machines make when they deliver a big payoff? She must have heard the whole dinging, ringing, honking, whoop-dee-doo payoff in her head when she heard me utter the "B" word, and she took that payoff, and she ran with it just as fast and loud and long as she possibly could.

"Oh, Mr. Goldman, I don't BEE-LEEEEEEVE that you just swore at me. I don't believe that you just swore at me." (She started walking around in circles.) "Don't even talk to me—you just swore at me? I'm trying to have a conversation with you out here, and you swear at me?"

This from a girl who uses language that would make a tattooed, barroom-brawling, barrel-chested, battle-scarred motorcycle gang member drop to his knees and start crying for his mommy.

At this point, Jim and Freddie came out of the classroom because Theresa ensured that her outraged comments were loud enough for the classroom to hear. They had big smiles on their faces. "He swore at you? What did he say?" "He told me that I'd better cut out the bullshit." "MR. GOLDMAN said that?" "Oooh, look, his face is turning red! HAHA! Mr. Goldman swore at Theresa!" "He did? What did he say?" "He said, 'bullshit.'" "No shit, he did?" "YEAH! He said it to Theresa!"

Naturally, at that moment, several of my colleagues happened to be walking down the hall. Mark, the program coordinator, said "Do you need some help?" I replied, "No, the situation is under control." They smiled at me and continued down the hall as I said, authoritatively, "Jim and Freddie, please get back into the classroom—this has nothing to do with you, it's between me and Theresa."

They did, thank goodness.

Theresa was still working on her Academy Award-winning performance in the hallway. She conveniently forgot about the time that she looked at me and said, "You fucking asshole" when I reminded her that her lack of working on an assignment would result in a poor grade. She also conveniently forgot about the time, when I asked her to please put her cell phone away, that she looked at me and said, "shut up, shut up, shut up."

I said, "Okay, Theresa, I'm sorry I used a swear word with you, but I was trying to make an impression on you so that you would get a better grade next year." This seemed to stop the histrionics, and she stood there looking at me, and then a smile came across her face. I said, "Are we past this?" She replied, "Yes, but I can't believe you swore at me."

I said, "Well, when I ask you to put your cell phone away, don't tell me to 'shut up, shut up, shut up.' Deal?"

Another award-winning performance ensued.

"Oh, Mr. Goldman, I wasn't talking to you when I said that! When you told me to put my cell phone away, just at that second it started to ring. So, I was looking at the phone and telling it to shut up, not you. I wouldn't tell you to shut up!" I looked at her with my best "oh, puhhh-LEEASE" face, whereupon she started to giggle, but she steadfastly stuck to her story and repeated her explanations of why she said "shut up, shut up, shut up."

I said, as I walked her back into the classroom, "Let's treat each other with more respect from this point on." She didn't respond to this, but she did sit down and began doing her writing assignment. I knew the whole thing was over when, later in the day, she saw me in the hall and said, sweetly, "Hi, Mr. Goldman!"

I describe Theresa's reaction to my use of a swear word as an Academy Award-nominated performance because at the time that's what I perceived it to be. It took quite a bit of self-control for me not to say to her at that moment, "Oh, give me a break. How about all the swear words you've used with me? How about all the times you turned your back on me and walked out of the room while I was in the middle of talking to you? Don't you think that's even more of-fensive than the use of one word?"

But, it's usually better to hold your tongue when you want to say something like that to a student.

Over the course of your life, you'll regret saying things hundreds and hundreds of times, but you'll probably be able to count on one hand the number of times you'll regret not saying something.

Later, as I reflected back on the incident, I realized that maybe it wasn't an acting performance; maybe she was genuinely upset at hearing me use the word "bullshit." How could this be; how could a girl out of whose mouth expletives flowed at a steady pace be offended by one use of a mild swear word?

Maybe it's because I did make an impression on her as somebody who doesn't swear. Maybe all the effort I put forth into presenting myself as a positive role model actually worked, and it upset her when she discovered that this lofty view of me might be unjustified; that even Mr. Goldman is a fake, that Mr. Goldman tries to sell himself off as a classy guy but is a trash talker just like all the other trash talkers in the world.

I decided that either reason for her outburst—that she didn't really mind the swear word but was using it as a way to avoid the conversation or she did mind and was offended and upset by what I said—was an excellent reason for never trying that tactic again.

Throughout my getting to know Theresa, one of the things that I could depend on was her performing very well academically. Her reading comprehension was good, her oral comprehension was good, and her writing ability was almost, or perhaps at, the Prep level. One of the chief complaints I got from her throughout the semester was that she was bored and that the assignments were "lame." She argued to me, in several conversations, that the reason why she was trying to sleep was that she was bored with the lesson and that the reason she wasn't doing the assignment was that it was too easy.

This brings me back to my comparison between Theresa and Bill.

Theresa, like Bill, could probably benefit by moving up to the Prep level, and one day I decided to sit down with Theresa and discuss this with her. Theresa's ability to read, comprehend, and write were excellent for my class, and with effort, she could get a moderately good grade in Prep. It was interesting to me, when I had this discussion with her, that her reaction was almost the same as Bill's; she acknowledged that the work was boring to her, but she refused to even discuss the possibility of moving up a track.

Of course, students say that they're bored for a variety of reasons, and only one of them is because the work is too easy. What was interesting about Theresa was that she refused to do work that was easy for her, even though completing the assignment would result in getting an A.

On the other hand, refusing to do the assignment did result in attention from me; it seemed that the reward of getting attention from me was more significant to her than the reward of getting a good grade on an assignment. She seemed to value a consistent relationship with an adult much more than schoolwork.

This ties in very well with what she revealed to me earlier about her feelings toward her father. She obviously felt a great deal of hostility toward him, and it made sense that she wanted to strike up a consistent relationship with other males in her life to compensate for the failed relationship she had with her father. Academic performance and good grades seemed to take a back seat to her interacting with me, regardless of whether or not this interaction was obviously unpleasant and stressful to me and counterproductive to the classroom environment.

Theresa, like Bill, would have none of the idea of moving up out of Special Ed. She said, "No way. No way am I moving up to Prep." I asked her why not. The answer she gave me at the time was vague, which puzzled and frustrated me, but upon reflecting on it later I realized that it was the only possible answer she could give.

Her reason for not wanting to move up to Prep was that she didn't want to "move into that lame class."

I said to her the same sort of things that I said to Bill, that her academic performance was good, her writing was good, her comprehension was good, and that she could do a great job and be more challenged if she went up to Prep. She continued to refuse but would not give me a reason why. I said to her, "But Theresa, you said that the reason why you didn't want to do today's assignment is that it was lame and boring. You said this to me more than once in the past, right?"

She acknowledged that she had said this before; in fact, we had spoken several times in the past about why she was sleeping, why she refused to do the assignment, and so on, and it was always because it was stupid, it was boring, or it was lame.

I said to her, "Theresa, this is your chance to get into a class where you're going to be more challenged, and as a result, you can become an even better writer, reader, and thinker."

She continued to say that she did not want to go on to that class and that she wanted to stay where she was.

I then said, "Well, I don't know what to do. You say that the classroom is boring and that the work is below your level, but yet you won't move up to a class that's going to be more challenging and more interesting. Tell me what I should do because I don't know. You can't have it both ways, Theresa. You can't say that you're not going to do the work because it's boring and yet refuse to leave the boring environment. You can't come in here every day starting next year and sleep, or talk, or text message people on your cell phone, or do all the other stuff you do from time to time that distracts the other students."

She looked at me thoughtfully, chewing gum and shaking her head slowly from side to side as if to say, "I have no idea what to tell you."

I don't think that she knew herself.

I had a feeling that this was one of the first times that an adult had showed her a clear picture of her behavior and given her the power to choose what to do to change it. Although she put on, as most adolescents do, an air of having centuries of wisdom despite an annoying lack of fine lines and wrinkles around her eyes, she was utterly at a loss to know what to do in this situation.

So, I'm going to have Theresa for English next year, and I find myself looking forward to seeing her. I wonder if she will have matured over the summer, I wonder how she will respond to the more diverse and more challenging requirements in twelfth grade English, I wonder how everything will have gone with her father, I wonder . . . the list could go on for pages. Theresa illustrates one of the strange paradoxes of Special Education: much of the time you find yourself looking forward to seeing the most challenging students.

18

SPECIAL EDUCATION— A PARADOX

When I was student teaching, I had a student named Muñoz. He forbade me to use his first name, which was a perfectly good, manly, gilt-edged name; for some reason he wanted to be referred to by his last name, Muñoz. This boy was only about five feet two and 120 pounds, but he more than made up for his slight physical stature with a mouth that could get him banned from the Jerry Springer show.

Muñoz had two parole officers, was known to be an active drug dealer, combined obscenities into expressions that were simultaneously horrifying and fascinating, dressed in an oversized black quilted jacket so he resembled a dark pincushion skewered by a lollipop stick, and threatened others without noticing (or caring) that the person he threatened was six feet one, two hundred and five pounds, trained in combat, and armed with a six-inch knife and a Beretta.

He was disobedient, he was disrespectful, and he was without a doubt the most intelligent student in any of my classes.

When he answered a question, he was nearly always right. When he asked a question, it was nearly always wholly relevant to the lesson and raised interesting issues. When he expressed an opinion, it was honest and was based on sound thought.

Within him was such value, such intellectual wealth, such potential, but it was inaccessible because of the fetid composition of what surrounded the sparkling and hidden core.

Most people wouldn't have much to do with him. His personality was like a diamond in a cow chip.

Those who did interact with him on a regular basis treated him like you would expect from the previous simile; he was kept at a distance, denied true affection and respect, but was feared. This seemed to satisfy him, and he returned the treatment in kind. Every day was a new adventure with Muñoz. Some days I had to ask him to please not exclaim, while reading Steinbeck's *The Pearl,* witty plot observations that went like this: "That is ONE FUCKED UP DUDE; I would have POPPED HIS ASS, and the game would be OVER."

Most days, I had to quietly ask him to not answer a few questions to give some of the other students a chance to think and answer the questions on their own.

Suddenly, Muñoz stopped coming to class. His attendance had not been perfect, but it wasn't bad. But, it was unusual for him to miss so many days in a row. During lunch, I asked my mentor teacher where Muñoz was, and he answered, "Oh, you won't see him for a while. He's back in jail, probably until the end of the school year."

I stopped eating my sandwich in mid-chew. I said, "Really?" My mentor teacher nodded. I said, "Oh, no!" Now, an outsider might think that I would be thrilled not having to get on the endless behavior-correction treadmill with him every day, but I was truly sad and disappointed upon hearing this news. My biggest behavior problem was gone, and I didn't like that one bit.

Such is the paradox of teaching students with behavior difficulties and emotional disorders; you sometimes grow most attached to the biggest challenges.

Maybe it's because teachers like attention, too. One of the worst things that can happen to you as a teacher is to passionately and effectively (as far as you're concerned) deliver a lesson that you find very interesting and look out on a sea of blank stares, heads tilted downward, and half-closed eyes.

We want attention, too.

We want an acknowledgment of our existence. We actually are relieved when Muñoz screams out, "That's BULLSHIT, man. That dude should have just TOSSED that NASTY-ASS PEARL into the ocean and then POPPPED his wife, smoked some DRO, and CHILLED the rest of the night. WHAT? Come on, man, it was MEXICO a hundred years ago! You don't think they were all smoking weed every single NIGHT?!" because it stimulates the other students to voice their opinions, too.

It's students like Muñoz that are challenging, that argue with us, that force us to think, change, grow, invent, and decide right on the spot; they're the ones that in some ways are the most fun to have around, because deep down, you know that if they didn't regard you well, if they didn't respect you to a certain degree, they wouldn't have anything to do with you.

Think of someone that you strongly dislike or you have no regard for at all. Would you talk to them? Would you ask them a bunch of questions? Probably not, and neither would a high school student.

This will help you through the rough days. When you're standing in the trenches, and you feel like the lesson isn't going the way you want because of Simon, and Jim, and Theresa, and Will, and Freddie; remember that you can do this.

You can control the classroom.

The very fact that your challenging students are interacting with you in the way they are means that they regard you highly enough to follow your instructions and do what's right. You'll find this to be the case over and over again. They seem to know when they've reached that point where they have to knock it off and get to work. Never underestimate your students' astute abilities to research teacher behavior.

They can read your tone of voice, the words you utter, the way you move, and a million other variables, and make stunningly accurate sense of it in real time.

They want to know your limits, your fears, your soft spots, the things that irritate you, the things that are absolutely off-limits, and the things that should bother you but don't. They will find these things out in a surprisingly short time; they have a reading disability, but there's plenty of sophisticated social analysis going on in their heads.

They make me laugh and make me think and make me blush and make me happy and sad and angry and proud, and I always like seeing them.

19

YOU DON'T HAVE THE PATIENCE TO BE A TEACHER

I've always viewed myself as not being a particularly patient person. My blood pressure goes up in crowded parking lots that are filled with dozens of people who have nowhere to go and nothing to do and who are insufferably and unforgivably overly polite to everybody within their field of vision. "No, no, go ahead, you go first, I have LOTS of time. I'm retired." When the person in front of me in such a parking lot moves at one mile per hour and taps his brake pedal every time he even *thinks* that a car *might* pull out from its parking space, yes, the veins in my neck start to bulge.

When I'm having trouble with my Internet connection and can't get onto the Web, and I call Comcast for technical support, and they put me on hold while playing an announcement that most problems can be solved by going to www.comcast.com, but that's impossible because I can't connect to the Internet, yes, my blood pressure goes up.

When my property taxes are extremely high, yet the traffic department of the town in which I live doesn't seem to understand the whole concept of traffic signal progression and that traffic signal controllers can actually communicate with each other and make it so that you can—GASP—get a couple of green lights in a row, and I get a red light, red light, red light, red light, red light, red light, red light, red light as I travel down the same busy street every day of my life, while at the same time this town publishes beautiful 4-color newsletters that talk about the problem with outdoor air pollution and smog in the Chicago area, yes, my eyes roll towards the sky.

When you make an appointment to bring your car in for service, and you inconvenience yourself to arrive at exactly the correct time, and your car sits there for an hour and a half before anybody works on it, and you realize as you sit in an ugly waiting area, forced to listen to pants-soiling, inane daytime TV, that the entire service department is overbooked beyond imagination for the sole purpose of making more money at the expense of the time and convenience of the very customers that make their entire existence possible, yes, I feel like giving somebody a piece of my mind.

You get the idea.

When I first told my friends that I was thinking of becoming a teacher, they said to me that I wasn't cut out to be a teacher because I am not a patient person. "You want to be a teacher?" one of my best friends said. "You don't have the patience to be a teacher! You get impatient if there's one person ahead of you in line at Kmart!"

Objections sustained.

But something is different when I work with my students.

I certainly get impatient if a student is deliberately being difficult, but this doesn't happen very often. Usually, my students are innocent with their questions, earnest when they put their mind to working, consistent in their desire to improve their abilities, and are genuinely clueless when they make statements in class that are inappropriate.

Here's an example. When I was in graduate school, I had to work with an eighth grade student named Tony who had a moderate cognitive delay. He was extremely friendly and willing to talk, and I looked forward to working with him. One of the things I had to do for my assignment was to teach him how to do a task and document how I taught the task. I decided to teach him the children's game of "rock, paper, scissors." I'll explain in detail in a short while how it works, in case you don't know. It's a simple game that allows two people to randomly decide who "wins," sort of like flipping a coin.

It's a simple game; you could take two ten-year-olds and show them how to play it in less than two minutes. So I thought I would teach this simple game to Tony. I didn't realize at the time that this would not be possible.

As we go about our lives, performing simple tasks like tying our shoes, making a sandwich, and locking the front door, we don't realize how complex these tasks are.

For example, the process of making a peanut butter and jelly sandwich, if broken down to a series of simple, explicit instructions, can take hundreds of steps. For some people with severe cognitive delays, just saying "Untwist the twist tie on the bag of bread" is far too complex; you have to give them explicit instructions, including which hand should do what, which finger should do what, and which wrists should rotate which way to break down the task sufficiently.

In the field of computer technology, there's something called an "input buffer," which is responsible for accepting commands quickly and putting them into a temporary storage space so they can be carried out later. The input buffer is what lets you type in your username and press <enter> a few seconds before the screen is ready and then watch your username zip across the field a few seconds later while your fingers are idle.

The purpose of the input buffer is to make the computer more efficient and more usable to human beings; rather than have to wait for the computer to finish completing step one before you can tell it to begin to perform step two, the computer will accept your instructions to do step one, step two, step three, and step four as fast as you can give them. Then, because of the input buffer, you are free to leave the computer alone and began eating your lunch while the computer gets to work on doing the tasks you instructed it to do.

We also have an input buffer in our minds.

If you would be told to walk over there to the desk, open the drawer, take out a pen, take out a piece of paper, write your name on the paper, put the pen back in the drawer, close the drawer, and give me the paper, you'd be able to do it. As you were being given the series of instructions, you were storing them in your input buffer, which is sometimes called your short-term memory.

Different people have different size input buffers, and it doesn't always have a direct correlation to your overall intelligence; a friend of mine who is a Ph.D engineer can't remember an entire phone number at once; if you want to tell him the telephone number 123-456-7890, you have to first say the "123," wait for him to write it down, then say the "456," wait for him to write it down, and then say the "7890." This limited input buffer coexists in the same brain that's capable of doing integral and differential calculus and understands, in detail, something called chromatic dispersion in optical fiber. Uh, okay.

(All I know about chromatic dispersion in optical fiber is that it has something to do with being able to call Aunt Mary, who lives in New Zealand, and get a loud, crystal clear connection, so you can hear her tell you about the darling little Maori souvenirs she recently purchased for her étagère without having to say, "What, honey? What? Mary, nobody ate a chair, you're not making sense again.")

Back to input buffers. People with cognitive delays, with very few exceptions, have very short input buffers. They can't handle more than one or two pieces of information at a time and may take a long time to gain an understanding of the relationship between these pieces of information. I didn't know this when I started working with Tony, or more accurately I should say that I kind of knew it in the back of my mind, but it was never made as clear to me as it would be when I actually started working with him.

As I started teaching him rock-paper-scissors, I had in my mind that it was a simple game, and I thought that teaching the rules to Tony would be something that I could accomplish. I promised I would tell you exactly how the game worked, so I will do that now.

This is a simple game played by two people, and the purpose of the game is to play an odd-numbered quantity of trials and win the majority of them; usually it's two out of three, or three out of five, and so on. Ultimately, the game is usually played to decide who has

Table 18.1. Rules for playing "Rock-Paper-Scissors"

First player	Second player	Winner	Reason
Rock	Paper	Paper	Paper covers rock
Rock	Scissors	Rock	Rock breaks scissors
Scissors	Paper	Scissors	Scissors cuts paper

to do an unpleasant task: "We'll play rock-paper-scissors, and the loser has to clean out the garbage can."

The two players face each other, and each player puts one hand behind his back. While a player's hand is hidden, he forms his hand to resemble one of three objects: 1) rock, which is signified by a closed fist; 2) paper, which is signified by a flat palm with all fingers extended all the way; and 3) scissors, which is signified by folding the third and fourth fingers back to your palm, putting your thumb over these folded fingers, and keeping your first and second fingers extended sort of like a pair of scissors.

One player says "1, 2, 3, go," and both players simultaneously and quickly move their hands from behind their back out in front of them so each player sees the other player's hand at the same time. If both players show the same sign, the trial is repeated. If two different signs are presented, the winner is decided by this truth table.

So, during each trial, a player has a 50 percent chance of being the winner or loser.

Let's say that either you or your sister has to take out the garbage. You play rock-paper-scissors best-of-three to see who has to do the dirty job.

Your sister won, two out of three. As a result of this competition, you'll be the one hauling out the refuse.

Table 18.2. Sample Game of Rock-Paper-Scissors with Outcome

Trial #	Your sign	Sister's sign	Winner	Reason	Score	
1	Rock	Paper	Sister	Paper covers rock	You: 0	Sister: 1
2	Scissors	Paper	You	Scissors cuts paper	You: 1	Sister: 1
3	Paper	Scissors	Sister	Scissors cuts paper	You: 1	Sister: 2

This was my task—to teach this game to Tony. You're a perceptive person if you realize now that I was in big trouble before I even got started.

Tony and I were seated in a sunny room free of distraction. I used all the teaching techniques that I had learned thus far in graduate school: I asked him about games he'd already played so he could use his previous knowledge about games to help him understand this new one. We did some exercises before the instruction to help him focus on the physical actions he was going to have to do. I told him that he was going to be learning a new game that was a lot of fun and that either he could win or I could win; this information gave Tony great pleasure and he seemed eager to begin learning how to play it.

As my students say, I was totally psyched, dude.

To make a long story short, I tried, and tried, and tried, but Tony did not get it.

I backed up, I simplified, I repeated, I demonstrated with my own hands, I helped him make the movements with his own hands, I praised him when small progress was made, I encouraged him when no progress was happening, I restated the instructions in different words, I role-played, and I remained positive.

Tony simply was not capable of understanding the game.

As I worked with him and tried to break down the game into simple rules, I began to realize just how complex the game was; moreover, I was introducing many new, higher level concepts to which he had not previously been exposed, such as the following. I'll bet you will be as surprised as I was, upon reflecting on the rules of this simple game, how many tricky, difficult-to-teach concepts exist within it.

1. The same hand sign that allowed you to win one trial would cause you to lose another trial; there's no connection between the hand sign you make and the outcome of the trial.
2. The game gives the illusion that you are in control of its outcome, but in fact the outcome is decided purely by chance. This means that regardless of how often you practice, you can

never become more skillful at this game. This concept runs counter to most of what all of us are taught as we grow up—that practice makes perfect.

3. The need to understand the concept of "best of three" or "best of five" and the underlying concept that a tie is impossible when playing an odd number of game trials.

4. If you're playing, for example, "best of five," you sometimes can win after three trials, but you sometimes have to play more than that to win. It's difficult to explain why.

5. Some trials count and some trials are discarded depending on the hand signs presented, but there's no correlation between particular hand signs and whether they will result in the trial being discarded. Whether or not your hand sign is discarded is dependent on your partner's hand sign.

6. It is essential that your partner not see the sign that you are making because this would allow him to make a sign that will beat you every time. This is a higher-level strategy concept that is outside Tony's ability to comprehend. (Tony kept showing me his hand before I said "go.")

We continued for about an hour. Much to Tony's credit, he remained cheerful and cooperative throughout the entire process. Finally, I told him that he had done a good job learning how to play the game, which put a big smile on his face. We engaged in some more small talk, and I returned Tony to his classroom.

This process might have frustrated many people, but it didn't have that effect on me.

As I reflected on what had happened, I realized that at no time when I worked with Tony did I become frustrated or impatient. I kept thinking to myself, "What can I do to help him understand this concept?" As I saw that Tony was not making progress, the experience became an intellectual exercise; it was like a game within a game; how could I get this concept across to my student?

What could I do, what props could I use, what could I say, how could I phrase the question, how could I give more contextual sense to my explanation, or how could I invoke his previous skills and knowledge to help him understand this new idea so that he would understand the game?

It wasn't Tony's fault; he was trying in earnest. Rather, I saw his lack of progress as a failure on my part, but this didn't cause me to be depressed, or to feel incompetent, or make me want to walk out of the room. It caused me to think, and it stimulated my interest in solving the puzzle that was before me.

Later, I was quite relieved when I realized that I was *not* impatient, but I always knew in the back of my mind that I didn't become impatient when explaining things to people because I was fascinated with making the journey of discovery with them and took great pleasure from seeing the smile that appeared on their face when they made the connection, accomplished the task, or got an A on the test.

It drives me nuts to be behind a slow driver in the left lane but makes me happy to work next to a student who's having a hard time figuring out how to improve her grammar.

Maybe my friends told me that I wasn't patient enough because they felt that they weren't patient enough. This could be explained by projection, one of Freud's famous defense mechanisms. Projection describes the phenomenon of your attributing characteristics about yourself to another person because you don't feel comfortable accepting that these characteristics are more attributable to you.

One of the classic examples of projection is an unfaithful husband accusing his wife of cheating on him. The same thing occurred when my friends insisted that I wasn't patient enough to be a teacher, and here's proof.

When I described the above scene with Tony to them, nearly all of them said that they didn't know how I did it, they didn't know where I got the patience, they didn't know how I could get through that for an hour without screaming, and so on.

You see? Projection.

Maybe my friends really wished that they had more patience and were frustrated when they heard that I was going into a field that required boxcars full of it. Yet, I still maintain that I am not a patient person overall. I change lanes on the highway too often, I think the boot-up time of my computer is ridiculously slow, and I almost never watch television because the incessant procession of vapid, vacuous, valueless commercials has almost made me throw the infernal tube into the back of a garbage truck with great force.

In the classroom, I won't tolerate childish misbehavior, which irritates me, and I feel angry when I know a student is lying to my face.

But when a student says to me, "I don't understand this," something different inside me takes over, and I have all the time in the world.

So if you're thinking of becoming a teacher, don't be dissuaded by people who insist that the only successful teachers are the ones who have limitless patience. It's okay to be a real person *and* be a teacher; it's okay to have things that get on your nerves, it's okay to have your own little personal idiosyncrasies, and it's okay to let your students know in a respectful, firm way that you're losing your patience and that they've reached their limit.

Just be sure that you enjoy explaining things—sometimes in several different ways; and remember that if students understood everything the first time, there would be no need for teachers.

The biggest part of your job isn't merely presenting the curriculum, it's *doing something effective* when you see a room full of kids with puzzled looks on their faces. Such a sight should spur you to creative action and not trigger frustration born of impatience.

20

WHY ARE WE LEARNING THIS IN ENGLISH CLASS?

You'll hear this complaint more than once from your students. You'll hear, if you're good, "Is this English class or consumer education class?" You'll hear sarcastic comments like, "Oh, I didn't realize I was in math class; let me find my calculator—hold on." When you try to bring some broad reading and some real-life situations into the classroom, you might be surprised to discover the extremely limited view your students have of what they are supposed to learn in English class, and, in the larger picture, what they are supposed to learn in school and what an education means.

There are many news articles that say that students in American schools are not adequately prepared for the workforce. In these articles, business owners and managers complain that newly minted high school graduates lack basic technical and literary ability, and they are begging schools to change how we teach and what we teach to allow the young American workforce to be more competitive in the global economy.

Also, many young people, although they can read and write, have a shocking lack of knowledge about the meaning of the words in a sweepstakes offer, a lease agreement, or the terms and conditions of a credit card, among other things. I said to myself that I'm going to teach my students more than what a gerund is, more than why Atticus Finch did what he did, and more than the startling similarities between the experiences of Elie Wiesel and Frederick Douglass.

Surprise! This would be met with surprise and some resistance from my students.

My students had very clear, specific ideas about what activities should happen within our English class.

These "approved" activities include reading classic, familiar novels and short stories, memorizing facts about them, regurgitating these facts on regular quizzes and exams, getting writing assignments that require them to summarize, compare, and contrast stories they had read, completing worksheets that strengthened their grammar and punctuation skills, learning the more than two dozen rules that govern the use of the comma, and engaging in limited classroom discussion that relates closely to the content of what was being read in class.

Of course, in their minds, English class also included watching many, many films and videos to "make the class interesting." Then you have a test on the movie that requires you to spit back a bunch of facts.

That's it. That's English class.

There were clear boundaries between English class and math class, and English class and consumer education class, and English class and history class. I must not have gotten the memo, but, in their minds, teachers are prohibited from crossing the boundaries between academic subjects and forcing them to learn a little about the intriguing, complex mystery of the way the world actually works, and by acquiring this learning, helping them to gain a little bit more control over the way the mystery affects them.

But no, I was not allowed to do this; it violated the rules in their minds.

Apparently, requiring my students to make the connection between understanding the meaning of words in Edgar Allan Poe's "The Tell-Tale Heart" and the meaning of the words in the fine print at the bottom of the alluring yet potentially harmful credit card of-

WHY ARE WE LEARNING THIS IN ENGLISH CLASS?

fer they just received in the mail would be a stressful and disorienting experience to them because it might remind them of the existence of the vast land named "Things I Don't Know," and this would subvert their efforts at convincing themselves that they are the wisest people on the face of the planet.

Keep in mind that one of your jobs as their teacher is to challenge their laissez-faire attitude and make them see things in a new way. So, tell them the same thing that they said on "Star Trek": "Resistance is futile." When you hear the objection, "Why are we learning this in English class?" tell them to open up their minds and broaden their view of what an education is.

Ask the objecting student, "What does it mean to be educated?" That'll make him or her think.

It's interesting to ask a roomful of teenagers what an education actually is. You'd be amazed at the number of blank stares you receive in response to this question. Once the windmills begin turning in their minds, you're sure to hear that education means learning "stuff," and by "stuff," they mean "facts."

I see this reflected in the exams that I was given when I was in school, and I still see the same tendency in some of the exams that I see my students having to take in other classes. I'm not being critical of this, mind you—we have to learn facts, and a lot of them, in order to survive in the world.

We have to know what a red light means, how we can get sick from eating undercooked pork, how to spot the early signs of breast cancer, and the list of common household dangers and what we can do to protect our children from being harmed by them.

At work, we must know an enormous quantity of facts. A friend of mine who is a Family Court judge must have a litany of facts at his immediate disposal in order to do his job with efficiency and compassion. Years ago, in Philadelphia, a man working at a riverside fruit terminal was instantly crushed to death by a massive crate of fruit as it was being unloaded from a Chilean freighter. Why did this happen? The crane operator did not know his facts about the capacity of the crane at different lean angles of the boom, and the crane toppled onto the man and killed him.

We as educators should develop our students' abilities to memorize facts. But education is much more than that—and this is something that many of my students don't realize.

I explained to them that the process of becoming educated does not only include learning facts but also includes the development of your ability to effectively use what you know. It's not enough to give you a sword in a fight, I have to teach you how to use the sword, how your opponent is likely to try to injure you, and how you can effectively counter these attacks.

How many young people can calculate what is 14.9 percent of $10,000, yet get in over their head with credit card debt?

How many young people can tell you the definition of a noun, a verb, and an adjective, yet find themselves spending too much money on a mediocre consumer electronic device that was advertised as "new" and "on sale"?

One of the lessons we did in class was to examine just what those words mean. The task seemed simple enough and was met with some derision at the beginning of the lesson; one student said, "What is this, first grade?" I said no, it's twelfth grade, so tell me what does "new" really mean?

We discussed how the word "new" can mean two things that are dissimilar yet related: it can mean something that has never previously been used by a consumer, like a "new" car as opposed to a "used" car, or it can mean that it is the first time that a product has been put on the market, like a "new" flavor of breakfast cereal. I made it clear that I was talking about the word "new" in the second sense of the word—the sense that told you that people have never seen this product before.

In response to my question about the meaning of the word "new," the student said, "Duh! Not old."

I said, "Right, it does mean not old. But be more specific. When does something change from being new to being old? How old does a 'new' product have to be before it's no longer 'new'?"

I was met with a classroom full of quizzical stares. This was good.

I told them that research has shown that the word "new" is one of the most powerful motivations to entice people to purchase some-

WHY ARE WE LEARNING THIS IN ENGLISH CLASS?

thing; that it has been inculcated into us that new is what people want; new is good, new is desirable—notwithstanding the hit show "Antiques Roadshow."

"New" gets people to buy things—NEW features! NEW technology! The NEWEST colors! The NEWEST styles! A NEW treatment for hemorrhoids! They all nodded their heads in agreement, whereupon I said to them, "Well, the question still stands—how old does something have to be before it's no longer new?"

Mumbled, diverse answers followed—a year, a month, six months, two weeks, and so on. I said, "Okay, let me ask a question a different way. Let's say that you work for Nike, and you're the head of the marketing department, the department that makes up all the advertising. Nike has just made a "new" style of running shoe that everyone at the company thinks will have big appeal to people who have mild arthritis because of the way that this particular running shoe is constructed.

"Now, you're going to put it on the market and of course, one of the things you are going to say is that it is—drum roll, please—NEW. For how long can you say that legally?" One of my students said, "Legally?" I said, "Yes, legally. You know that there are truth-in-advertising laws, right?" I saw a roomful of nodding heads. I said, "well, you can't say that something is new when it's not new any more than you can say that something is made out of genuine leather when it really isn't. So, the question still stands: for how long can you legally say that your new running shoe is new?"

The class was silent, staring at each other with puzzled looks on their faces, which gives me no end of pleasure because it means that the gears are all turning in their heads at maximum speed.

They then did a short writing assignment where they had to pretend that they were officers at the Federal Trade Commission (FTC), and their job was to review Nike's advertising practices.

(I had to digress for five minutes to explain to them what the FTC was because most of my students didn't know. This is one of those instances where you have to use your wisdom to know when to stop the lesson for good reason. Later in the semester, they had to do some research and some writing on the FTC, find a print advertisement that was misleading, and write a well-crafted letter to the advertiser which detailed the violation and what the advertiser had to do to prevent a large fine.)

As an officer of the FTC, they each had to make a personal decision as to whether or not words are misleading in advertising, including the use of the word "new" in Nike's ad for their never-before-seen brand of running shoes. Again, the written responses I received back from my students differed greatly. The students found it very interesting to hear each other's opinion of what constituted abuse of the word "new."

I explained to them that, in fact, there is no law which restricts the use of the word "new" in the sense of the word where it describes that something has just been introduced to the market for the first time. This is interesting to me because the FTC's rules are very clear for the use of the word "new" in the other sense of the word; the sense that says that no other consumer has used this product.

For example, tires that have been retreaded may not be advertised as "new," and fabric that contains material that has been reclaimed or respun cannot be advertised as "new." Along the same lines, retailers such as automotive dealerships make it an extremely clear point that once you drive the car off the car lot, they may no longer legally sell the car as "new," which of course will result in a very sad day for your wallet if you decide you're unhappy with the car after a day or so.

But, as long as the manufacturer is using the term "new" in the sense that it's the first time the product has been seen on the market, no law requires them to withdraw the use of that term in their advertising.

The manufacturer may continue to use the term for as long as they want to with no threat of legal repercussions, and they do so on a regular basis. Walk down the aisles at Kmart, especially the aisles where they sell snack foods and other products with a lot of words on the packaging, and watch how many times you see the word "new."

Good teachers will explain to their students that this whole exercise is very much part of a good English class because it requires them to examine, analyze, compare, and evaluate the use of words; and it doesn't get any better than that when it comes to improving students' minds and furthering a good education.

There may be a few naysayers within the classroom, which might unnerve you; but you'll learn as the months elapse that these students complain all the time. I joked with a few colleagues that Kyle, one chronic complainer in particular, would find something to complain about if I held a party in the classroom complete with the Rockettes themselves, free food, and a premium sound system.

I joked that if he were there, he would frown and say, "These girls are all too old for me, I'm not crazy about your caviar hors d'oeuvres, and would you please fix the equalizer on this sound system as I can't hear the middle frequencies."

Kyle miraculously paid attention when we did another English lesson that—God forbid—crossed the border between one subject and another.

This time the forbidden subject I was breaching was consumer education; we were learning all about what the fine print really means at the bottom of credit card solicitations. I said to him, "Hey Kyle, we're all going to do a little bit of reading, but first I want to ask you a question. Now, don't get upset and don't get angry; just answer the question. How would you like it if I called you a complete and total loser?" (I had a good enough relationship with Kyle at this time that I could get away with doing this.)

He played right into my hands, as did the rest of the class, by causing a small commotion. Kyle joked, "Well, if you called me a loser, then I'd have to call you a . . . hmmmmm . . . mmm.mmmm.MMMM .mmmmm." His friends were amused; the mood in the classroom was good.

I continued, "Do you see the reaction you just showed? You're not very happy with that word, are you? Of course, I don't think you're a loser and would never call you that. But, what would you do if you were in the mall, and some guy came over to you and called you a loser?" Kyle said, "I don't know, but it wouldn't be too good for him." I said, "I don't blame you; I don't want to know what you would do because it probably would break the law in all fifty states.

"What about a credit card company? What would happen if they called you a loser?"

Kyle responded, "Well, I wouldn't get a credit card from them, or if I had a credit card, I would tell them that they could shove it in . . ."

"THANK you, yes," I interrupted, "I'm sure that that's what you would do, which is probably what I would do, too. But what if the credit card company was calling you a loser using a code word; a euphemism." I wrote the word "euphemism" on the board and defined what it meant. I continued, "You know, credit card companies do this all the time—it's in the bottom of this credit card offer." I then handed out a photocopy of a credit card solicitation that I had received in the mail recently.

All my students looked at it with interest. Had these knowledgeable financial experts never seen one of these documents before?

At the bottom of the credit card solicitation was language referring to the "preferred rate" and the "default rate." I told them to read through the fine print of this credit card solicitation and find the code word for "loser." I clarified what I meant: "When I say 'loser,' I mean somebody who doesn't pay their bills or somebody who pays the bills late, goes over their credit limit, or does any other irresponsible thing that makes them look bad, financially, in the eyes of the credit card company." This was something that I don't think any of them had ever done before: to read the fine print.

Fifteen sets of eyes started reading the fine print with varying degrees of interest, but at least all of them showed some interest.

It was amusing to see several of these very youthful eyes having to squint and move the page closer or farther away so that they could actually read what it said. The credit card companies know that virtually nobody will read this fine print, either because it's so small as to be barely noticeable, and/or it's so small that a large percentage of the population cannot physically read such small print.

Credit card companies do an excellent job of communicating information that might decrease their income in ways that comply with the law but result in very, very few people receiving the message being communicated about the terms and conditions of the offer.

Of course, credit card companies make a lot of changes—big changes—in the type size of their written communication when you violate any of the terms of their agreement. Then, their messages change from four-point Arial in light gray on the bottom of the back of the piece of paper to sixteen-point Bold Arial in red, centered prominently in the middle of the front of the paper.

But, by the time you read this information, about how you have been charged $30 for going over your credit limit, regardless of your past credit history, it's too late—the damage has already been done, your credit has already been harmed, and there's very little you can do about it. You need to teach your students this.

I'm sure that at this time, the credit card company marketing professionals want to stand up in unison, indignant over my comments, and insist that everything they do is perfectly legal.

This is the shady defense used by those who know what they do is less than ethical. It's legal for me to eat at a restaurant, receive excellent service, and leave a nickel for a tip, but I don't do it. I believe that the marketing of credit card offers is a business rife with misleading yet legal tactics, and my job as a teacher was to arm my students with knowledge—the best weapon to defend themselves against the real possibility of falling heavily into debt as a result of credit card misuse.

After a few minutes of reading the fine print, nobody could understand what they were reading; they could understand the English words, of course, but they didn't know what the words *meant*.

This is what is called a practical education, and all teachers should do this to some extent. Make sure your students can generalize their knowledge to real world situations.

We focused on the distinction between the preferred rate and the default rate. The preferred rate was 9.9 percent annual interest. The default rate was 21.9 percent annual interest. I put these two facts on the board and asked them again which word is the euphemism for "loser"? They got it immediately—"default rate." I shouted out, "YES! DEFAULT RATE!" I wrote on the board:
"DEFAULT RATE = LOSER"

I asked them, "How many of you have seen ads for bankruptcy law firms on television? How about ads to get out of debt, reduce your debt, and so on?" Every student raised his or her hand. I said to them in a loud tone of voice, "Why do you think that these companies that help people get out of bankruptcy are doing so well? Why do you think there are so many of them on television and on the radio?

"Where are all of their clients coming from?" More blank stares from my students. They began looking at each other.

"Do you realize how much money it costs to run a thirty-second commercial on television? Maybe $10,000, $20,000, $50,000, or more! Where are these law firms coming up with the money to pay for all these television ads? To pay for all of these radio ads? Hundreds and hundreds and hundreds of them every day times $10,000 each!" My students were sitting in stunned silence; they never thought about how much those ads cost.

"Where DID they get the money?" they wondered and couldn't come up with an answer to this question; it intrigued them because it does seem counterintuitive that it is possible to make a tremendous amount of profit by dealing with people who are desperately short of money.

There was a brief discussion back and forth between some of the students, along with some prompting from me, but not much forward progress was made. I finally told them something that startled them: bankruptcy attorneys make money by charging the people that they represent—the very people who have gotten themselves into a desperate financial situation.

I asked them if they knew anybody who's been through this situation.

What followed next was a delight because controlled chaos broke out.

Students were raising their hands left and right to tell a story about someone that they knew that got in trouble with their credit card, or someone that they knew who had declared bankruptcy, or a credit card that they had where they were charged outrageously high fees for minor violations, such as being late with a payment, going a few dollars over a credit limit, and so on.

This is one of those moments as a teacher where you feel good about what's happening in your classroom even though it doesn't follow strictly with the curriculum. I'm sure there are stuffy administrators out there (thank goodness, not at this school) who would walk into my classroom at this moment and say, dryly, "So, what novel are your students learning about?"

I would say to this administrator that the students aren't learning anything about a novel at this very moment, but they're learning about how to function effectively when we give them their caps and gowns and kick them out the door in six months.

I would tell this administrator that our purpose as educators is to educate, and this sometimes requires breaking from the script. We need to give our students precious time to communicate with each other in a safe environment, listen to and evaluate each other's ideas, relate what they hear to their own experience, and grow wiser as individuals.

Of course, you're their teacher, and one of your jobs, regardless of what you teach, is to help your students improve the way they read, write, and think.

So, always try to work reading and writing into your assignments as much as possible.

In this lesson, once the students were worked up into a frenzy over the less than honest tactics used when credit card companies design their offers, we engaged in a writing assignment where the students had to identify misleading characteristics of advertising that were displayed on the projector.

As I'm sure you've figured out by now, this whole subject is of great interest to me, and I enjoyed spending the time necessary to obtain a good cross section of ads that were misleading and credit card offers with particularly fine print. Over the next class or two, the students were given color copies of some of these ads, and some of them were shown on the projector.

They had to read the ads thoroughly, including all text enclosed within them, identify the misleading aspects of these ads, record these aspects in writing on a worksheet, write a justification for each misleading aspect that was recorded, and what could be done, specifically, to change this misleading aspect so that it did a better job of disclosing the true terms of the offer.

At this moment, I would hope that the aforementioned stuffy administrator was still in the classroom. He would see a room full of students reading with great interest, collaborating with each other regarding the assignment, writing with clear intent, and completely focused on the lesson.

My students were skillful at separating the wheat from the chaff within the ads and completed the assignment with a high degree of accuracy.

As I said earlier in this book, my students have good heads on their shoulders and, once pointed in the right direction, can exceed both others' and their own expectations. But, you have to stimulate their interest; you have to introduce topics which are going to motivate them to work, and this sometimes requires that you step outside of the standard English curriculum and introduce lessons that broach other subjects.

(Bringing out Virginia Woolf's "To the Lighthouse," masterpiece of stream-of-consciousness that it is, won't do it for my kids.) Once you get their interest, and they can relate the lesson to events in their own personal lives, and you can make the lesson relevant for them, the "Why are we learning this" objections fade away.

There's something else very important to keep in mind when teachers and educators design a curriculum—the learning standards listed by your state's Department of Education.

Each of these standards is for a particular subject area, like mathematics or English language arts. Within each of these standards are a series of overall goals and associated skills that are surprisingly varied and fully support teachers who implement diverse, academically broad lessons that may overlap other core subjects. When one reads these state learning standards, one realizes that English class should be much more than reading about Ishmael, Queequeg, and Captain Ahab.

In the state of Illinois, the English language arts learning standards cover five broad goals: reading, literature, writing, listening and speaking, and research. Here's a sample of *some* (there are more than seventy for early and late high school) of the subgoals and skills listed under these goals that support broad reading and diverse class activities (taken from the website of the Illinois State Board Of Education at www.isbe.state.il.us/ils/ela/standards.htm.)

You'll notice there's *much* more to them than reading novels and taking Scantron tests on their content.

Goal One: Read with Understanding and Fluency

- compare the meaning of words and phrases and use analogies to explain the relationships among them
- analyze the meaning of abstract concepts and the effects of particular word and phrase choices
- read age-appropriate material with fluency and accuracy
- preview reading materials, clarify meaning, analyze overall themes and coherence, and relate reading with information from other sources
- use questions and predictions to guide reading across complex materials
- analyze and defend an interpretation of text
- interpret tables, graphs, and maps in conjunction with related text
- evaluate how authors and illustrators use text and art across materials to express their ideas, such as complex dialogue and persuasive techniques
- summarize and make generalizations from content and relate them to the purpose of the material

Goal Two: Read and Understand Literature Representative of Various Societies, Areas, and Ideas

- evaluate relationships between and among character, plot, setting, theme, conflict and resolution and their influence on the effectiveness of a literary piece

- describe the influence of the author's language structure and word choice to convey the author's viewpoint
- analyze and evaluate the effective use of literary techniques (e.g. figurative language, allusion, dialogue, description, symbolism, word choice, dialect) in classic and contemporary literature representing a variety of forms and media
- discuss and evaluate motive, resulting behavior and consequences demonstrated in literature.

Goal Three: Write To Communicate for a Variety of Purposes

- produce grammatically correct documents using standard manuscript specifications for a variety of purposes and audiences
- using contemporary technology, produce documents of publication quality for specific purposes and audiences; exhibit clarity of focus, logic of organization, appropriate elaboration and support and overall coherence.
- Evaluate written work for its effectiveness and make recommendations for its improvement
- using available technology, produce compositions and multimedia works for specified audiences

Goal Four: Listen and Speak Effectively in a Variety of Situations

- use techniques for analysis, synthesis, and evaluation of oral messages
- follow complex oral instructions
- deliver planned and impromptu oral presentations, as individuals and members of the group, conveying results of research, projects or literature studies to a variety of audiences
- use strategies to manage or overcome communication anxiety and apprehension (e.g., developed outlines, note cards, practice)
- use verbal and nonverbal strategies to maintain communication and to resolve individual, group and workplace conflict (e.g., mediation skills, formal and informal bargaining skills)

Goal Five: Use the Language Arts To Acquire, Assess, and Communicate Information

- design and present a project (e.g. research report, scientific study, career/higher education opportunities) using various formats from multiple sources
- evaluate the usefulness of information, synthesize information to support a thesis, and present information in a logical manner in oral and written forms

Did you notice how few of the standards and goals specifically mention novels, short stories, and poetry?

Most of them use words like "literature," "text," and "authors," which implies they are granting educational freedom to the classroom teacher to use the materials that he or she believes will be relevant and motivating to students.

I love classic literature, and my students have read and will continue to read masterpieces like "Night," "Narrative of the Life of Frederick Douglass," "The Tell-Tale Heart," "One Flew Over the Cuckoo's Nest," "Frankenstein," and many others. Don't get the idea that my students aren't interested in the classics; when they've read these books, they've thoroughly enjoyed them, engaged in highly interesting classroom discussion about them, and handed in written materials that showed thoughtful and insightful analyses of the characters, plot, themes, and so on.

Of course, some books are more motivating than others. It's easier to get a room full of students from diverse cultural backgrounds to learn about the plight of Frederick Douglass than it is to motivate them to read about privileged, rich, whiter-than-white-bread Jay Gatsby and his not-particularly-interesting-to-a-teenager secret for weeks and weeks; they'll do it, but they're less likely to get excited over it.

It's just as important for them to read and understand a lease as it is to read and understand what Hamlet meant when he said, "To be or not to be."

If your student would get an unfair parking ticket, she should be able to understand how to read the fine print on the back and defend it successfully.

If your student's landlord violates the terms of his lease, he should be able to write a powerful letter that gets the results he wants.

Your students should know how to sift through all of the misleading nonsense in department store advertising so they can get the best deal on a computer. They should know how they are influenced by pictures in newspapers. They should know that the words "regular price" are virtually meaningless and why retailers use them to the consumers' disadvantage.

Yes, you need to teach them healthy skepticism if it means that they're going to read the ad more closely, listen to the newscast more carefully, and think about the newspaper article they're reading just a little bit longer. When they graduate from your class, you want them to know the difference between an adjective and an adverb as well as the difference between a well written and a poorly written police report.

21

KYLE'S OBSERVATION

Kyle, round-faced, disappointed with anything less than fifty-five minutes of nonstop entertainment, sat in my tenth-period class.

Usually morose and sardonic, when the class interested him he could be intelligently funny, highly insightful, and shockingly honest with his feelings. One of the things that entertained him the most was to say controversial things that would disrupt the class and get a reaction out of me.

His favorite was talking about drinking alcohol and smoking marijuana. Some of the expressions that would regularly come out of his mouth were: "kegger," "party this weekend," "sit back with a cold one," "I don't smoke . . . cigarettes."

I addressed these comments immediately because I felt it was important to send a message to the other students that it was not okay to drink and smoke drugs. Even though I had a feeling that Kyle enjoyed pushing the button and hearing the bell ring, in other words, making comments that he knew would get a reaction out of me and then watching the reaction, I still felt that disregarding his comments would send an implicit message to the other students that it was okay to break the law and get drunk at seventeen years old.

I would react with comments like, "Kyle, please don't talk about illegal things in class" or "Keep the discussions about drugs and alcohol out of the school and out of this classroom, please." He would comply, but then in a few days he would blurt out another one of those comments. I wrote him up for it once, and he seemed happy to be sent out of the classroom. In addition to comments about drugs and alcohol, Kyle would make a large number of minor distracting vocalizations, or MDVs. Here are some of the most common MDVs:

- [A loud sigh of boredom.]
- [Loud "TSK" sound by the tongue with skyward eye roll] followed by [deep inhalation] followed by [loud sigh of boredom]
- [Audible yawn.]
- "Oh God."
- "Oh, great. Writing. Woo Hoo."
- "Why are we doing this?"
- "What's the point of this? (Directed to no one in particular.)
- "When does the bell ring?" (Directed to no one in particular.)

Clever, clever man.

None of these individual comments were grounds for a write-up or were, by themselves, worthy of a hallway conference. He was highly observant of my behavior and saw when he was getting to be too much. When this happened, he backed off. But when things calmed down a little bit again, Kyle simply had to stir the pot. As always, I treated him with respect and encouraged him to continue to contribute because mixed in with his inappropriate comments were many highly insightful observations and true stories that interested the other members of the class and helped foster discussion about the topic at hand.

Yet, his misbehavior continued at a steady rate, like a squeaky shopping-cart wheel.

Discussions with him about it helped a little bit, and these discussions had to take place on a regular basis. Sometimes I had to send him out of the classroom and was highly irritated (but did not show it) at his superficial expressions of joy at being able to leave early. His attendance started to suffer. Unfortunately for him, he cut class on several days when we were having an important exam, and he found himself with a failing average about three weeks before graduation.

All of a sudden, Kyle had an epiphany and realized: no English class, no diploma.

I suddenly became an extremely important person to Kyle.

He looked at me after class one day and said, with new honesty, "Straight up—tell me, tell me right now—is there any way of me passing this class?" I told him that there was. I told him that there were several assignments that he could make up because they were not too old. I told him that his poor attendance was hurting the class participation component of his grade.

He said, "You mean, if I turn in these assignments and I behave myself in your class, I'll be able to pass?" I said, sure you will. He was highly relieved and extremely pleased at this news.

From then on, his behavior was much better. For the most part, he sat there without making the aforementioned MDVs. He turned in his back assignments. And, ultimately, Kyle passed the class.

On the last day of school near the end of the period, I said to Kyle that I was impressed at the remarkable improvement in his behavior. He smiled quietly. I said, "Kyle, let me ask you a question. It's the last day of school and the last class of the day. If I ask you a question, will you tell me the truth?" He said, "Shoot." I said, "Why'd you act that way in class? Why'd you always have to give me a hard time every day? The past few weeks you've been so much better; why couldn't you do that during the rest of the year? You probably could have gotten an A."

He looked at me with complete honesty and said these exact words, which I believe were completely honest and from the heart: "I don't know, Mr. Goldman, I really don't. You'd probably have to get a psychologist to figure it out."

Keep Kyle's honest statement in mind when a student starts misbehaving. Don't get paranoid. Don't get angry. It's not a deliberate, calculated attack on you personally. Most times, the student doesn't even know why he's doing it. Just address the behavior, forgive the person, and move on.

22

YOU'RE DOING THIS FOR FREE?

Stupid, underachiever, special, slow, retarded, can't do it, can't read, can't write, dumb, different.

A discipline problem, no good, delinquent, difficult to deal with, argumentative, acts out, can't sit still, doesn't pay attention, watch that kid, a knucklehead, a worthless piece of shit, probably won't make anything of herself, probably will end up in jail, probably a drug dealer.

A bad kid.

My kids get the message. They hear these generalizations that form captions at the bottom of the picture they see when they look in the mirror. They are generalizations that hurt.

Some of the students I teach do genuinely have a difficult time understanding certain concepts. Some of them have a hard time writing a plot summary of a film. Some of them find it very difficult to read a page of text and understand the subtleties of what they read, even though they often behave with great prudence and sensitivity within the complex social structure of friends, boyfriends, girlfriends, moms, dads, bosses, and police officers.

The proper use of "their," "there," and "they're" challenges some of them. All of them are teenagers, and a teenager's brain is not yet developed. This lack of development can result in disrespectful impulsiveness towards adults and the making of decisions that seem funny at the time but that result in a 2 a.m. trip to the emergency room or the local jail.

They hear the generalizations, and they believe them.

They see themselves as "bad." They seem to take a certain pride in this label, although I believe that usually this outward pride is a smoke screen to hide the discomforting truth that there are aspects to their intellectual functioning that don't measure up to the majority of the people in the world around them.

We are social animals, and we form our identities partially by whom we are grouped with. If you get accepted to an Ivy League university or win an Academy Award, you become a member of a subgroup of people. This subgroup itself possesses a reputation that is generally known by society as a whole, and you begin to attribute to yourself those characteristics normally associated with the group.

For example, if you win the Pulitzer Prize, you know, deep down, that you're a competent writer. Similarly, when you're told that you're going to be in special education classrooms for most of the day, you attribute to yourself the characteristics associated with that group of people by the general public, and you start calling yourself the names that are listed at the beginning of this chapter. This continues for years, forming a large and durable part of your self-image.

Sometimes the innocent words coming out of the mouths of these children illustrate the disturbing pervasiveness of this negative self-image.

This was illustrated in the following narrative of what happened when I was student teaching. When you're a student teacher, you're sort of a teacher and sort of not; it's a difficult situation to be in because the kids know that you're not really the boss.

But you can overcome this by being yourself.

One day when I was student teaching, I was in the middle of teaching a lesson to a ninth-grade English class, and we began talking about a concept discussed in the book we were reading. It was toward the end of the period, and the discussion became more general as more and more students contributed their thoughts. Suddenly, one of the students asked me, "So, what are you, a teacher? Are you actually a teacher? Do you work here at the school?"

I replied, "Well, I'm actually a student teacher. I'm in graduate school to learn how to be a teacher, and one of the things I have to do is to actually teach."

The student looked at me and said with a puzzled look on her face, "Why are you teaching here? I mean, why this school? Why this class? Why us?" I said, "Because I'm going to be a special education teacher, and this is a special education classroom." This answer only partially satisfied her. She continued to look at me, and then she asked, "Do you get paid to be a student teacher? How much are you getting paid to work here?"

I told her that I wasn't getting paid anything; in fact, that my teaching her was actually part of a course that I had to pay for.

I am reasonably confident that if I had told her, instead, that I was a space alien who ate electric lightbulbs for breakfast and produced piles of diamonds and rubies when I sat on the toilet, she would have not presented a more stunned and incredulous expression on her face. She leaped to her feet. I am not exaggerating. She didn't stand, she leaped.

"WHAT?! You AIN'T getting PAID?! To be HERE?! To be with US BAD KIDS? Are you FOR REAL?"

"Yeah I'm for real. I'm not getting paid. In fact, I'm paying to work with you."

"WAY-WAY-WAY-WAY-WAIT a minute. YOU telling ME that YOU AIN'T getting paid to be here, not one cent, and that you PAY money to teach in THIS CLASSROOM."

"That's right, I'm not getting paid. This is part of what you go through when you want to be a teacher. You have to actually teach, but it's part of going to college, and so you have to pay for it."

"Yeah, but why HERE? Why you wanna work with US? Why you wanna work with us bad kids?"

(Esteemed reader: At this point, give yourself a few moments, reread that last statement, and let its significance sink in. What was she revealing about her self-image?)

"I don't think you're bad kids. I actually like being here. I like working with you."

At this point, the student sat back down in stunned silence, just as a few other students wanted to hear it yet again, from my own mouth, that I actually was not getting paid anything to work with them. I heard from several other students' expressions of disbelief that I actually WANTED to work with them because they were "bad kids."

I repeated that I didn't think that they were bad kids and that I enjoyed working with them. Why did they have such a difficult time believing me? I was truly surprised and quite disheartened to hear these expressions of self-deprecation out of the mouths of such young people.

Months after my student teaching assignment was complete, another thought later crossed my mind. Why did some of these kids say to me, why do YOU want to work with US?

What did they mean by the word "you"?

Did it mean "you," a man? Did it mean "you," a white person? Did it mean "you" a person who insisted that they do the assignments and use their brains? They obviously perceived me as different from them in some way, and this difference that they perceived was a valid premise to what they believed to be a logical conclusion of my not wanting to work with them.

What was the premise? Was it gender? Was it age? Was it race? You could look at this in a different way, that I had broken a rule in their mind when they saw that I showed up every day, treated them with respect, and showed a genuine desire to be in the room with them. What was the rule I had broken? Was it sexist? Was it racist? Who taught it to them?

23

RACISM, THERESA, AND THE BIG-BOX STORE

"Racism" and "racist" are dangerous words, and heaven help you if they are unjustly tattooed on your forehead by people who are quick to judge but slow to listen and think.

They are words with poison barbs, words that stick to you with fearsome tenacity, words that divide people, wreck careers, ruin friendships. Few people want to be called "racist." To avoid being labeled with this term, we're supposed to treat everybody equally. We're not supposed to see a person's color or cultural background when we interact with them because doing so would be "racism," and then we would be labeled a "racist," and people would be whispering about us behind our back and filling out our performance review with the words "does not meet expectations."

Yet, members of minority groups celebrate their differences from mainstream culture, and rightly so.

When I was in elementary school, I learned that the United States was a "melting pot," in which many cultures, races, and ethnic backgrounds mixed together to the overall benefit and enrichment of the country.

CHAPTER 23

In Philadelphia there is a large, highly visible Puerto Rican community that is extremely proud of its cultural heritage and which contributes much to life in that city. There are many neighborhood organizations whose purpose is specifically to help those in the Puerto Rican community. The people who are involved in these organizations are deeply concerned with enriching the lives of people from Puerto Rico.

There are community centers, parades, charitable organizations, scholarships, and other systems in place to help people from Puerto Rico feel rooted in and proud of their heritage as well as to help them become successful members of the larger Philadelphia and American community in general.

Are the people that operate the Puerto Rican community centers racists? Would it be fair to point your finger at them and scream, "You treat Puerto Ricans differently! You discriminate against people who aren't from Puerto Rico! Racist! Racist! Racist!"

Of course not.

The people who operate the community centers, fund the scholarships, and organize the parades are doing these things because they understand the disadvantages of not being a member of the dominant culture and feel compelled to take steps to help secure the success of the members of their community in that dominant culture.

Can you imagine what would happen to a community leader if he looked upon recent immigrants and understood the cultural dissonance they are experiencing, the difficulty they are having in finding work because of a language barrier, and the manifold miscellaneous stressors that burden them and say that he is not going to do anything to help the immigrants because doing so would be racist?

This community leader would be ostracized by his peers; he would be seen as uncaring, as turning his back on his own people. His defense of trying to avoid racism would be seen as foolish because the actions that he chooses not to do are designed to help, not to hurt. I believe people would say to him that racism is when you hurt people, not when you help people.

Let's turn the focus of this discussion to the classroom.

The special education classroom has a disproportionately high percentage of minorities. In educational literature, this is referred to as overrepresentation of minorities in the classroom. A discussion of why this exists is beyond the scope of this book, but I want to make sure that you know that this overrepresentation is not—I repeat NOT—the result of a difference in intelligence or ability.

There are many factors contributing to this overrepresentation, including economic pressure, crime and the stressors it creates, language barriers, a higher incidence of single parent homes where the single parent must work multiple jobs, and others that are difficult to identify and more difficult to remedy.

Cultural diversity in my classroom is a very good thing because it exposes students to a broader range of opinions and perspectives during class discussion. Also, it helps acclimate students from the dominant culture with students who are minorities and vice versa, which is invaluable because such an environment is what they will experience when they enter the world of work.

Part of your job as a teacher is to prepare your students for life in the real world in addition to teaching them about when to use a comma, and having a diverse student body helps to achieve that goal.

Because you should expect all of your students to work together, put equal pressure on all of them to do their best.

Most students balk at schoolwork from time to time, and I don't see a correlation between skin color and likelihood of balking, but for some reason it bothers me when minority students slack off, refuse to do work that they are perfectly capable of doing, act in a difficult or uncooperative way, and by doing so, perpetuate the racist stereotypes that are unfairly attributed to them. I want all of my students—especially the minorities—to break through the prejudice and barriers that hold them back and prove to themselves and everyone else that they are perfectly capable of doing whatever career they choose.

Is that racism?

This entire issue occupied a large part of my brain during one or two days in about the middle of the semester. Theresa, one of my students, suddenly began a pattern of behavior that included trying to sleep in class, handing in frivolous or partially completed assignments, and being difficult and argumentative with me. I was thinking about her and how to handle the situation when I had stopped into the local big-box store to buy some things I needed.

As I approached the front of the store to pay for my purchases, there was a shift change taking place. Seven young, nearly identically dressed young black women stood at the front of the store waiting to relieve the young black women who were finishing their shifts. I stopped dead in my tracks, and I looked around at all the employees at the front of the store.

Every single one of them was a young black woman.

Every single one of them was probably making between seven and ten dollars an hour. Every single one of them likely had poor (or no) health insurance, little job security, and little hope of making a decent living wage regardless of how tirelessly they worked at their jobs. They were all friendly, all smiling, all, I'm sure, capable of moving up the corporate ladder into a more meaningful and rewarding career.

I am not disparaging cashiers or those who work in retail; I was a cashier for almost three years when I was in college, and it helped pay for my education. It's hard work. I remember what it was like for me; I stood on my feet for hours and hours on end, making a low salary, was given no financial reward for working hard and being pleasant and helpful to customers, and was reprimanded severely for the slightest infraction of rules by a manager for whom I have very few kind words. I was treated as a commodity, not as a person. I was given no respect by my managers; they never asked me how the store could run better, and when I offered some opinions, I was tartly told that my suggestions would be "discussed" and that I should get back to work.

My store manager enjoyed showing existing employees a stack of job applications waiting in the personnel department's inbox. He would say to us, "If you don't like the way things are run around here, I have a stack of twenty-five applications here of people who would love to trade places with you."

I'm sure that most of these women deserved more than this; they were capable of moving on to more challenging and rewarding work.

Why were they working at the big-box store?

Why was such a disproportionately high number of cashiers at this store young minority women?

If I ask these questions, am I racist?

I don't think so; there's no malice in my heart. These questions are fueled by my desire to see Theresa realize her potential. I was thinking about this issue the whole time I was in line, especially the next day when Theresa walked into third-period English in the same sullen, uncooperative mood she had been in for the past few days.

Her grade was slipping, and if she continued this behavior, there was a real danger that she would fail the entire class. In order to get a diploma, you need to pass my class. Failing my class has the real potential to delay your graduation date or make graduation impossible.

I was angry with Theresa, not because I took her visible disdain personally, but because I knew that she was beginning to screw up royally, and I didn't want her to waste her potential, struggling to make enough money to put a meal on her table and a roof over her head.

I wanted to—oh, what is the expression—get into her face about this.

I wanted to take her into the hallway and tell her what I really thought, that she was pissing me off because she was perpetuating unfair racist stereotypes by putting her graduation in jeopardy. I was angry at her. I felt as though she was, in a little way, hurting all minority women by slacking off in my class. It looked like another job application was going into the in-box at the local big-box store.

If she's lucky enough to get a full-time job in one of these retail stores, she'll make on the average about $11 an hour. After taxes are removed, she will be left with $.70 on the dollar, or $7.70 per hour. This comes out to be about $1,300 a month, which makes it very difficult to rent an apartment *and* buy food and clothing *and* have any money left over for any sort of pleasure. $1,300 per month makes it virtually impossible to provide for a child. As of the time of writing this book, a friend of mine is paying $1,200 a month for day care for her three-year-old daughter.

I wanted to tell all these things to Theresa.

I wanted to tell her that it was within her power to rise up out of poverty, do well in school, get a good job, and make enough money to achieve all the goals she sets for herself. I wanted to tell her that if she wants to help fight racism and prejudice, the most effective way is by graduating and becoming successful, and by doing so, proving to those with small minds that she is equal and possibly superior to them.

I wanted to tell her that actions speak louder than words, and if she tired of not being taken seriously by adults, it was her duty to stop acting like a difficult child and begin behaving like a mature adult and earn other people's respect by displaying character strength, competence, and a cooperative, pleasant personality.

But I didn't. Why? I was concerned about being labeled a racist.

I was concerned that she would misinterpret my statements, march herself down into the principal's office and tell him, the administration, and all of her friends that I was prejudiced and racist . . . that I was talking to her about how she was different because she was black . . . that I was focusing on her and making her life difficult because she was black . . . that I was putting academic pressure on her and not tolerating misbehavior because she was black.

I was frightened that, in her immaturity, she would accuse me of saying that "black people are all cashiers at the big-box store." (Hoo-BOY, can you imagine what would happen if the reporters get a hold of that sound bite?)

I was afraid that she wouldn't understand that what motivated me was to see her get her act together and realize her full potential; that the purpose of my lecture was to light a fire within her, to help her look in the mirror, and respect what she sees. But, I remembered that Theresa was not yet grown up. By virtue of this, her immaturity could result in her, intentionally or not, misquoting and misunderstanding me and severely harming my new career.

So I remained silent.

I restricted my discussions with her to her specific behaviors and what she needed to do to change them for the better. In doing so, I stayed safe, but did I miss an opportunity to have a positive impact on her? Did I miss a chance to make her think a little more about the power she had over where her life went?

Another episode happened in the classroom that had to do with racism, and I think that this is a good time to tell you about it.

24

FAIRNESS AND EQUALITY

She said I was racist.

Not only did she say that I was racist, but she put it in an e-mail and threatened to file a complaint with the assistant principal.

She was a paraeducator in my classroom, assigned to work with one particular student with mild autism whom she followed through the day as the student went from class to class. This responsibility put her in my classroom for only one period per day. Her duties are to support the student, give him additional instruction when needed, give him emotional support if he starts having a bad time, keep him focused on the assignment, advocate for his needs, and in general, do what she needs to ensure that the student to whom she is assigned learns as much as he can in my classroom.

She was born in Mexico.

Her accusation stunned me. One of my closest friends for many years was born in Puerto Rico. I took Spanish in high school. At the end of the semester, all of my students know who Aretha Franklin and Scott Joplin are and the incomparable contributions they have made to American music. My music teacher's husband was born in Argentina, and I've worked with him closely for years organizing charity concerts in the Chicagoland area. I insist that my students read the books "Narrative of the Life of Frederick Douglass" and "The House on Mango Street."

She said that I had treated David, whose parents were born in Mexico, differently than I treated Gordon, whose parents were born in Chicago, and when she saw that difference in treatment, she accused me of racism.

She told me that I treated David more harshly for misbehaving than I did Gordon. She said that they both were misbehaving about the same amount, but that I was more harsh with David than I was with Gordon because David was Mexican, and she said that I had better stop that or she's going to take this complaint to the assistant principal.

At once upon reading her e-mail I felt anger, dread, and fear. How dare she, how dare she, how dare she accuse me of possessing and putting into practice one of the most insidiously base and illogical patterns of thinking–thinking that results in human beings chopping off the arms of other human beings and throwing them in an oven, which results in a man being able to purchase another man, and then to whip the skin off his back while quoting the Bible as justification for doing so.

It was outrageous, it was unspeakable, it was unbelievable that she would say something like that to me.

She barely knew me. We had never had informal conversation outside of the classroom. She knew nothing about my point of view. She only saw me for about an hour a day. I knew that what she had said was false; I remember writing Gordon up in the past, writing Simon up in the past, writing plenty of white students up in the past just as much as students of other races.

My God, I knew when I got into this job that I was going to be working with minority students during most of the day, and that was one of the things that appealed to me about the job and still appeals to me.

I love the fact that the multicultural background within my classroom more accurately reflects life in the world of work.

I enjoy telling my students a true story about dinner a few years ago at a friend's house. Around the table was a woman born in the

Philippines who was married to a man born near Paris, France; a person born in China; a couple from Kiev, Ukraine; and another couple from Moscow, Russia. I was having dinner near Chicago, and I was the only person in the house who was born in the United States! Many times, in the classroom, a white person will make an inaccurate comment about another culture, and a member of that culture, sitting five feet away, will open up his or her mouth and set the student straight.

This "What the heck are you talking about?" reaction from a student upon hearing a bizarre statement from another student is a beautiful thing to behold. When an issue is raised in the classroom, regardless of what it is, I think it's invaluable that there are representatives from different cultures and races in the room with me. The students really listen to each other and educate each other about the differing points of view based on different cultural perspectives better than I ever possibly could.

Cultural diversity in the classroom is a good thing; it enhances sensitivity and prepares the students to be more tactful and more knowledgeable about the people they will likely be encountering when they leave high school. And here was this person calling me a racist.

But wait. Could there be truth in what she said? I like to think of myself as somebody who is self-aware, but maybe I'm wrong; maybe I do treat minorities differently. After all, my accuser is a member of a minority group, and being in such a group makes you more sensitive to the subtle signs of racism than somebody who is not.

I, for example, a Jew, am hypersensitive to anti-Semitic comments and drawings and still see them on a regular basis.

When I point these things out to another Jew, they agree with me that it's anti-Semitic. When I point these things out to somebody who is not Jewish, they tell me that I'm overreacting.

This brings me to my second emotion, dread. I started worrying to an extreme degree that there was truth in what she said, that I was treating the minority students differently. Is this why some of them were misbehaving? Is this why some of them seemed to be angry at me? It's true that some of the white students were angry at me from time to time when I was enforcing the classroom rules, but

I forgot about that for the moment and was focusing only on the unhappy minority students

I began asking myself the question, "Do you know who you are?" which is a very upsetting thing to ask somebody who prides himself on believing that he knows himself.

It was like one of those moments when you've stopped at a red light just next to a large truck. The truck begins to inch forward, and you don't know, just for the moment, whether you're moving backward or the truck is moving forward. You push your foot harder on the brake pedal, but you think you're still moving backward. Red lights flash, and sirens blare in your brain as billions of circuits try to figure out just what is going on.

Your brain doesn't know what to do. It's receiving discordant inputs, one from your foot on the brake telling you that you've stopped and one from your eyes telling you that you're moving, and you feel disoriented.

It's not a good feeling, especially because you know that you just began your career and you begin to dread that there may be deep-seated, fundamental flaws in the way that you think that will prevent you from becoming successful in this new career.

Fear.

The fear of getting a call from the assistant principal. The fear of a meeting with the administration where specific incidents are reviewed and painfully unpleasant, untrue conclusions are drawn. The fear of not being tenured. The fear of knowing that the administration can say, "Thanks, but no thanks" at any moment.

The fear of rejection.

The fear of having to explain to your family and friends that you no longer have a job.

The fear of shame; the fear of embarrassment. You're an educated, intelligent, forty-one-year-old professional who is not fit to stand in front of the classroom. You have self-loathing, the disorientation and depression of not knowing who you are. You fear all these things from a one-paragraph e-mail.

I know what it was that made this paraeducator write the e-mail. I was teaching a senior English class which had a number of colorful characters in it. Two of the most, oh, how shall I put it, "behavioral" students were David (who knows what "chanclas" are) and Gordon (who does not).

Yes, they exhibited inappropriate classroom behavior. Yes, I handled their behavior differently.

Of course I did. When you're a teacher, especially in Special Education, you handle every student's misbehavior a little bit differently, depending on what behavioral intervention is effective for that student. Of course you're going to give all of your students respect, kindness, and patience. Of course you're going to do whatever you can to help your students understand the material and help them trust and respect you as a fellow human being on whom they can depend and feel safe and comfortable around.

But when things go wrong, when the student has a meltdown or hasn't yet learned the right way to act, that's the point at which you must handle different students a little bit differently. Handling them all the same might have undesirable consequences.

The same response to misbehavior that will help one student calm down might infuriate another.

Understanding how to treat each student differently to get the most out of him or her is what makes a good special ed teacher.

Here's an example of how you must sometimes treat different students differently. Suppose that you have two students, John and Chris.

Let's start with John.

You know that his father was just arrested for public drunkenness. When he walks into the classroom in a bad mood tomorrow morning, you give the guy a break. Does he say something grouchy to you? Let it go. He doesn't normally act like that, he's having a hard time, and he's a seventeen-year-old who doesn't have an arsenal of strategies at the ready to help him pull through this. When he makes a grouchy statement, you let it go, and you don't make a big deal about it in the middle of class because you are reasonably certain that doing so will push an already volatile teenager over the edge and will likely incite him to do something that will get him in real trouble.

Some educators might say that this is hogwash, that a child has to understand that he must treat all of his elders with respect regardless of the circumstances, but we must remember that John is in this class-room in the first place because he has a difficult time with handling his emotions.

Because you gave him some room, he comes up to you the following day, apologizes for the way he acted, and you just built a relationship with him that's going to make it more likely for him to do more work for you and to finish that research paper on time when he doesn't want to. If you had taken the strict path and acted in a way that triggered an obscenity-filled tirade from him in the middle of class, it's unlikely that he would do any real work for you in the future.

In addition to John, you have another student named Chris.

He has a long history of challenging the teacher inappropriately as a method for getting attention from his peers. You had a series of discussions with him about it, but his inappropriate behavior persists. You've spoken with his other teachers and with his parents and have determined that he's doing this to get attention. All of his teachers, as a team, decide that each of them is going to employ the same strategy that will result in his being excluded from the classroom for a short while if he challenges the teacher over the next week, and you're going to report on the effect of this intervention on his inappropriate behavior.

The general thinking is that he will learn that challenging the teacher will result in being excluded from the classroom, therefore making it impossible for him to get the attention that he so desperately wants. Simultaneous with this intervention will be the employment of a secondary strategy of praising him when he is behaving appropriately. The result of this will likely be a reduction in the number of times that he challenges the teacher.

Now, imagine that you didn't know anything about John and Chris, but you were placed in this classroom the following morning to observe what was going on, and you see the following two events:

Event 1. You witness John telling the teacher that he's a hypocrite because he saw the teacher making a cell phone call in-between periods earlier; yet the same teacher enforces the school policy of no cell phones visible during the day. The teacher says, "John, we can talk about this later."

Event 2. Ten minutes later, you witness Chris saying to the teacher, "What does this homework have to do with the lesson? We're reading a story about a diamond necklace, so why are you asking us to write a stupid paragraph about something that happened that was ironic? I don't even remember what 'ironic' means!" The teacher says, "Chris, you're challenging me, which we've been talking about. Please sit in the hallway for five minutes."

An unknowledgeable observer might immediately become indignant at seeing the different way that you treated Chris and John.

How dare the teacher, the observer would think, treat John with patience and treat Chris with impatience and embarrass him, demean him, insult him by putting a seventeen-year-old boy into the hallway like somebody in kindergarten? Outrageous, the observer would think; he would think to himself, this teacher should be at a calculator and a computer all day long, not in front of a bunch of teenagers.

The unknowledgeable observer's thinking is misguided. The interventions he saw were effective and appropriate.

They might not have been the ideal teacher reaction; there may be room for improving the interventions, but they are based on sound behavior research and are wholly defensible. A short conversation with John after class elicited an apology, and he didn't make any grouchy comments for at least four to six weeks after that. Chris, as a result of all of his teachers' excluding him from class for three to five minutes after challenging the teacher, reduced the quantity of times he engaged in this behavior to a noticeable extent.

Yes, there is racism, intolerance, and bigotry in the world. But there was no racism in my classroom that day.

Everybody is forgetting the answer on the psychology test: "It depends." When a teacher handles misbehavior differently between different students, you must know the background of the students and the history of the teacher-student relationship before passing judgment.

Let's get back to what happened in my classroom that day. David was talking. And talking. He was doing it for the attention of his peers, who looked up to him and liked him, and also to get my attention. In some instances, you can ignore misbehavior, and it will extinguish itself.

But in this case, this day, his talking was out of control. He was making it impossible for me to teach the class.

So, I asked him to walk down the hallway, go get a drink of water, do whatever he needs to do to get this energy out of him and then come back, sit down, and participate in the lesson. Once he left the classroom, the rest of the students in his vicinity quieted down and got to work. David was a student who seems to have been goofing around most of his time in school, but I saw intelligence and capability that belied his playful and sometimes exasperatingly immature exterior. I did what all good teachers do: I pushed him. I made him finish the assignment. I didn't let him get away with acting like he was six years old.

Once, he decided that he was going to start calling me by my first name instead of the usual way of addressing me. He wouldn't stop this behavior, and it took a meeting between me and him and several administrators to convince him to stop it, which he did. His thing was to do things that got attention and made him feel like he was the funniest, most clever guy in the classroom.

One of the big payoffs for David was when a teacher would come over and give him a lot of attention in the form of scolding. Therefore, if every time David started talking excessively, I were to go over and give him a long lecture about expectations and how he was behaving inappropriately, I would be dispensing a glittering reinforcer that would simply increase the likelihood that he would talk even more in the future.

So, the most appropriate response for David, when he misbehaved, was to exclude him from the classroom for a short while, something he truly disliked.

What I don't think he realized is that he actually was one of the brightest students in the classroom, and I knew that he had the ability to do work far above the level that he was turning in. So I pushed him, as I said. I let him get away with very little.

I wasn't always like that with David, but as I got to know him, I saw his ability, and I knew what was needed to do to get him to reach his potential.

During the first month of the class, David's work was terrible. He was failing the class.

The result of my relentless pushing, my relentless insistence that he do better? His truancy dropped, his work improved significantly, his grade improved to a C, and he knew—he knew in his heart—that I didn't just give him that C, that he earned it with every sentence he wrote and with every paragraph he read. His misbehavior dropped. The number of times I wrote him up almost dropped to zero. I'll never forget the looks on his face the few times he was able to do A level work. He stared at the grade with a smile on his face, and he looked up at me. I said, "You earned that, keep it up." Of course, from time to time, he still had his high-energy days, but they were now the exception rather than the rule. I watched him mature many years within a few months.

Gordon, on the other hand, was a different sort of person entirely. Gordon was in my classroom primarily for behavior reasons. He was a good reader and a very good writer—probably the best one in my class. I believe that he was perfectly capable of moving up out of the special education class into a prep level class except for one thing: his behavior, which was troublesome yet different from David's.

Gordon was doing all the work, and the work that he turned in was top rate. He was getting an A in the class. I didn't have to push him to do the work. His attendance was excellent. He was almost never late for class.

The primary inappropriate behavior of Gordon's was his occasional, low-volume, expletive-filled comments to nearby students about a variety of topics.

Unlike David, Gordon did not like teacher attention. He basically wanted to be left alone to provide his play-by-play commentary to those near him. When I let him know I heard what he said and that his behavior was inappropriate, he looked surprised and embarrassed. For this one behavior, at least, I'd found something that was aversive to him and I used it with some effectiveness. (If only I had found effective behavioral interventions for his other inappropriate behaviors!)

There is another important difference in characteristics between David and Gordon that is essential that you know. David's misbehavior was frequent, and Gordon's was only occasional. Therefore I was more sensitized to David's misbehavior. This is a normal human reaction, and it's not fair to say whether it's fair or not.

Fair does not mean equal.

If two people of the same age come before the same traffic judge with a speeding ticket for going 20 miles an hour over the limit, one of the first things the judge is going to do is to ascertain the drivers' ticket histories.

If Driver A has never had a speeding ticket before and this is Driver B's fourth speeding ticket in the past six months, driver B is going to lose his license and Driver A is not.

Driver B can complain about this "unfair" treatment all he wants, but it's not going to be taken seriously because it's not a valid basis for an allegation of unfair treatment. The reason? Society's tolerance of misbehavior reasonably and fairly decreases significantly with habitual offenders. It's a fundamental characteristic of human nature, and it is reflected in our laws.

State law in Illinois permits easier treatment of minor traffic offenders through a system called "court supervison." If you are convicted of a minor traffic offense, have had no other traffic offenses over the previous year, and commit no future traffic offenses for the next year, the ticket is removed from your record as if it never happened. This option is not available if you have been convicted of a traffic offense over the previous twelve months. Another example is the "three strikes and you're out" law, where a person who is convicted of burglarizing four homes on four separate occasions is treated very, very differently than a person who is convicted of burglarizing only one.

Yes, it's true. I'm a human being. I was more sensitive to David's misbehavior than Gordon's because David's was an every-ten-minutes episode, while Gordon's was less frequent. So I reacted more quickly and more significantly to David's misbehavior than to

Gordon's. It's not because David's skin is brown, it's because he was misbehaving more often than anyone else in the class.

I can imagine what it was that the paraprofessional witnessed in class that day. She saw me send one student out of the room for talking and not send another student out of the room for talking. She never gave me the opportunity to explain why I was doing what I was doing; instead, she simply fired off an e-mail which upset me very much.

I won't go into details of how this was resolved, but I will tell you that it was resolved successfully and she and I enjoy a cordial professional relationship to this day. I think as she got to know me better as the months went on, and as she learned more about me, she realized that she was mistaken.

In a way, in retrospect, I think that perhaps she may have done me a favor because that memo is always in the back of my mind when a student suddenly begins to misbehave. It's almost like she installed a little supervisor in my brain, and the supervisor asks me questions like, "Are you being fair? Could your behavior be misinterpreted as racist? Can you justify what it is that you're about to do?"

Although on the whole I think it was a good experience, at the time it was one of the most upsetting things that happened to me during my first year of teaching. I ask you, dear reader, that if you witness a teacher-student interaction out of context, and you know nothing of the history of the relationship between the student, the teacher, the administration, and the family, and it seems like the teacher may not be treating all students equally, please withhold judgment and try to learn a little bit more about what you see: there's much more fairness and professionalism below the surface than you might think.

This is especially true for a special ed teacher; behavioral interventions that are marvelously effective for one student are completely ineffective for another; we must pull from a wide variety of techniques and individualize the way we educate each student in order to ensure the success of all of them.

Individualized education and behavior intervention is a cornerstone of special education; remember to view it as skillful teaching, and make sure you know the whole picture, in depth, before you come to a conclusion that unfair treatment is going on.

25

THE CRASHING AND BURNING OF A GROUP CONTINGENCY

An ice-cold water balloon dropped on the head is the appropriate punishment for any education professional who believes he or she has identified something that always works to control behavior.

In graduate school, my professors extolled the foolproof and fail-safe virtues of a group contingency. A group contingency occurs when a group of students all get the same grade or all receive the same reward or punishment based on all the students working together as a team. If one or more of the group doesn't carry their weight, the entire group gets a failing grade. This is, in fact, the way it is in most real-life situations, such as being on a football team, being a member of a group of soldiers on the battlefield, even being in a committed relationship.

You may learn something during your first year of teaching: when you ask a group of students to work together for a common goal (in other words, implement a group contingency in the classroom), be sure that the students involved are capable of behaving like adults.

If they are, then everything should work out fine. But if they aren't capable of doing so, you're doomed to failure.

All education professionals, from teachers to administrators, should rethink the wisdom of implementing group contingencies on populations of students with behavioral and emotional disabilities.

I make this request as a result of the utter failure of an attempt to improve behavior by establishing a group contingency between three students who exhibited disruptive behavior on a consistent basis. Here's how the students were acting, the group contingency that I implemented to try to improve the behavior, and the spectacular failure of the contingency within three days.

The players in the drama were Alice, Freddie, and Jim.

Each provided fuel for the other two engines. Each provided irresistible stimulation for the other two to talk. Every day, the three of them would walk into the classroom and begin some sort of verbal interaction. Sometimes it was Jim and Freddie doing the talking, with Alice listening. Sometimes it was Alice and Freddie doing the talking, with Jim listening.

Sometimes it was all three of them doing the talking, with nobody listening.

It was always distracting, always disruptive, and, over time, always irritating and frustrating to me. These students simply could not resist talking to each other. When they were faced away from each other, they turned their seats to face each other. When they were placed in chairs and told not to move them, they turned their bodies in the chairs to face each other. When I would remove one of them from the classroom into the hallway for a brief conference, the same ritual took place. It was as if they had been secretly trained in the Disruptive Student Academy, and here was the procedure they were told to memorize when asked to step into the hallway for a conference with the teacher:

1. Loudly say, "WHAT? WHAT IS YOUR PROBLEM? YOU NEED TO CALM DOWN!" to the teacher when asked to go into the hallway. (Note to reader: "Calm down" is teenage code for "Let me do whatever I want without negative consequences.")

2. When asked the second time to go to the hallway, loudly say, "WHY? I WASN'T EVEN TALKING! I WAS JUST ANSWERING A QUESTION!" (Note the contradictory statement.)

3. Continue arguing with the teacher, asking questions, and refuse to move until you see the teacher walking toward the disciplinary referral slips by the desk.

4. Say, loudly, "GOD, ALL RIGHT ALREADY! JESUS!" and walk out into the hallway.

5. If you are one of the members of the group that has not been asked to go out into the hallway, loudly take the role of defense attorney for the person being escorted into the hallway. Loudly say statements like, "SHE WASN'T EVEN TALKING! WHY DO YOU ALWAYS PICK ON HER; [insert another student's name] WAS TALKING, TOO! YOU HAVE TO CALM DOWN! WHAT ARE YOU GOING TO DO, SEND US ALL INTO THE HALLWAY?!"

6. When you are brought into the hallway, begin a preemptive strike by refusing to let the teacher finish a sentence; interrupt as frequently as you can and as early as you can with repeated denials of the charge.

7. Alternatively, if you do not feel comfortable with employing the previous strategy, you can adopt a childish, surly attitude—stand there with your hands folded in front of you, turn your head to the side, frown, and roll your eyes up to the ceiling. Say, "WHATEVER" about every ten seconds or so, regardless of whether or not the teacher is in mid-syllable.

8. If you are one of the students who remained in the classroom while the other student is out in the hall for the conference, get up out of your chair and go into the hallway to interrupt the conference. When the teacher out in the hallway asks you to return to the classroom, ignore him. Eventually, move to the classroom.

9. If you are one of the students who was kept in the classroom while the other student was brought out in the hallway, loudly

ask the student, "What did he say? What did he say? Did you get written up?" when that student returns back to the classroom.

Many of you might read the above exchange and ask yourself why in the world would anybody want to become a teacher.

But, I want to say to you that, although these disruptions are frustrating, they have an unexpected characteristic—there is almost no hostility within them. All throughout the time that this game, for lack of a better word, is being played in the hallway, you are aware of an unwavering affection and respect for you, despite the surliness, rolled eyes, and "whatevers."

And, throughout this entire transaction, your affection for the student and your paternal instinct never fades. I used the term "game" earlier, and it is almost like a game. It's a series of behaviors that are controlled by rules, guarantees entertaining conflict with an opponent, and is designed to achieve a substantial reward. The reward is an interaction with you.

The student is being difficult with you, but at the same time they care enough about you to go to the trouble of being difficult.

They are engaging in behaviors that are surprisingly effective at getting you to pay attention to them, even though it's what my college professors call "negative attention." Attention, positive or negative, is attention nonetheless to many of my students. They need it, they crave it; it's highly rewarding to them. It fills a deep void in their lives.

A number of my students have home lives that are filled with hardship and dysfunction: absent parents, ineffective parenting, emotionally abusive people living in the home, alcoholism and drug use, poverty, discrimination, violence, fear, and gang influence. The school is a strong stabilizing force for Mr. "whatever"-rolling-his-eyes-up-to-the-ceiling standing before you, and you, as his teacher, are an integral component of it.

When your student engages in behavior that's guaranteed to elicit your response, in some ways it's his or her way of saying, please show me that you care about me.

Please show me that I'm important enough for you to get upset over.

Please take me in the hall, please let me talk with you for a minute; let me talk with somebody who I can depend on, somebody who I can look up to, somebody who I know will be there for me every day; somebody who won't punch me hard in my ribs, who won't call me a waste of life in front of my girlfriend, who won't throw my clothing on the front lawn and lock me out of my own home in a drunken stupor, who won't compare me to others who have superior ability to me.

Let me talk to someone who sees my potential, my strengths, and my abilities. Let me talk to someone who will make me believe that I really can reach goals that I previously believed were out of my reach, who will forgive my bad behavior today—behavior that was mostly the result of my stepfather punching me in the jaw this morning—and smile and shake my hand when I walk in the classroom tomorrow morning.

The contradictory nature of this dichotomy—of seeing challenging behavior from a likable, affectionate student—is not immediately apparent to those outside of education. A school visitor might see the exchange in the hallway and say either that he sees a rotten lousy kid, or a teacher who is unliked, and would probably say both if he were interviewed further.

Even though as a teacher you understand the nature of this somewhat dysfunctional interaction, you still have an obligation to your other students to eliminate it.

Your responsibility as a teacher is to maximize the amount of instruction that each student gets, and you have to do what you need to do to get all of your students with the program and eliminate disruptive behavior. This is not only good for the other students, as it allows them the peace and quiet they need to think and concentrate on the task at hand, but it is also highly beneficial to the disruptive student as it helps them to develop new and productive behavior patterns that will help prepare him for life as an adult.

And so, in order to change the student's disruptive behavior, we must employ strategies. Reason with the student, you say? That's not always effective. Reasoning with a chronically disruptive student can be difficult, mostly for the reasons previously discussed (that the negative attention is rewarding in and of itself) but also because such students often have not had enough time to develop proactive, socially acceptable ways of acting in a classroom. Some students genuinely do not know how to control their behavior.

Simon may be six feet one with a beard, but when it comes to maintaining focus, he's potty training.

I decided to put one of the techniques I learned in graduate school into action, namely, employing a group contingency.

I decided that if the Three Musketeers—oh, pardon me, I mean Alice, Freddie, and Jim—could hold their act together and behave well for the first forty-five minutes of the class, they would all be permitted to leave ten minutes early to go to the library and read whatever magazines or books they wanted.

The term "behave well" meant that I would be redirecting the three of them, taken as a group, no more than five times per class period. Once I redirected any of the three of them the sixth time, they lost the option of leaving the classroom early for that day. I chose the option of leaving to go to the library because in previous discussions I discovered that this was something that was highly desirable to them, or at least they said that it was desirable.

Now, I realize that at this moment you're probably noticing a contradiction between what I'm saying and what I said earlier, namely, that the students misbehave to get my attention. You probably want to say, and rightly so, that if the students are misbehaving to get my attention, they're not going to want to leave this attention, and anything that results in their being removed not only from my attention, but the attention of their peers, is a poor reinforcer.

This is indeed a valid objection, but you have to remember that these three students were being highly disruptive in the classroom and making it impossible to teach on a regular basis.

I simply had to find a way to motivate them to keep quiet and compliant so that I was able to teach the class. Even though my attention and the attention of my peers was highly rewarding to them, I had to find some other reinforcer that would allow them to get some sort of payoff from a more socially acceptable set of behaviors.

The fact is that they told me that they liked the idea of being given the autonomy and trust of being sent down to the library to read for ten minutes.

The first rule of behavior modification is to find something that is desirable to the person whose behavior you're trying to modify and use it as a reinforcer for exhibiting desired behavior.

Another objection that you may raise is against the whole plan of allowing the students to be removed from the classroom as a reward for behaving well. You probably want to tell me that doing this does an excellent job of teaching my students that time spent in the classroom is oppressive drudgery, in the same way that teachers who assign extra homework as punishment do an excellent job of teaching their students that schoolwork is a bad thing.

Again, this is a valid objection worthy of discussion, but you have to remember that this was a desperate situation.

My job was to teach a complex curriculum to my students, and Freddie, Alice, and Jim were making it impossible for me to do this.

Literally every single day there were a series of arguments and almost constant disruptions in the class. I had to do something quickly. I had to find some way of getting them to be quiet.

Detentions, phone calls home, reductions in grades—all of these were not effective at changing their behavior. The stimulus of the classroom in each other's presence was a powerful contextual trigger to their disruptive behavior. So, I started to try what I thought was a good idea. I told them to wait when the bell rang one day during class, and they did. I told them of the contingency after class. I told them that if they were all redirected five times or fewer in one class period, all of them would be able to leave and go down to the library.

Their faces lit up with surprise and happiness.

The next day came. Alice, Freddie, and Jim found at their desks a small 3 × 5 card that said "Five times or less as a group, and you may leave at 10:20." No other student in the classroom knew of this contingency. Sure enough, when I asked the students to settle down so we could get started, Freddie and Alice continued laughing and talking to each other.

I drew a small green dot on the board as I told this group of three students I would each time I had to redirect them. Three sets of eyes flicked to the circle as it was being drawn, and all three went silent.

I was delighted.

A few minutes later, Jim laughed out loud at a face that Freddie was making, and another green dot went up on the board. As I drew the dot, Freddie said, "Why are you drawing that dot? He didn't say anything?" I drew another dot. At that moment, Alice said to Freddie, "Man, shut UP!" and Freddie shut up.

Alice was my unwitting assistant.

Did I tell you that I was delighted? If I didn't tell you that I was delighted, I was delighted.

I thought to myself, oh my God, it actually works. I saw the brilliance, the genius of it. Freddie might not listen to me when I asked him to be quiet, but he was certainly going to keep his lips juxtaposed when his friend and compatriot ordered him to do so.

Sure enough, the three of them behaved in a much more mature manner for the rest of the period, minimizing extraneous conversation, answering questions in class, contributing to the discussion, but not doing any of the immature, disruptive behaviors that I had grown used to seeing. When the clock showed 20 minutes after 10, I said Jim, Freddie, and Alice, it's 10:20. They gathered up their belongings and left the room. None of the students that remained asked me what was going on, although there were some puzzled looks on their faces. However, within a few moments, most of them realized what was going on, and the puzzlement vanished.

The next day, the behavior of Jim, Alice, and Freddie was excellent. I only had to redirect the three of them two times total. At 10:20, they all got up and went to the library. I was pleased with myself. I was proud of myself. I felt like I was the most effective behavior manager the school building had ever known.

In actuality, I wasn't effective—I was lucky.

There's a reason why there are dozens of lineal feet of shelf space devoted to classroom and behavior management at your local library or bookstore. There's a reason why there are dozens and dozens of alternative schools in the Chicago region alone. There is a

reason why highly intelligent teachers with thirty years of experience are sometimes unable to reach a kid and get him to stop acting
like a schmuck.

The fact is that changing the behavior of a teenager is often a
maddeningly intractable problem.

I would discover this the following morning when the students
came in to class as usual, and Freddie, Alice, and Jim took their seats
and displayed desirable, mature behavior. In the middle of the class,
we entered into a discussion about a book that we had recently been
reading. I don't know what happened; maybe it was the relatively
unstructured class discussion, maybe it was the day of the week,
maybe it was Jim's blood sugar level, but Jim began displaying his
old behaviors. He was tapping his pencil on the desk. He was making faces at Freddie, who was responding with utter delight.

The two of them had completely tuned out of the discussion and
started playing the "ignore the teacher" game when I asked them to
please pay attention to what was going on in class. I started writing
dots on the board as I repeated my instructions to Jim and Freddie.
One green dot, two green dots, three, four, five.

As the fifth dot went up on the board, Alice stood up and exclaimed, "This is bullshit! Why do I gotta be punished because Jim
can't control himself?!" She glared at me and said, "Is that fair? I've
been sitting here quietly, I've been sitting here doing everything I'm
supposed to do, I'm doing everything you told me to do, I didn't say
one word, and now because he is acting crazy, I'm being punished!
This is completely ridiculous! It's completely unfair!"

Jim and Freddie were so out of touch with what was going on in
the classroom that even during this impassioned speech, they continued their immature back-and-forth "I make a face and you laugh"
game. The rest of the students switched their gaze between me and
Alice, Alice and me, me and Alice, as if they were watching a tennis
game. What was the teacher going to do?

I stood there, mute. Alice was right. What had just happened was
completely unfair to her.

She did everything she was supposed to do and was unable to obtain the reward. I had made a serious error in judgment by assuming

that Jim was able to control his behavior. He wasn't. The stimulus of the classroom and his friends was a trigger far too powerful to be overcome by ten minutes of library reading or an after-school detention.

As I said, even during Alice's spectacular speech, he still was unable to focus on what was going on in the classroom despite the extremely high interest level of an angry student blowing off steam in front of the teacher. A student losing his or her cool with a teacher is guaranteed to earn the rapt attention of nearly every high school student with a pulse, but even this was not enough to stop Jim from acting like a child.

My instinct was to tell her the truth, so I stopped class and pulled her out into the hall. I told her what I was trying to do; I told her that I didn't know what else to do to try to improve her behavior and the behavior of her two friends. This conversation I had with Alice in the hallway taught me an unforgettable lesson about the value students place in being treated in an honest, respectful manner by a teacher. It also clearly illustrated the process of a teenager growing up just a little bit.

In the hallway, I got one of the biggest surprises of my first year. She didn't give me a surly, eye-rolling "whatever."

She said she understood.

She said she knew that Jim acted like a little kid and that it drove her crazy a lot of the time. I said to her, "Alice, I need your help. I can't stop all three of you from talking and acting silly and making it impossible for me to teach. Do you see how Jim acts? That's how you act sometimes." Alice said, "I know, but I don't mean to disrupt the class." I told her, "I know you don't mean to disrupt the class, but you do. I can't do this without your help. I can't stop all three of you from acting like this. Look, go to the library today, go down there, and think about this whole situation. Will you come in the class tomorrow and try to act more mature? Will you try to talk less and help me out?"

She said that she would, and I believed she really meant it.

We came back into the classroom, then Alice got her belongings and left. Jim and Freddie looked at her and looked at me to try to figure out what was going on. I continued teaching the class and gave the students their homework assignment, answering a few more questions from the other students about the day's lesson.

The next day, Alice's behavior was a little better. By getting her to calm down and talk a little bit less, Jim was given less fuel for his fire, and we actually had a good day. At the end of the day, I brought the three of them together and told them how pleased I was about how they acted, and I wanted them to try to act that way every day.

They actually listened to me for the ten seconds it took me to say those words.

From that day on, the three of them had good days and bad days. Some days Freddie was calm and Jim was bouncing off the walls, and sometimes it was reversed. But it seemed as though on the whole, their behavior was somewhat more manageable than before and there were longer and longer stretches of time where I was able to teach without having to ask one of them to stop talking.

But the group contingency? I never employed that again, at least not with those three. I never found another behavioral situation where I thought that it would be a good idea to employ a technique that brought on a student's involuntary outburst. This resulted in justifiable anger from another student who felt as though he or she had no control over receiving desirable consequences and avoiding undesirable ones.

26

WORTHLESS PIECE OF SHIT

Y^{ou} may be surprised to learn who said that.

When I was student teaching, I observed on a daily basis a ninth-grade regular education English literature class that contained a student named Jerome who was receiving special education services.

Jerome had an Individualized Education Program (IEP) with a diagnosis of Attention Deficit Hyperactivity Disorder (ADHD), which seemed to be an accurate diagnosis based on my observations of his behavior.

He was seldom on task, spending the majority of his time looking around the room, tapping a drumbeat with his hand, wrist, and pencil, and running his fingers along, and tapping, the rows of tightly braided hair on his head. Jerome was popular with his peers and friendly and cooperative with the teacher but had a difficult time staying on task.

This class was an American literature class with two teachers presenting material: the regular education English teacher and my mentor, a special education teacher. The regular education teacher primarily presented the material, but my mentor would also participate in the presentation. Also, my mentor would circulate through the room, offering assistance to students who needed it and monitoring the students receiving special education services to ensure that things were going smoothly.

Jerome was nearly always off task, and the attention of my mentor and the regular education teacher was minimally effective at helping him focus on the current activity.

When I observed Jerome not being on task, I felt a strong desire to go over and help him with whatever the current activity was. I wanted to try to give him the additional help he needed to stay on task—individual attention that was nearly impossible for the other two teachers to provide, given the twenty-eight students in the classroom. But, my primary role in that classroom was to observe and not to help, so I simply monitored the situation.

Also, I realized that my going over to Jerome on a frequent basis might be stigmatizing to him, and the resulting reactionary behavior to the stigma might result in a disruption of the class, ultimately resulting in my doing more harm than good. But, on a few occasions, I had the opportunity to lead the class in an activity as part of my student teaching duties. I took this opportunity to work more closely with Jerome and give him some more individualized attention than he was used to receiving. This was easy to do without his feeling as though he was being singled out because of my active role in the teaching of the lesson.

I found that when I did work with him, the percentage of time that he spent on task and the amount of work that he completed increased significantly. He had difficulty understanding some of the concepts presented in class, such as the symbolism within a poem, and he also had difficulty writing with fluency at grade level, but he seemed to appreciate the attention and was cooperative with me at all times. He accepted redirection, such as when I reminded him that it was inappropriate to drum his fingers in class.

Working with Jerome was sort of like working on a complex puzzle.

I hope that nobody, including Jerome if he happens to read this book, takes offense at my comparing the complexity and dignity of a live human being with an inanimate puzzle. I don't mean to reduce him to a game of checkers, yet I believe that all educators are puzzle solvers, or at least puzzle solution attempters, at heart. We must disconnect our emotions when trying to find the best solution to complex challenges in a systematic and scientific way.

This is the sort of approach I took to Jerome. What could be done in this particular classroom environment to help him focus a little better? Perhaps his seat could be moved, or he could sit next to less desirable students, or he could be given some sort of a timer on his desk, or perhaps the instructions needed to be made clearer in a more step-by-step fashion, or perhaps . . . well, other ideas popped into my mind, but that's not the purpose of this chapter.

The purpose of this chapter is to tell you about a short, shocking conversation I had with a new teacher at the school about Jerome.

One day, when the bell rang at the end of the period and the students filtered out, a new, young teacher named Laura came into the room. Laura was full of energy, intelligent, cheerful, and had a passion for English.

I had never observed her teaching directly, but I had walked past her classroom on a number of times while she was teaching and saw an energetic teacher that engaged students within the classroom. I knew that Laura had Jerome in one of her other classes. It might seem strange to an outsider that a student would be taking an American literature class and an English class within the same semester, but this happens frequently when students fail classes that are graduation requirements. I had a sudden desire to ask Laura what she thought of Jerome; if she had come up with any ideas to help him focus and demonstrate more of his ability.

I asked her, "Laura, you have Jerome in your English class, right?" She replied, "Uh-huh," and she looked at me steadily with a fake smile on her face. I said, "What do you think of him?"

She replied, "He's a worthless piece of SHIT" and continued her steady gaze at me along with continuing the fake smile.

I stood there with my mouth hanging open, speechless. I stammered, "Jerome Johnson, with the braided hair." "I know who you're talking about," she continued, "Jerome Johnson with the braided hair, and he is a WORTHLESS PIECE OF SHIT."

At that moment, the respect that I had for Laura evaporated.

At that moment, my brain moved her to a very different compartment, from one of the top floors, all the way down, down, down into a moldy box on a low shelf at the end of a long, dark, damp basement hallway. Within a few seconds, she went from a spirited, gifted, sublime educator to a common, loudmouthed, opinionated fishwife who managed to memorize a few lines of Longfellow.

I truly could not think of anything to say to her at that moment.

I felt like coming to Jerome's defense. I felt like telling her how sad it was that she had only been teaching for a year or two and should already be thinking about retirement due to burnout. But, by that time, the class had already become half filled with students filtering in for the next class in that classroom. The only thing I could manage to say was, "Wow." A student came up to her to ask her a question, and I left the classroom.

Then, I went into the faculty lounge and looked out the window. It was fortunate that I didn't have a class to observe or to teach that period because I needed some time to collect my thoughts. Laura's comment about Jerome upset me more than I would have anticipated, and I was trying to figure out why it upset me as much as it did.

At that time, I really wasn't able to put my hands around this problem. However, after reflecting on it over the next several months I realized what it was that made me feel as disoriented as I did. The trouble lay within the *person* who was making the comment: a young, energetic, highly competent educator, and not simply a random person on the street.

When a person tells you something, a significant component of the message being communicated to you consists of the very person who communicates the message. If a five-year-old child would come up to you in a drugstore and tell you there was a lion outside in the street, you'd probably look at the child's parents and share smiles with them at her precociousness. But, if a police officer came in the store and said exactly the same thing, you'd listen with rapt attention.

This illustrates why I was upset; it was because I had respected Laura, that I had been impressed by the multiple shelves of classic literature she had brought in to the classroom, that I had marveled at her energy, that I had smiled at her sense of humor. These inspiring characteristics of her personality, and my desire to emulate them when I had my own classroom one day, put a razor-sharp edge on her words.

Laura's short sentence to me was so disturbing because it brought up fears in me that my dreams of enjoying my job for the rest of my life and making a difference in the lives of my students were unattainable.

It was the hand of reality whacking my head out of the clouds.

Her words arose fears in me that my energy and my passion for teaching were of little value and that I was working very hard, and spending large sums of money, to enter into a career where I would be nearly powerless to make any significant positive change in the lives of my students because they were, deep down, worthless pieces of shit, and it was only a matter of time before my rose-colored glasses fell off and I discovered true, grim reality.

Some might say that such doubts should never have entered my mind, but remember that at that point I had no experience with students in special education. I had never raised children of my own, and even if I had, being a teacher is not the same thing as being a parent, from what I have been told. Thus far at grad school I had only taken a few semesters of academic courses and had little or no opportunity to actually be responsible for the academic progression of a crew of seventeen-year-olds. So, at forty years old, with a few decades of adult life experience, I had no context in which to frame Laura's comment.

So, the paranoia, the fear, the uncertainty, the questioning, and the second thoughts had free reign inside my head.

A few days later, I had the opportunity to talk to Jerome after school. I was assisting my mentor with his duties in the Photography Club, and Jerome walked in to spend some time with a few of his friends. This impromptu visitation was actively encouraged because students spending time in a supervised, safe classroom after school with their friends are not on the street getting shot because they forgot where one gang's territory ends and another's begins.

I asked him how his classes were going, and he responded like a young man and not a worthless piece of shit.

He told me about which classes were easier for him and which were giving him difficulty—and English was one of them. He told me that he had a very hard time understanding what he reads and because of that, it's difficult for him to stay focused. He told me that he's tried for years and years to do well in English, but the words jumble up and he has a hard time understanding what he reads and what it is that he's supposed to do.

We talked about girls and we talked about cars, and I must tell you all that it was a thoroughly enjoyable conversation. He was polite, he was friendly, he spoke in a mature manner, and I got to see a side of him that really made me like him. I saw him as a student, and as a man, and as a teenager as he flirted with a few of the girls in the classroom. Of course, he is a person with ADHD, and it was hard to keep his attention sometimes; but then again, his attention was being distracted by his friends, and if I remember my high school days correctly, I probably wouldn't be paying much attention to a teacher's questions if those distractions were in my immediate vicinity, either.

If only Laura were in the room with me, observing what I observed, and listening to our conversation. Perhaps she would spend a little bit more time helping Jerome focus during the next class.

Jerome was easy to deal with; I wonder how Laura would have reacted to having to teach my student named Garth.

Of all my students, I liked Garth the least. The only thing that I could depend upon in Garth was a disdainful attitude towards me.

Regardless of my approach, Garth almost always rejected it. If I praised him for good work, he remained silent and was no more likely to do good work subsequently than if I had not praised him.

He would consistently do things that he knew would result in a response from me, including using a cell phone during class, talking to another student loudly enough to disrupt the class, moving his seat without permission, and so on. His persistence and his consistency in driving me absolutely up the wall and out of my mind was remarkable.

It was particularly maddening because he was one of my most intellectually capable students, yet he used his intelligence and his resourcefulness to develop his maladaptive behavior, which made him particularly vexing. When a challenging assignment was given to the class, he would finish in half the time of the next most capable student, hand in a paper that was well written, well thought out, and virtually free of grammatical mistakes, and then would do something—and what that something was could be almost anything—which would interrupt the classroom and interfere with the train of thought of students who were in serious need of a quiet environment to finish the assignment.

When I would remove him from the classroom for these infractions he would not go without a diatribe against me personally, the school, my teaching, my shoes—anything that would allow him a few extra glorious moments of time in the spotlight.

I must admit to you that over time this all got very old, and I began to dislike him.

My perception of him changed from that of a troubled child who engages in maladaptive behavior as a result of forces beyond his control to that of an intelligent adult, fully aware of his behavior and the effect it has on those around him, who coolly plans beforehand to engage in specific, targeted, effective behaviors that are known to result in entertaining reactions from me and then engage in these behaviors and obtain pleasure from witnessing the result.

I never yelled at him; I almost never allowed him to engage me in an argument and control the situation.

I would remind him of the class rules, bring him out into a hallway meeting if necessary, and explain to him the benefits of behaving in the right way and the consequences of behaving in the wrong way. In most cases this sort of reasoning and reminding was effective, but when a student is being so disruptive that it's impossible for you to teach or for the other students to learn, the teacher must remove the disruptive student from the classroom, and that's what I did on a consistent basis.

Some might say that if I had worked harder on coming up with an intervention strategy that was effective for Garth, I would have been able to reach him and would have eliminated the situation. But, I don't believe that was possible with him; he seemed to make a conscious attempt on a daily basis to disrupt the classroom environment, and as a result, slowly over time, my opinion of him went way south.

However, throughout all of this, even when Garth was at his most irritating, and even if I was on vacation with my friends hundreds of miles away from the school district so that no coworker could hear me, I still would never have said that he was a worthless piece of shit.

When you're faced with a student like Garth, talk to your friends about this kid Garth who drives you out of your mind. Try to get some insight from them as to why he behaves the way he does and what you could possibly do to get him to realize that these maladaptive behavior patterns will result in a very bleak employment outlook. Think about the way that you handle his behavior and try to come up with ways of improving it. Pat yourself on the back for maintaining a sense of humor and not losing your cool when he asks you in front of the class if you got your teaching degree from a box of Cracker Jack.

It's been a year, and I've experienced great joy in the classroom and have gotten to know some wonderful young people. Sometimes (actually most of the time) dealing with them all day long might require your taking a nap as soon as you get home from school, but when you wake up from the nap, you'll probably start thinking about tomorrow's lessons because you'll know that all of your students deserve it. None of them, even Garth, are worthless pieces of shit. Garth got a job with FedEx right around the time that he was graduating. I really, truly hope that he succeeds in this job and that he finally learns to keep his mouth shut when something happens that's not to his liking. I'll tell you honestly, in a few years, if he would show up at my classroom door, I'd be happy to see him. I'd want to know how he was doing, where he was working, and who he still talks to from high school. I hope that I never look at a student and think that he is a worthless . . . well, I've used that expression enough for this book.

27

NO DRINKS IN THE CLASSROOM

The school handbook has a lot of rules. A lot of them. Many of them. A large list. A long litany. A comprehensive compendium. An exhaustive, extensive, expansive, extended, excruciating explanation.

What you shall wear; where you shall be; what you shall do; with whom you shall talk; when you shall arrive; when you shall leave; why you shall obey; what shall take place if; no guns; no objects that look like guns in any way; no knives; no sharp or dangerous objects that could be used as a weapon or could pose a hazard to other students or staff; no drugs; no substances that look like drugs; no gang references; no gang colors; no gang graffiti; no gang hand signals; and no gang-influenced clothing selections or styles of wearing such clothing, such as one pant leg up and one pant leg down. No food or drinks in the hallways or classrooms; no yelling or running in the hall; no physical intimidation; no fighting; no threatening; no yelling; no demeaning glances, no unkind comments; no excluding others from your peer group, no practical joking; no inappropriate, vulgar, indecent, prurient, ribald, racist, elitist, ethnocentric, misogynist, homophobic, or otherwise offensive or disparaging language, and no backtalk. No delay in completing the request of a staff member; no littering; no tardiness; no food of any kind deposited in the water fountain drains; no disobedience; no cleavage; no thighs; no navels (except for oranges and then only in the lunchroom during the designated lunch period in an area designated by the lunchroom supervision staff and in a manner befitting the code of conduct of the school and not eaten in a way so as to disturb, harass, or interfere with the enjoyment of the other students in the lunchroom); no visible underwear; no visible shoulder blades; no text or images on clothing which refer to any kind of alcohol, violence, or drugs; no blocking of exits; no congregating near the main office; and no depositing of paper towels on the bathroom floor.

Wait, wait . . . give me a moment to catch my breath.

There's nothing wrong with these rules; they make sense, but you have to admit that there are a lot of them. When a teenager sees them, you can guarantee he will roll his eyes to the sky and say, "Oh, puh-leese, what do they think I am, a child?"

Now before you label me as an antiestablishment modern-day hippie who advocates the questioning of authority and believes that if it feels good, you should do it, I want you to understand that I believe in rules and laws. They allow me to drive to school without getting killed in a car crash. They prevent the electric company from telling me that although I'm a customer in good standing, I have to pay a $5,000 security deposit within five days or else they're going to disconnect the power to my home.

I know why the school has an exhaustive list of rules; it reflects the larger desire of the members of nearly all civilizations to live in peace and safety. Furthermore, I understand that it's our responsibility as educators to do more than simply explain what a prepositional phrase is; that it's incumbent upon us to inculcate into our students a respect for rules which, if followed, guarantee the maximum opportunity to live a contented and happy life.

Rules are enforced in my classroom; I write tardy slips when students are tardy, I take cell phones when I see them being used during class, and I send students down to the assistant principal's office for dress code violations. I agree that if students don't learn respect for rules, they're likely to get into legal trouble and not be able to hold a rewarding job when they get out of school.

But on the other hand, I don't want to turn my classroom into a minirepresentation of Victor Hugo's *Les Misérables*, in which Javert insists on enforcing the law to the letter regardless of the circumstances.

Even the most dogmatic and conservative career person in the criminal justice system would agree that it is not appropriate to throw a man in a squalid prison for five years as punishment for stealing a loaf of bread to feed his starving children.

Doing so would result in an imprudent expenditure of scarce taxpayer dollars, the starvation and death of the man's children, and the lamentable embitterment of the imprisoned man to judges, juries, and police officers—ironically, all of whom are employed in these occupations so they may protect the very man they have harmed from that which would do him harm.

A classroom is an autocracy, and an autocracy without wisdom and compassion from the autocrat will, in short order, disintegrate and explode in a spectacular display of student anger, threatening e-mails from parents, a flurry of student rescheduling, and a teacher being "asked" to work in another school district.

Notice to my administrators: I do not enforce all the rules all the time, and I say this with a clear conscience as a mature, moral, law-abiding person.

I further say this as a teacher with one year of experience under my belt who has discovered that minor bending of rules from time to time has resulted in improved relationships with my students—not because they see me as somebody who'll let them get away with things, but because they view me as somebody who is capable of recognizing them as mature individuals capable of making wise decisions and who will treat them with forgiveness and compassion when they make honest mistakes.

This desire within me to give my students a break and treat them as adults was challenged this year with a memo from the assistant principal.

Will, my student, was likable but immature. One of the most significant incongruities you experience as a high school teacher is the fact that the person standing before you, who is six feet tall and can probably bench press more than you can, is very likely to act in the same manner as your friend's four-year-old son.

Such was the case with Will; on a regular basis, depending on the phase of the moon or the day of the week or the relative humidity within the classroom or whatever other mysterious combination of factors, he would behave in a childish manner. My students are going through an awkward and challenging transition—from that of children to that of adults.

Just as a boy who is going through puberty experiences the uncontrolled cracking of his voice, where his vocal cords can't decide whether to sound like a child or sound like a man, five years later he experiences the cracking of his behavior patterns. He uncontrollably switches between acting like he is four and acting like he is forty, and he has as little control at seventeen over the maturity level of his behavior as he did over the pitch of his voice when he was five years younger. Our jobs as teachers are to bear with this waywardness and continue to give our students guidance.

Will needs a lot of guidance.

As you most likely know, public schools are generally not air conditioned. When you take a massive un-air-conditioned building, cram it with two thousand hypermetabolizing teenagers and bake it in the hot noonday sun, you have on your hands what most teachers would say is an educational obstacle.

Most of the students, especially the boys, of which I have a majority in my classroom, complain about the heat with vigor. No descriptive expression of the heat is too over-the-top for them.

If they are able to put into your head a shocking and gruesome image of a classroom full of putrid globules of melted flesh, on top of which are scattered charbroiled ribs and cooked tibias here, blackened femurs and bleached skulls there, all floating in a foot-deep pool of fetid human sweat, it would still not satisfy their need to describe to you exactly how blisteringly, volcanically hot they are.

Further adding to the amusement factor you experience when hearing these stories is the fact that many of the complainers are wearing sweatshirts.

That's right, you heard me. Sweatshirts. Long sleeves. No, even better: three—count 'em—three shirts.

I am not making this up.

Normally I don't make comments about the clothing that students wear, but when the three-shirted heat and humidity complainer finished expressing himself, I almost reflexively stammered, "Why are you wearing three shirts, for God's sake?" The result was silence on the part of the heat-prostrated student.

A second later I heard, meekly, from another student, "because that's the style."

I couldn't help myself. The image of this poor kid wearing three stylin' shirts with sweat trickling down his forehead was too much. I laughed out loud, and fortunately the other students laughed with me. I said, "You mean the style of wearing three thick shirts when it's 88 degrees in the classroom?" The One With Three Shirts laughed a little more. I said, "Style is good, my man, but find a style that doesn't result in so much sweat."

He compromised The Style, took off one of the shirts, and sat close to the fan for the rest of the period. See what I mean about six-feet-tall people needing adult guidance about all kinds of surprising things?

I imagine by this point you get the idea that it was hot in school, and under these conditions the lure of a cold drink of water is too much for high school students, especially when they have just come from gym class. The school rule is that there is to be no food or drink in the classroom, but I had so many students asking if they could go get a drink of water that I realized that this rule is not practical, and I was going to disregard it.

Don't get the idea that I just casually disregarded a school rule. The fact is that many students were missing important parts of the lesson because they wanted to leave the classroom to get a drink of water. These students weren't asking for a drink because of a frivolous attitude toward the class; their faces were red from the heat, and I could literally see sweat on their foreheads.

Some teachers and administrators might say to me that I should tell my students to get a drink during the passing period, and if they didn't use the time effectively during the passing period and were unable to get a drink at that time, that it was tough patooties, and they would have to simply wait until the bell. Case closed.

Case reopened. Rules are made to be broken, to wit:

When I was the information technology director for a large national retail chain, we were permitted to bring—gasp!—food and drinks into meetings; in fact, people regularly brought doughnuts, coffee, soda pop, and water with them.

We consumed the food and drinks like adults, of course; there were no food fights, there were no smears of doughnut jelly on the walls, and there were no puddles of cold coffee on the leather seats.

Nearly all of the employees at the company had some sort of coffee cup, soda can, napkin with cookies on it, or some other combination of water, sugar, caffeine, and carbs at their desk, and management did not have the slightest objection to this because they knew that a hungry, cranky, caffeine-deprived employee takes much longer to produce accurate financial statements and is less likely to spot a vendor who is charging more than the contracted price.

All of my professors at graduate school—all of them—permitted you to bring drinks and food into the classroom. In fact, a particularly memorable event at grad school was when one of my first professors brought in a collection of cookies, pastries, and juice during the first day of classes; this food was her way of conveying her desire to make us feel at ease with her and with the entire graduate program.

It worked; I immediately felt much more relaxed about being in graduate school, and I still remember her simple gesture with great affection.

At the faculty meetings at my high school, food is served on a regular basis; during meetings with parents, there is usually an assortment of light snacks, candy, and bottled water in the meeting rooms; when the superintendent of the district himself calls a meeting with faculty members, there are granola bars, popcorn, and an assortment of beverages on ice at the side of the room. Even the receptionist of the director of human resources has a large bowl of candies on her desk, which I referred to earlier in this book.

Keeping all these things in mind, could you, the reader, come up with any reasonable explanation for the school rule of absolutely no food or drink in the classroom? Please remember that I said "reasonable." We're supposed to be treating our students like adults; in most circumstances adults are allowed to snack on a granola bar if they feel hungry.

Sure, some of you will say that if we let the kids bring food and drink into the classroom, the floors and walls will look like the inside surfaces of a restaurant's garbage dumpster within a few hours.

This is not true. I learned something important when I relaxed the rules.

Nearly all of the time, seventeen-year-olds return respect with respect.

I told my students that they are permitted to bring food and drink into the classroom but to keep the room neat and clean. The students know that they must throw away all wrappers and juice bottles, and they may not drop crumbs on the floor or leave crumbs on the tables—everything must be cleaned up completely when they leave the room. The small percentage of students who do bring food or drink into the classroom comply with these requests; I give them the responsibilities of being an adult, and they have not disappointed me yet.

Yes, yes, yes, the mice.

It is a fact that there are mice in the school; what a surprise—mice in a one hundred-year-old building with five cafeterias! I've seen mice in my own classroom, sneaking out quietly as I was sitting there after school grading papers. One of the little guys was walking around the floor, as nervous as a moth in the testing room of a flamethrower factory, trying in vain to find something to eat. After a few moments he decided the quest was pointless and disappeared under the gap in the built-in shelves.

The Gaping Maw (I called him) was disappointed because not only is my room kept clean, but the waxed tile floor is swept thoroughly every night and the plastic bag within each trash can is replaced every day right after classes. The Maw will find no morsels in Room 231.

CHAPTER 27

You may have forgotten about Will, and if you have, which is understandable after having to read the Adventures of the Educated Rodents, I will remind you that he was the likable, perspiring, thirsty, immature student mentioned about a hundred pages ago.

Near the beginning of the year, I was giving a lesson on English grammar and had turned to write something on the board. I heard giggling and turned around to find a surprising sight that I'm going to try to describe to you now.

Will was sitting in his seat with his head tilted back about 45 degrees. He was holding a half full Gatorade bottle high in the air with both hands, and was squeezing the bottle as it was tilted down. The lid on this bottle had a small hole in it that Will had somehow created. The result of this was a steady stream of purple Gatorade flowing from the bottle down into his mouth. My first reaction upon viewing this was amazement because I must say that his aim was remarkably accurate. After a second or two, the amazement died down and was replaced by the same feeling of mild irritation that a parent might feel when he discovers that his three-year-old daughter has drawn on the wall with Mommy's lipstick.

I said, "Will, knock it off, please, that's really immature and really inappropriate." A few more seconds went by of this bizarre Gatorade commercial outtake, and for some reason, I suddenly got angry. (He later said that he was unable to stop because if he did, purple Gatorade would have ruined one of his two stylin' shirts.)

Usually when you ask a student to stop doing immature behavior, they do it. They may complain about it and have a little minor temper tantrum, but they know they have to knock it off and they do— usually.

But this behavior persisted past the time frame of childhood innocence and extended into the category of a conscious, premeditated act of a student who wishes to deliberately disrupt the class. My class.

No sir. It's not going to happen in my classroom.

I said, "Will, put the bottle down right now, or I'm going to write you up." I was quite angry at this point, but I was not showing it. The

---

CHAPTER 27

You may have forgotten about Will, and if you have, which is understandable after having to read the Adventures of the Educated Rodents, I will remind you that he was the likable, perspiring, thirsty, immature student mentioned about a hundred pages ago.

Near the beginning of the year, I was giving a lesson on English grammar and had turned to write something on the board. I heard giggling and turned around to find a surprising sight that I'm going to try to describe to you now.

Will was sitting in his seat with his head tilted back about 45 degrees. He was holding a half full Gatorade bottle high in the air with both hands, and was squeezing the bottle as it was tilted down. The lid on this bottle had a small hole in it that Will had somehow created. The result of this was a steady stream of purple Gatorade flowing from the bottle down into his mouth. My first reaction upon viewing this was amazement because I must say that his aim was remarkably accurate. After a second or two, the amazement died down and was replaced by the same feeling of mild irritation that a parent might feel when he discovers that his three-year-old daughter has drawn on the wall with Mommy's lipstick.

I said, "Will, knock it off, please, that's really immature and really inappropriate." A few more seconds went by of this bizarre Gatorade commercial outtake, and for some reason, I suddenly got angry. (He later said that he was unable to stop because if he did, purple Gatorade would have ruined one of his two stylin' shirts.)

Usually when you ask a student to stop doing immature behavior, they do it. They may complain about it and have a little minor temper tantrum, but they know they have to knock it off and they do—usually.

But this behavior persisted past the time frame of childhood innocence and extended into the category of a conscious, premeditated act of a student who wishes to deliberately disrupt the class. My class.

No sir. It's not going to happen in my classroom.

I said, "Will, put the bottle down right now, or I'm going to write you up." I was quite angry at this point, but I was not showing it. The

226

purple fountain continued. Out came my pen and the disciplinary referral slip and down he went to the assistant principal's office.

The laughter died down, and the lesson continued. Actually, as I think back about it the whole event probably lasted no more than ninety seconds. The event was over, I thought, but it wasn't.

I found out that Will received, I believe, two consecutive Saturday detentions for disrupting the class and for insubordination. But the thing that irritated me probably more than a Saturday detention irritated Will was the memo I received from Mr. Dunbar, the assistant principal:

Dear Mr. Goldman,

I wish to remind you of the school policy that no food or drinks are to be brought inside of classrooms. I direct that none of your students may bring food or drink of any kind into your classroom. If any of your students have a problem with this policy, tell them to make an appointment to see me.

Sincerely,

R. D.

This memo stirred up a lot of emotions in me. Part of me was nervous because I was not a tenured teacher, and letters like this could be used as justification for not inviting me to come back to teach the next year. I feared that my violating the school policy had to a small extent put my job in jeopardy at the school.

But, the other part of me wanted to tell him that I get more out of my students when I treat them like adults and to let me do my job with a reasonable degree of autonomy. I wanted to tell him to keep some healthy perspective on the situation; I'm letting my students eat granola bars and drink orange juice as we read Poe; I'm not passing out loaded guns, snorting cocaine, and showing porn movies involving various breeds of farm animals.

In a short time, the part of me that was nervous about keeping my job somehow took the upper hand, so I made an announcement to all of my students the next day, with the temperature in the classroom at approximately 76 million degrees Fahrenheit, that they are not permitted to bring in drinks or food of any kind from this day forward until death do us part, which I feared might happen at any moment upon making the announcement.

The death of which I speak could either be my students' or mine because some of them made it clear that if they could not drink water in class they would die and because some of them glared at me with an expression that foretold the unspeakably horrifying methods they were formulating in their minds of murdering their English teacher.

Every educator will do well to understand that a large part of a teenager's mind is devoted 24/7 to making mountains out of molehills and ensuring its owner's experiencing a fresh crisis every day at a minimum.

One might discount their objections as simply another expression of teen outrage over the "totally, totally bogus" rules we impose upon them. But, I'm telling you that there was more to their objection than that; they felt truly insulted by the new rule.

One student, Bob, glared at me and pointed to a water bottle I had in the front of the class and said, "Okay, okay I get it. We're not allowed to have water, but you are. We can't be trusted with drinking a bottle of water. Why do you get to have a bottle of water and we don't?" Here was my answer, which was absolutely not good enough for Bob: "I'm not allowed to leave the classroom during class, and you are. You're allowed to leave any time to get a drink, but I'm not."

Bob responded, "What does the rule say, Mr. Goldman? What does it say? 'No food or drinks in the classroom,' including that water bottle. A rule that's put in place for students should be a rule for teachers, too."

He was right.

There was no way I could win the argument because the rule was an insult to my students. So, I tried to move on; I said, "Look, if anybody wants to read the memo that I got from Mr. D. after class, I'll be very happy to show it to whoever wants to see it. Now, the assistant principal has told me that I'm not allowed to have any food or drinks in the classroom, and I'm going to enforce it. I know you're not happy with it, but that's the end of it. Now can we please move on to what we were going to do today? Thank you."

Some of the students didn't really care, but some of them felt so deeply offended that they sat there glaring at the wall and at me, and the only thing that would heal their wounds would be time.

My resentment of the memo from Mr. Dunbar continued, and I decided that I was going to somehow let him know about it, but in a mild, untenured way.

When I saw him later in the day, I said, "Mr. D., was that memo because of Will's behavior with the Gatorade bottle?" His answer surprised me very much, and it only served to reinforce that one should never assume the motivation for people's behavior.

I fully expected a tart admonishment from him that reminded me that if I had been doing my job and enforcing the rules and if I had the slightest hint of the beginning of a clue in my vacant skull about how to manage a classroom, that none of this would have happened.

Instead, he said something that was almost the opposite in tone and intent: he told me that he sent the memo to me to support me in the classroom; he sent the memo as an authority figure of the school to show my students that the administration of the school stands behind the teachers.

I wasn't sure what he meant, and I told him that. He further explained that he sent the memo so that I would have backup evidence validating my request that the students not eat or drink in the classroom. He said, "This way, if any of your students give you a hard time, you just show them that memo and tell them that if they don't follow your instructions, they'll have to deal with me." As I recovered from the surprise of hearing his highly appreciated expression of support, I thanked him and told him I appreciated what he did, which was entirely true.

Nevertheless, the rule still did not sit well with me for the reasons I gave near the beginning of this chapter.

You will find that, time after time after time, as you give your students your trust, they will come through for you.

They are so appreciative of being given the freedom and the choice that an adult would receive that they receive this expression of trust in almost a sacred way, and it will be rare indeed that one of your students will fail you.

I soon decided that I was not going to enforce the rule.

I didn't bring out the trumpets and make a proclamation about my mini-episode of political activism. I simply said nothing when the students inevitably began bringing snacks and juice into the class after a few days. The first few times they did, they eyed me warily. I looked at the drink, I looked at them, I gave them a short nod of permission, and I moved on. Bob knew what I was doing. I wished that I could snap a picture of his smiling face when he realized that I viewed him as a capable adult.

It was more than just a water bottle, it was a symbol of my trust and my affection, and it helped forge a rewarding bond between us.

From that point on, Bob always gave me his best work. He always tried to write with his best grammar, he always cooperated, and he was always pleasant. Bob and his water bottle—I'll never forget either of them.

28

THE LBS-I
IS A GOOD THING

When I was in graduate school at the University of Illinois at Chicago (UIC), I was enrolled in a program within the College of Education that grants a master's degree in special education. Completing the program authorizes you to take an examination which, upon passing, would allow you to call yourself a Learning Behavior Specialist I (one) and would also grant you a valid certificate to teach most special education classes anywhere in the state of Illinois.

Some people, upon hearing that the LBS-I permits you to teach any special education class, want to ask some follow-up questions.

For example, people ask if there is a grade limit for the LBS-I. The answer to that question is "no," the LBS-I permits you to teach any grade level, from kindergarten through twelfth grade.

People also want to ask if there is a limit to what population of students can be taught with an LBS-I, and the answer to that question is also "no." The LBS-I permits you to teach any disability category except for students who are deaf and blind.

You would be legally permitted to teach a class of first graders with cerebral palsy, eighth-graders with significant cognitive delays, or eleventh graders with learning disabilities and emotional disorders.

It is a broad certification indeed, and the breadth of the certification surprised me while I was in graduate school. This surprise was also expressed by the faculty, who told us that it was a difficult job to put together a graduate school curriculum that would ensure each graduate student receiving an education broad and deep enough to gain competence in whatever classroom they would eventually teach. They told us that part of the challenge was to design such a program so that students could finish within a reasonable period of time. It seems to me that they succeeded; I felt prepared to go into a high school classroom when I graduated from the program.

This educational model differs from many other states, where people who wish to be special education teachers select a specialty and enroll in a program that is tailored to that specialty.

For example, in some other states, if you wanted to work with young children with autism and cognitive delays, you would be presented with a different graduate school curriculum than if you wanted to work with, for example, teenagers with reading disabilities. This resulted in graduate schools minting out teachers with relatively limited special education certification areas. This limitation would result in significant scheduling problems and additional school district expense in all but the largest districts.

Smaller school districts would not be able to combine disabilities in one classroom and staff them with one special education teacher. If a district had, for instance, two children with autism, three children with cognitive delays, and three children with learning disabilities, these children would have to be taught by at least two different teachers, which would create scheduling problems and additional expense for the district.

Illinois, and other states, decided to combine the special education certification so that all of the students detailed in the above example could be taught in one classroom by one special education teacher. This saves the district money and classroom space, and anything that saves money and classroom space is very popular with school boards, taxed residents, and elected officials.

Are the hypothetical students with autism, cognitive delays, and learning disabilities well served by such a classroom/teacher arrangement?

The answer is yes.

The curriculum that the teacher candidates were exposed to in graduate school, the coursework they had to complete, and the on-site direct service requirements of the educational program gave all of us significant knowledge and training with students who had a wide range of disabilities and needs. Some might criticize this all-encompassing approach as having the undesired effect of turning out multitudes of new special education teachers that know a lot about a little but who do not have adequate in-depth knowledge and experience to effectively teach students with particular disabilities.

In my experience, this is not a valid complaint.

Yes, there are different disabilities within the classroom, but the students' educational needs in that classroom are not so different that they cannot be served well by the competent efforts of one well-trained teacher. Even though the LBS-I program turns out teachers who are legally qualified to teach at any age level and to nearly any disability, in reality, these teachers will specialize in a specific grade area and a particular disability category that reflects the personal interests and calling of each teacher.

This is particularly true in secondary schools, where a special education teacher will usually focus on teaching one or two core subjects to classes of students with an age range of only a few years and who have similar educational disabilities and instructional needs.

In a very short time, by virtue of experience and the professional influence of their colleagues, these new teachers will become experts in their area—whether it is with students with significant cognitive delays, students with emotional disturbances, students with learning disabilities, or any other disability category.

After teaching eleventh and twelfth grade students with learning disabilities, mild autism, mild cognitive delays, and behavioral disorders, I would have to say that the graduate-teacher training program did an excellent job of preparing me for life inside the classroom with my students.

At some point, after you have spent years filling a future teacher's head with educational theory, you have to toss that teacher into the deep water of the classroom and let him or her learn how to swim.

Every day presents different challenges; every student requires you to use a different approach. No amount of graduate school education can prepare you for an environment where literally each separate minute over the course of your career is different.

Giving teacher candidates more background in educational theory will not help them deal with student sleepiness any better. I was given many books filled with graphic organizers proven by research to improve reading comprehension; I have an absolute arsenal of them, though I doubt I'll use even half of them throughout my teaching career.

Giving teacher candidates more detailed knowledge of cognitive delay and mental retardation will not help them be better politicians when speaking to parents. These parents persistently enable their children's disability by asking school personnel what they are doing to help their child succeed, rather than asking themselves what they could do to better teach their children the critical life skills and survival strategies they will need to negotiate the complex game of life, once the parents are no longer alive to vigorously advocate for their children's welfare.

Giving teacher candidates more information than they already have about clever, engaging, effective manipulatives that can be of great assistance when teaching math will not help these candidates figure out what they need to do to keep the academic momentum going when it starts snowing heavily during the middle of the lesson.

You can talk to teacher candidates from today until tomorrow about classical and operant conditioning, unconditioned and conditioned stimuli, effective and ineffective reinforcers, and group contingency models. But, even an encyclopedic knowledge of this information that would make B. F. Skinner himself shed a tear of joy will not give these candidates any guidance about what in the world to do when they hear from a security guard, during the middle of a lesson, that one of their case management students just physically attacked another student with almost no provocation and will likely be expelled.

Giving prospective teachers a solid background in educational theory is a necessary prerequisite to turning out competent educators.

So is letting them hear the personal stories of professors who were previously teachers.

So is requiring the prospective teachers to spend hundreds of hours in practical situations with real students, observe them in these real situations, and give the student teacher detailed feedback about their behavior, their attitudes, and the choices they made in these real situations. Graduate teacher education programs provide all these things, and many more that are invaluable.

But, at some point, providing more and more teacher education results in reaching a point of diminishing returns. After a prudent period of time, you have to kick the future teachers out of graduate school and put them into Real School University, the place to get the ultimate on-the-job training.

Each student; each lesson; each call to a parent; each homework sheet you have to grade; each angry outburst; each plaintive request for help; each handshake, thank you, and smile from a student—all are different. It's the teacher's intelligence, character, morality, and wisdom—just as much as knowledge of pedagogy—that will allow him or her to interact with students in such a way that both the students and the teacher are better off than before.

You could give me years more specialized training with the sorts of disabilities represented by the populations of children I'm responsible for; yet, even this additional training would not have made a significant difference in preparing me for the startlingly diverse educational needs required by my students.

You can only train a teacher so much at college; then, you must put him or her in front of the class and let them learn from experience and shine. Just keep in mind that during the first year, it's more likely to be a flicker than a steady light.

29

DON'T FEAR
THE HIGH SCHOOL

When I was at UIC, I spent many hours talking to my fellow teachers in training and to other teachers in the field. During these conversations, the same theme recurred—fear of teaching high school.

"Oh, I would never teach in a high school—that would totally intimidate me," said one elementary school teacher I met. "You want to teach high school? Why?" said another elementary school teacher. Another teacher said, "at least you can control the little kids, but how can I control a student who's six-feet-two?"

Wait, it gets better. Listen to what people said to me when I told them that I want to teach high school students with learning, behavioral, and emotional disabilities:

"What?!" (Look of amazement on face.)

"Why do you want to do that?!" (Look of hostility on face.)

"High school BD? Of all the teaching jobs you could take, you want to work in high school BD?!"

"Oh my God, my sister knows somebody who worked in a high school class with emotionally disturbed kids, and last year he had to go to the hospital because a kid threw a chair at him."

"God bless you for wanting to work with those kids."

These sorts of comments continued throughout my teacher training. To be fair, there were others who offered encouragement and support and who said that they could never work with elementary school kids. It all comes down to what sort of thing appeals to you at the gut level.

(Please don't be offended by what I'm about to say if you're an elementary or middle school teacher. I have great respect for all educators; all of us have difficult jobs, and all of us get tremendous rewards out of what we do. I merely am expressing my own personal opinion, to help you understand why I chose to work with high school students.)

For those of you who cannot understand why anybody would want to work in a high school setting, I'm going to tell you some reasons why you should do it.

Prior to my beginning my teacher education, I was aware of a preference to work with older students. The graduate teacher training program at UIC requires you to spend literally hundreds of hours in a variety of settings—schools for children with severe physical handicaps, schools that specialize in children with serious cognitive impairments—and the ages of these students can vary from elementary through middle and high school. So, I was exposed to a wide variety of students requiring special education.

This exposure strengthened my desire to work with high school students with learning, behavioral, and emotional difficulties, and here are the main factors that engendered this desire. Again, these are my opinions, and they aren't intended to diminish nonhighschool students and the professionals who work with them.

In My Opinion, High School Students Are More Interesting Than Younger Students

High school students are interesting because, by virtue of their cognitive development, they are able to express more intriguing thoughts about the world around them and the experiences that they have been through. The statements they make are sophisticated enough to make the gears spin in your head at a high speed. I enjoy speaking to people who make me think, and every day my students do just that. Here are some examples of what I mean.

At the end of class one day, the students had a few minutes to talk among themselves. Some conservative professors in teaching training programs would say that I'm supposed to teach from bell to bell and take advantage of each and every single microsecond of education time. I agree with this for the most part, but not completely. I usually teach from bell to bell, but not all the time.

Sometimes giving your students a few minutes to relax and communicate with each other allows you to glean valuable insight into their lives and their perspectives of the world around them. Don't get the idea that I am interested in their lives outside of school because I'm nosy and I like to butt into other people's business; I find these conversations interesting because they help me understand my students better.

When Tricia comes in and she's in a bad mood, it helps to know that she's been having a really hard time getting along with her mother recently.

During this conversation, my students were talking about—what a surprise—romance and dating. One of my students said that he was having difficulty with his girlfriend because he was in a band and had to spend a lot of time practicing. He said that his girlfriend expressed frustration about not being able to spend more quality time with him.

The student reflected upon this and said, "This is just a high school romance; it's not something to be taken so seriously. It's not like this is going to be the only relationship in my whole life." How interesting that this student was able to engage in a metacognitive analysis of a relationship that he's currently involved in; in most cases, people are rarely able to maintain a clearheaded perspective on a current relationship, especially when the relationship is going through rocky times.

A female student said to him, "Well, girls are like that. We want you to spend time with us because we worry that if you don't spend a lot of time with us, that means you don't like us." The first student replied, "But I'm in a band. We get paid for what we do. If I get paid to show up at a gig, I've got to be sure that I'm ready to do a good job." A fellow classmate who also plays in a band said, "That's right." The female student said, "Well, what if you bring your girlfriend with you to practice?" The first student replied, "No, that wouldn't work. If she was there, nobody would get anything done."

I decided at that point to open my mouth and say, "This happens all the time in relationships; things you have to do in your life make it hard to find enough time to spend with each other." The first student said, "Yeah, that's what I mean. What am I supposed to do—quit the band? Like I said, this is a high school romance; I'm not going to let it bother me too much."

This conversation continued on for a few minutes prior to the end of the period. During this conversation, I was sitting at the table (my classroom has three large tables rather than individual student seats) where all the students were talking.

You should feel honored when students welcome you into their conversation and are clearly comfortable with speaking freely while you are listening to what they have to say. A good way to get this to happen is to rarely criticize or judge them.

This whole conversation was interesting because it revolved around a very adult topic with no clear answers. Answer me a question, esteemed reader: do you feel that you have a perfect balance in your life between work, hobbies, and relationship and family obligations? If you don't, join the club of untold millions who don't, either.

This sort of student conversation makes me think about my own life, and as I said, any conversation that makes me think and reflect is a conversation I enjoy very much.

The enjoyment that high school teachers get from working with their students comes not just from listening to them talk about their personal lives but also from the unexpected events that happen during instruction time. Here's an example.

We were discussing parts of speech in English class, and the subject turned towards abstract nouns such as love, hate, fairness, and so on. The class and I were in a brainstorming session, coming up with as many abstract nouns as possible. They had not yet mentioned justice, and I wanted that included on the list. I said to the class, "What's associated with the courts? What's associated with the court system and the judicial system?"

A student blurted out "corruption!"

It was an unexpected, amusing, and very correct abstract noun. It took more than a few seconds for the laughter to die down in the classroom; much of the laughter was coming from me.

In class, we frequently talk about what's going on in the world around us; on a regular basis, I bring in news articles about topics of interest that are taking place that day for the purpose of discussing and writing about the news item.

A lesson plan can be delayed for a little while if something is happening in the world that is of high interest to your students. Introducing impromptu discussions like this invariably is met with an enthusiastic response from the students, and spirited discussion and much writing and analyzing follows.

(An educational benefit to this activity is the requirement that students read and analyze a sometimes lengthy news article. But, don't reveal my secret to them.)

You'll discover as a teacher that sometimes the real world outside of school has an eerie way of following the lessons going on in the classroom.

For a few days we were talking about race and racism in preparation for reading a sublime autobiography entitled "Narrative of the Life of Frederick Douglass." That night, as I was reading the news, I discovered a troubling series of events that was happening in a public school in my hometown, Philadelphia.

A small number of Liberian immigrants had taken residence in a predominantly black neighborhood in Philadelphia, and these immigrants began attending their nearest public school. Ironically and unbelievably, some of the black American children were taunting and assaulting the black Liberian children with racist epithets and telling them that they should "go back to Africa."

The problem had become serious enough to cause the formation of Liberian quasi-gangs, the purpose of which was to protect the safety of the Liberian immigrants.

The students were truly surprised and upset upon reading this article and the associated pictures during class when I showed them on the projector. As you may know, minorities are well represented in a special education classroom, even in a predominantly white neighborhood like the one in which I teach. I have white kids, black kids, Hispanic kids all mixed together, and all getting along very well with each other indeed, thank goodness.

Never since the beginning of the year had my students read an article with such fascination as they did this article about black-on-black racism.

A spirited and lengthy class discussion followed. We discussed concepts such as, what is racism? What would you do if you were the principal of the school or if you were the parent of one of the American boys who was assaulting the Liberian boys? How would you calm the situation down? The students were required to write a letter to the community as if they were the principal of the school, and this letter had to have a series of potential solutions to the problem. Something about this article struck a nerve with them, and they wrote some beautiful ideas that illustrated the good and the kindness within their hearts.

I learned just as much that day as my students did.

We all learned about the black perspective and the Hispanic perspective on these events.

We all saw a variety of races coming together in the classroom to solve what they all saw as a deeply troubling situation. The comments they made and the viewpoints they shared gave me a respect for them that makes my hair bristle when I subsequently hear someone call them "brats."

Their plans to address the racial tension in Philadelphia included community meetings, one-on-one counseling, informational pamphlets and films made about how hard life was in Liberia in an effort to educate the American children, peer mediation, and others. As the suggestions came forth, others critiqued the advantages and disadvantages of each; they analyzed which were viable and which were unrealistic. It was truly a fascinating few days' discussion. I'm reasonably confident that a stimulating discussion like this would not be happening in a third-grade classroom.

Aside from the tremendous intellectual stimulation you'll receive from your students, as well as the endless hours of amusement at hearing their naïve yet refreshingly simplistic suggestions of what could be done to solve the world's ills, there's one other major reason why you should choose to work with high school students.

Your Life Experience Allows You To Offer Real Help to High School Students That Would Otherwise Be Wasted on Younger Children

Question: What's older than old?

Answer: Thirty years old.

Question: When do they put you in adult diapers, sit you in a wheelchair, and ask you, slowly, "DO YOU WANT TO WATCH A NICE TELEVISION PROGRAM OR SIT BY THE WINDOW, DEAR?"

Answer: When you turn forty.

Of course, the above opinions are those of my high school students, who live in a world where, often, you're old if your age doesn't end in "teen." But don't allow yourself to believe the popularly held view that teens are really creatures sent from another planet and are mistrustful of and disrespectful toward anybody over twenty-five. Nothing could be further from the truth. In fact, your students will almost constantly look to you and all the other members of the faculty for opinions, advice, support, assistance, and encouragement.

When I talk, they listen to what I say, and that makes me glad that I am forty-two and not twenty-two. My students benefit from my age. There is so much, so much, so much that they don't know. (Me too, by the way.)

Students have remarkably sophisticated viewpoints towards complex social issues. Yet there's so much that my students don't know. How can this be?

Ah, the teenage years, the years of duality-fueled angst: the duality of being able to be pregnant but not being able to vote; the duality of having facial hair while skateboarding at the mall and discussing the latest, totally awesome video game with your buddies; and the duality of needing to work until midnight but still having to go to school and do well in the chemistry test tomorrow morning.

There's more: the duality of a desperate search for one's independent identity coexisting with an irrepressible desire to blend in with the crowd; the duality of being able to drive but being prohibited from doing so because you were grounded when your father is "majorly pissed" at you from your expressing your feelings a little bit too well. There's also the dichotomy of being told by your father to grow up and be an independent man, yet being punished when you think a little too independently from his worldview and critique his sacred perspectives.

And, don't forget the dichotomy of knowing a lot, yet really knowing very little. This is where a middle-aged teacher comes to the rescue.

There's more to the teacher-student relationship then simply unscrewing the top of a kid's head and dumping in the difference between covalent and ionic bonding, why nobody can say what the slope of a vertical line is, and why a defense mechanism has nothing to do with a black belt.

Naturally, the transferring of knowledge is important, and perhaps even more so is the instruction of how to remember, analyze, and summarize that information.

But just as big a part of being a teacher is giving advice that extends beyond the classroom. Every day, you're given what seems like a million opportunities to give your students some guidance in life. Each one of the following statements or questions was actually said to me by students, and I tried my best to use their exact words here. When these sorts of statements or questions are said to you, you could choose to not address it, or choose to give a trite, glib answer, or, in my case most of the time, choose to take the opportunity to tell the innocent, needy child in front of you what they need to know to make a smart decision.

- Which college should I apply to? What should my major be?
- My ex-girlfriend is dating a guy that I can't stand, and I think one day I'm just going to knock his fuckin' head off.
- My father and I got into a fistfight last night, and I'm sleeping in my car— sorry I'm late. Any idea where I can sleep tonight?
- I can't stand vocabulary lists; I can never remember the words when it comes time for the test. Can you help me with that?
- I have two papers due in two days, and I have to work tonight and tomorrow night. What should I do?
- What do you think about the death penalty? Yeah, I know you don't want to tell me, yeah, yeah, yeah, I know that I've got to have my own opinions, but did you ever think for one minute that maybe I look up to you, believe it or not, and I respect you and because of that I want to know what you think? Why do teachers always say "it doesn't matter what I think" or some other ridiculous statement? Why do they always make excuses when I ask them for their opinions on this kind of stuff? (I talked about this elsewhere in this book.)
- How old are you?
- Do you make a lot of money?
- What's the fastest you've ever driven on your motorcycle? Why won't you answer my question? What are you trying to be, a good influence on me or something?
- My buddy's brother dropped out of school, and now he's making $16 an hour at a construction company, so what's all this bullshit about how diplomas are worth half a million dollars?
- I know we have to do a PowerPoint presentation, but I never used PowerPoint. I hate computers. Can you help me use it?
- I don't know how credit cards work, but I know I can't wait to get one.
- I can't wait until I drive. I don't think I need insurance, do I? What's insurance for, anyway?

- Why do I have to write correctly? What's the difference whether or not I say "I ain't going" or "I am not going." You understood what I said, didn't you? Isn't the whole point of writing about communication? So if I communicated, what's the difference how I communicated as long as you understood me?
- Why can't I wear my hat in the classroom? It's totally ridiculous. All these rules are ridiculous.
- We had homework last night?
- I was filling out a job application online, and I got to the point where it asked me about my previous employment. I was fired because I got sick and didn't go and didn't call in, but I just told them that I quit.
- When I do a Google search, the information I get will be right, right?
- The first time I got high was with my father.
- You drive better when you're drunk. No, really! It puts you in a better frame of mind.
- Last month I got a $920 cell phone bill, probably from talking to my girlfriend. (Not a typo: nine hundred and twenty dollars. That's what the student said to me.)
- Cops are all a bunch of pussies.
- My buddy wants to drop out and work for his family. What do you think about that? He could make $16 an hour!
- What time did I go to bed last night? Oh, about four.
- Weed is harmless; everybody knows that. How many people do you know that jumped out of a window or started bashing car windows when they were high on weed?
- You know the Pledge of Allegiance we say every morning? What does "allegiance" mean?
- Why should we help out the people in Iraq? They never helped us.
- God, I drink this Jolt Cola every morning, but I still fall asleep first period.
- I can't finish the assignment by the due date; I have to work.
- I'm late to class because I have to go from gym all the way to the third floor to go to my locker, and then I have to go all the

way down to your room. What's that? You can change my locker so that it's right outside of this classroom? Nah . . . that's all right, don't worry about it.

- Don't sit me next to that girl because we had some problems last year, and I don't want there to be any trouble in the classroom.
- We had homework last night? What did we have to do? Oh yeah! Oh, wait . . . I did that! Where is it? I left it at home. By the way, why are you giving me a D in this class?

How would you respond to the above statements and questions? Remember that the student is looking at you intently, so you only have a second or two to think of the response, and the answer you give will be remembered, possibly for the rest of his or her life. Also keep in mind that the above list of statements and questions represents what you would be exposed to not in a year, not in a month, not in a week, but in one day, and possibly less than one day.

Because of my age and because of the things I've been through, I feel qualified to be the person who responds to all of these questions.

I've loved. I've lost. I've dumped, and been dumped, multiple times. I graduated from high school, graduated from college, and graduated from two master's degree programs. I purchased and sold three homes. I've gotten myself into financial debt and gotten myself out of it. I worked as a dishwasher and felt the sweat run down my face as I cleaned out the stinking garbage in the sink trap. I worked in corporate America for fourteen years and had to deal with a Mount Everest-sized pile of office politics, unjustifiably over-inflated egos, incompetent chief executive officers, annoying supervisors, and petulant, whiny, backstabbing subordinates.

I felt great pride at seeing software I slaved over for months be used by 1,500 retail employees for almost ten years. I've been promoted, I've been given huge bonuses, and I've been fired. I've traveled around the United States and felt culture shock when I traveled to Russia and couldn't understand a thing that was being said. I've been threatened, I've been cheated, I've been honored, I've been robbed, I've been admired, I've been loved, and I've been resented. I learned the hard way how to treat other people in the workplace. I've been in a car crash. I wrecked my motorcycle because I didn't know what I was doing. I'm currently discovering how difficult it is to play a viola.

As my friend Ken would say, "So what's your point?"

The point is that students can and do benefit from an older teacher's knowledge. Older teachers don't know everything and make a lot of mistakes, but they know a lot more than their students do about a lot of things.

If you're an older teacher, you'll know what to tell them when they come to you for advice on how to deal with a teacher with an ego the size of a Mack truck; you'll be able to give them pointers on how to try to get what you want without offending another teacher in any way.

You'll have thousands of personal stories to tell them during class to help drive home the point of what you're reading in the book, and your students will be old enough to be able to relate to what you say about work, parents, school pressures, love, and other mature topics. You'll very much enjoy telling your students these stories and listening to what they have to say in response and listening to their take on it, their perspective, and their analysis. More often than not, when your students tell you jokes, complain about their science teacher and how he makes them do "so much work," and tell you what they feel would be the proper punishment for the child murderer in "M," you'll truly understand where they're coming from. When you ask them follow-up questions, you'll find they truly reflect upon and analyze their position.

This meeting of the minds takes place between teachers and students much of the time—not all the time, not most of the time, but much of the time, which is all that any reasonable person could expect between a middle-aged person and a teenager.

But why is this meeting of the minds so satisfying? I can't explain why, even after quite a bit of reflection. Perhaps it has something to do with a desire to be respected and accepted, but that can't be a wholly satisfactory explanation because I feel justified and right when I set and enforce limits and experience the inevitable resulting anger and resentment.

More careful reflection produces no results in an attempt to come up with an explanation. I would have to say that working with older teenagers is elementally satisfying. I use the term "elementally" in a chemical sense. An element can't be broken down further into other elements, and some likes and dislikes can't realistically be broken down further. I love butter pecan ice cream and strongly dislike the taste of beets, but if you ask me why, the best I would be able to do is flash a vacant smile and reply in a brilliant display of intellect, "I don't know, I just do."

I enjoy giving them my knowledge, I enjoy helping them make smart decisions, I enjoy watching them "tsk" their tongue and roll their eyes towards the sky when I give them some advice, and then watch them take that same spurned advice a week or two later, and as a result, get the job. Even though I don't have any children of my own, I understand how parents feel when they see their children get the A.

It's a mixture of pride and satisfaction that tastes even better than butter pecan ice cream. With chocolate sprinkles.

30

THE MYSTERIOUS KANGAROO AND HIS INDICTMENT

It was just another day in English class. It was about five minutes after the late bell had rung, and I was actively engaged in a lesson. I was asking the students to give a summary of what had happened in the section of the book that we read yesterday. Some of the students were raising their hand and/or calling out answers to the questions I was giving; everything was going relatively smoothly, with the usual interleaving of insightful answers and mildly inappropriate behavior.

Suddenly, a student I had seen before, but whose name I did not know, entered the room and started jumping up and down near the door. He spoke not one word but started to jump up and down, almost in place, and then started to spin around as he jumped. He deliberately knocked over a few books from a portable book cart and continued jumping around, in about a three feet radius, wordlessly. His behavior reminded me of a kangaroo in the zoo as he was hopping around and waving his arms in the air.

For about five to ten seconds, I was too surprised to do anything.

I'm sure most of you have experienced that peculiar mental state where you're faced with something that's so novel, so bizarre, and so unexpected that you stand and observe the bizarreness in stunned silence. I glanced over at Mrs. Grimaldi to see her reaction. Thank God for working with someone who has much more experience with the sometimes truly intractable and bemusing behavior of seventeen-year-old human beings.

The look on her face was unforgettable; her jaw was partially open and moved to one side, but her lips were closed, her eyes were rolled up to the ceiling, and the whole expression at once conveyed irritation, impatience, and thank goodness, composure. It was the same sort of look that a weary mother might have in the supermarket as she is holding her crying, diaper-soiled infant daughter in her arms, while her three-year-old son whines for the fifteen millionth time that he wants a candy bar, he wants a candy bar, he wants a candy bar, he wants a candy bar.

My students, too, watched in stunned silence for a few moments, which was unexpectedly relieving because their surprise communicated to me that this was not a group-sponsored premeditated event. After a few seconds, of course, some of the students started giggling, and one student who is normally quite mischievous said very honestly, "Oh my God," as if he was truly surprised at what he was seeing.

Well, being a man, the testosterone and adrenaline started surging through my body, and I started to say to myself, "There's no way this little snotnosed pischer is going to come in to my God! Damned! classroom and act like a fool without me opening up a can of whoopass on him."

My first instinct was to move over to the classroom door and close it, trapping him in the classroom, and stand by the door with my hand on the knob. If he wanted to leave the classroom, he would have to put his hands on me, which would be assault and battery. I could stand there and have Mrs. Grimaldi call for security.

But then, a second or two later, I realized that being a teacher is not about getting into a power struggle with a student. I realized that this was a meaningless prank that the student was probably put up to, and it was not intended to be personally offensive. Plus, I also realized that my job was to teach my students and maximize the amount of instruction that they had. If I got into a situation with this student, it might result in a lengthy standoff which would cheat my own students out of the instruction to which they were entitled.

Also, of course, you don't know what goes through the mind of another person, and it was possible that such a physical confrontation from me would, in the heat of the moment, incite the student to do something stupid which could result in him, me, or both of us, getting hurt. This particular student was about six feet three and was probably much stronger than me, but I would not have physically confronted any student, regardless of his stature.

So, I did what I believe was the wise thing, although at the time it felt like I was backing down. I stood there with a blank expression on my face, staring at the back of the room.

The students' attention was equally divided between watching the spectacle and watching my reaction. They observed in me patience and restraint, which I hope made some sort of a positive impression on them after the fact, though I admit to you that at the time I felt utterly ineffective and at a loss for what to do.

My heart was pounding with anger and, to a lesser extent, fear—fear of what might happen next, fear of what would be the administrative consequences if I didn't handle this like a professional.

Suddenly, he stopped and left the room. Mrs. Grimaldi said, immediately, "Okay, that's over. Let's all continue with what we were doing before we were interrupted."

Bravo to her.

I gave the students a little bit of time to stop giggling uncomfortably and saying, "Oh my God," and I continued on with what we were doing. The students, not surprisingly—or surprisingly, I don't know which—seemed to want to continue on with the lesson, and the rest of the period continued as usual.

At the end of the period, one of my students came up to me and said, "Mr. Goldman, did you know who that was?" I couldn't tell at the time if the purpose of the question was to learn the identity of the jumping kangaroo or whether it was to determine whether or not the jumping kangaroo, a person known to the student, was going to evade consequences for acting in an outrageous and highly offensive manner because I simply did not know who he was. I said to the student in the most confident tone I could muster at the time, "I don't know, but I'm going to find out who it was, you can depend on that." The student left with a weak smile on her face.

My next period was a prep period, therefore, down to the assistant principal's office I trotted. My intent was to pore over the last edition of the yearbook to try to match a face with a name. (In our high school's yearbook, every single student is pictured each year.) I felt like I was at a police station looking over pictures, like you see in the movies.

I very much wanted to stand up, point to a photograph, and shriek, "He's the one! He's the one who did it!" Ah, but no. Do you know how difficult it is to look through 925 one-year-old, postage-stamp size, black-and-white photographs to try to identify one student who has grown quite a bit over the past year and who has a different hairstyle? "Impossible" is the word. Just when you think you have your man, you see another photo that looks even more like your man, and then another photo six pages later that is definitely your man, and then another thirteen pages later that is definitely, positively your man.

I gave up the quest after forty minutes. "Oh well," I said to myself, "no harm done. Just a teenage prank."

Adopting that forgiving attitude so soon after I've had someone thumb their nose at me in front of a large audience is satisfying to only part of me; the part that could be a rabbi, or a priest, or Mother Teresa's helper.

But there's another part of me, the small-town sheriff, that kept saying, "Y'all kin betchur gal-danged boots ah 'mon git that sumbitch, yessirree Bob."

Nothing happened the rest of the day regarding this matter until the end of tenth period when a few students innocently said, "Hey, I heard what happened earlier! Did you ever find out who that was?"

I remained silent for the moment. I learned a long time ago that silence is a powerful technique to get people to open their pieholes and spew facts.

Another student said to the first group, "What happened?" A member of the first group said, "You didn't hear?"

The other student said, quietly, "Oh yeah, Jasek" just above my threshold of hearing.

This was one of those sweet, sumptuous, oh-so-delectable, every-cell-in-your-body-has-a-tongue-and-they're-all-licking-honey moments. The student told me the name of the kangaroo. Thank God for not going to a lot of heavy metal concerts when I was eighteen.

It was said so quietly that the other students did not realize that I had heard that name—"Jasek." The bell rang, and at that instant in time I sprinted to my computer with such speed that my wake suction almost pulled books out of a bookshelf. I typed in the name and up came the puss of Mr. Pouched Marsupial High Jumper himself— name, address, locker number, schedule, the whole thing.

If I had had a ten-gallon hat I would have whipped it up into the air and yelled out "YEEEEEE-HAAAAAAWWWWW!"

What to do, what to do. I could've written him up. I could have called his family and arranged a meeting at school. This offense of interrupting a class, deliberately interfering with instruction, and knocking books to the ground, was grounds for suspension. But, I didn't. Something tells me deep down that he really didn't think about what he was doing; he didn't know me, he didn't know most of the people in the class, and he was probably put up to it at the last minute by one of the students in my class, not in a malicious way.

So, this is what I did. I saw his schedule on the screen and, the next day during my prep period, went over to the classroom he was in. I apologized to the teacher for interrupting the class and said that I needed to speak to Jasek for just one moment. He said that it was no problem and called him to the door. The look on Jasek's face when he saw me was truly priceless. I've never seen pupils dilate so quickly and so dramatically in my whole blessed life. I shook his hand and said, "Jasek, I'm Mr. Goldman, up in room 231. I believe we met yesterday." He gulped and said, "We did? I don't think so."

I said, "OH YES WE DID, Jasek, yesterday at about 11:00, up in room 231." He stared at me silently with a look of moderate shock and fear that satisfied me to the extreme. I said, "Do me a favor. Don't do that again, please."

He paused, staring at me, and said, very quietly, "Okay." He meant it. There was sweat on his forehead, and it wasn't warm in the room.

I said, "Good, thanks. Have a good afternoon," and walked away.

A week or so later he saw me in the hallway and immediately looked down at the floor upon our making eye contact. I always feel sad when I get into a situation with a student that interferes with our having a good relationship, and this situation was no exception.

However, on the other hand, I was glad to see that he felt a little bit of contrition upon seeing me; it told me that he had an intact moral sense, which made me hopeful for his future. I'm glad I didn't write him up and engage the traditional "How DARE you!" reflex re-action of many teachers. Sometimes the most effective thing a teacher can do when faced with misbehavior is to try an unorthodox approach. By doing so, you might very well break through all the noise, make an impact on the student, and actually change behavior for the good.

Jasek, if you're reading this, it's okay, man. No harm done.

31

STUDENT TEACHING: INTRODUCTION

This is the more controversial part of the book.

This section of the book reveals the experiences I went through as I performed my student teaching internship in one of the Chicago public schools. I don't mean to imply that the events that I'm going to reveal are unique to the Chicago public schools; it's likely that these sorts of things are taking place throughout our country, and likely the entire world.

I'm about to tell you about some good and not so good experiences. The ones that aren't so good might surprise you. Some of you might even be upset by my decision to reveal some of the events that took place during my internship.

I decided to include these events in this book not for the purpose of being sensational, not for the purpose of upsetting people, not for the purpose of selling more copies of the book, but because I feel the general public should know some of the bad—and good—things that took place within the school. I hope that telling people about these situations and these events will encourage discussions between students, faculty, administration, and families that will improve the quality of the school.

As is the case throughout the rest of the book, all of the names have been changed.

What Student Teaching Is

In every profession, as you go through training, you need to have a significant opportunity to practice doing the real thing while being supervised by experienced people. You can't call yourself a plumber unless some experienced plumbers have watched you replace dishwashers and fix sewage ejector pumps and unclog drains, and these experienced plumbers have all agreed that you did these things right.

The same thing goes with unclogging minds, replacing rusty study habits, and installing sparkling new ways of thinking.

If you wish to become a teacher, you have to practice. The most significant opportunity you will have to practice is during what is called the "student teaching internship" that is a requirement of (I imagine) all graduate-teacher training programs. During this student teaching internship, you are actually a teacher. You are actually standing in a classroom with fifteen sets of eyes focused on you, wondering what you'll be like, hoping you'll be on their side but fearful that you won't, and determining with rapidity and accuracy your strengths and weaknesses.

One of your main jobs is to come up with a lesson that's interesting and engaging, that actually teaches a concept aligned with the state learning standards, and that contains a way of checking to ensure that the students "get it" (also known as the "assessment"). To put more spices in the soup, there's a good possibility that your professor from graduate school will suddenly show up and sit in the classroom, observing what's going on.

While you're student teaching, you can't work days because you're teaching during the day, so you have to work nights. But then, you can't work nights because nights are when graduate school happens to be taking place. So your income will drop approximately to zero, and the amount of restful sleep you get will also drop approximately to zero.

But, what an exciting time it is!

It's the first time you have an opportunity to try out what you've learned with real, live kids. You forge your first relationships with students, and they can fascinate you and make you laugh before you know it. For the first time, you experience the satisfaction of helping a kid read a little better, understand a plot with a little more depth, and write with just one less spelling error. Most times, notwithstanding the occasional behavioral issue, they are receptive, friendly learners who will give you a break if you make a mistake because you give them a break when they screw up. It was a stressful, exciting time where I learned an enormous amount in a very short time. I'll never forget it.

32

A GLOBE

I was teaching a history class, and we were discussing maps. The classroom was a cross categorical, self-contained special education classroom, and all the students were diagnosed either with a specific learning disability or a mild cognitive impairment. I was showing my students maps of Europe within the textbook, and one of them asked, "What happens if you travel off the edge of the map?"

I blinked at him and said, "What?"

He said, "What would happen if you were in an airplane and you flew off the edge here," as he pointed to the edge of the map. He either believed that the world was flat or knew that the world was round, but he didn't get the relationship between a flat map and the hot-centered oblate spheroid on which we live.

He truly wanted to know what happened if you flew off the edge of the map. He was hungry for the answer; he looked at me intently and awaited my response. I had to teach him that nothing bad would happen, because . . .

Now, stop think about this for a moment. "This map is flat, but Earth is round" is a difficult concept to get across. Here's a kid who's looking at a flat map on a page, and you have to explain the relationship between the page and the world. Go ahead and explain the mapping of a plane onto a sphere to a student who's unaware of the fact that if you're at the edge of the map and you take one more step, you won't fall straight down toward the center of the universe, shrieking in terror, until the end of time or the moment when people stop thinking and doing what celebrities tell them to think and do, whichever comes first, although both describe immense periods of time. No, there's no time to think, pal, the kid is looking at you right now. How are you going to do it?

The first thing you're going to need is a globe. You already have the map, but you need an actual model of the Earth. Once you're able to put the flat page up against the round globe, the kid's sure to get the concept.

All you need is the globe.

Go ahead, take it down from the shelf.

Wait a minute, there is no shelf.

Wait another minute, there's no globe, either.

Duck out of the classroom into the next classroom and ask, "Do you have a globe?"

An incredulous "A GLOBE?" is the response. To get the same effect, go out on the street right now and ask the first person that walks past you, "Excuse me, but do you happen to have a plutonium and faux-lapis-lazuli encrusted stainless steel Australian emu toenail clipper?"

I rush back into the classroom and tell my student that I will explain the concept to him tomorrow. Soon after that, the class is over. Fortunately, right after this class I have about a forty-five minute break, which will give me the opportunity to find a globe and free my student forever from the mortal fear of taking that last fatal step.

I begin my quest: the quest for a globe. It should be easy to find in an enormous public school.

I try a few more classrooms, but I get the same blank plutonium toenail clipper stare as you got from the guy you stopped on the street just now. Some of the teachers offer a faint glimmer of hope; their heads tilt upwards, their eyes dart back and forth as they reach back into their dusty memories of many years gone by when a globe, that marvelous modern model, existed in the school.

No luck. I try the office of the head of the science department. I said the *head* of the *science department*. No globe.

I try the main office. No globe. I literally walk up and down the halls while classes are in session, peeking into classroom after classroom after classroom, scanning the shelves, the windowsills, and the teachers' desks. No globe. I try the library. Pay dirt—the only globe in the school. I ask the librarian if I may borrow the globe to show something to a student. She allowed me to take it only after showing my identification and forcing me to swear, under the threat of the pain of the whip, to return the globe within twenty-four hours.

The next day, I meet my student in the classroom and show him that it's okay to take a really long walk this weekend.

We talk about maps for a while and how the edge of the map doesn't mean the edge of the Earth and that each map is like a little piece of an orange peel. The flat map is what you get after you peel all the peel from an orange and press all the pieces flat on a desk. The student gets the concept, or more accurately, he does a convincing job of telling me that he gets the concept —it's quite hard to distinguish which—and that, by the way, is what makes tests necessary.

It doesn't matter; while we were talking about it, he was concentrating—really thinking about what it's like to live on a big marble, and that if you throw a baseball hard enough in just the right direction and wait long enough, it'll hit you on the back of the head.

If I can get a student to furrow his eyebrows, look at a page, look at me, look at a page, look at me, and then say, "OOOHHH!" I've done my job.

I returned the globe and said to the librarian, "You know, I think this is the only globe in the school." She said, "I think you're right." Am I the only teacher who needed to show a student a model of the Earth? Was my student the only one who didn't quite get the concept that flat map does not mean flat planet?

33

METAL DETECTORS

The school has big walk-through metal detectors. Every single student must go through the metal detector before coming into school. The detectors are there to prevent the introduction of dangerous weapons, such as knives and guns, into the safe learning environment. As you walk through the metal detector, it beeps if you're carrying too much metal on you, such as if you're carrying a large set of keys, a knife, or of course, a firearm of any kind.

There is a security guard stationed at the detector whose job it is to ensure that all students walk through the metal detector and to detain any student who sets it off. As I researched walk-through metal detectors on the Internet, I see their price ranges from about $3,500 to about $5,500 each.

Every day, every student walks through the metal detector. Nearly every student causes it to beep.

I never saw a single student detained at the detector.

In the school's defense, I want to say that I was not there every morning all morning; some mornings I wasn't there, and some mornings I was there watching for only ten minutes or so. So, I am not telling you that nobody was ever stopped. Every morning I heard beep-beep-beep-beep hundreds and hundreds of times as the students flowed into the school. Who knows what was setting off the detectors; maybe it was keys, maybe it was cell phones, or maybe the detectors were set to be too sensitive; I don't know.

Maybe the detectors were there as a deterrent. Maybe their existence discourages students from bringing dangerous weapons to school. Maybe I was misunderstanding the beep that sounded and the red light that flashed at the top of the detector for four out of the five students who walked through it. Maybe there are different levels of alert, and if a student actually did bring a switchblade or handgun to school, a different sort of alarm would sound on the detector. Maybe they were there because lawmakers or local parents twisted the arms of the school board and forced them to spend the money for them. But it seemed to me that they really weren't doing much good. The beeping was so prevalent that it was ignored.

I wonder how much money the school actually paid for these detectors.

34

THE PERPETUAL
ASSEMBLY

Each day, as I traveled from classroom to classroom to do the thousand and one things that I had to do each day, I walked past the auditorium on several occasions. Nearly every time I walked past, I heard the jovial voices of students inside.

One day I walked past, and the voices were surprisingly rambunctious; I wondered just what was going on in the auditorium. I poked my head into the door and about ten students turned around and looked at me blankly. They were the only ones in the auditorium. Oh well, I said to myself, maybe it's for a drama class, or maybe they're members of the band.

A day or two later, I walked past the auditorium and heard giggling and laughing, and it was loud enough so that I almost reflexively walked over to the door and peeked inside.

A different group of students was inside, about ten of them, laughing with a member of the security staff. It was about nine o'-clock in the morning.

The next day, in the middle of the afternoon, I again hear voices coming from the auditorium. I walk inside, and yet a different group of students are sitting there, this time there were about twelve to fifteen of them, all sitting together in the far corner from the main entrance, laughing and talking. They see me standing there and one of the students waves at me and says, "Hey, how are you doing?" I respond, "Doing good!" I let them return to whatever they were talking about, and I go about my business.

A few days later, the same thing. The next day, the same thing. It seems to be that randomly, throughout the day, there are groups of students in the auditorium. Sometimes there is a security guard there, and sometimes there isn't. I never saw a teacher accompanying them. They weren't playing any musical instruments, they didn't have any schoolbooks with them, and they weren't working on any kind of a dramatic undertaking. They were just sitting around, chatting with each other. Each time I looked in the auditorium, some of the faces remained the same, and some of the faces were different.

After a while, after seeing this about ten to fifteen times, I became more and more intrigued by the situation. What in the world were these students doing in the auditorium? Why weren't they in class?

I half jokingly asked one of the security guards, "What is that, a class?" She responded with an unsatisfying and vague "No, it's not a class," rotated her head 90 degrees from me, focused a disinterested stare on a distant object, and remained silent.

This taciturn, over-coiffed security guard wasn't a Rhodes scholar, but she launched at me a brilliantly crafted combination of silence and body language that got the message across loud and clear: turn around and walk away and don't ask any more questions.

Half of me wanted to say to her, "I beg your pardon then, ma'am, but could you please explain to me why those students are sitting in the school's auditorium with no teacher in sight at 9:30 in the morning while you just stand there and clearly ignore the fact that they are not in class, even though part of your job description is to ensure that students are where they're supposed to be?"

But, as I said, only half of me wanted to say that. The other half of me was intimidated by the treatment she gave me, which had a subtly unsettling flavor to it. I grew up in a big city and that experience taught me that sometimes it's a good idea to mind your own business.

So, I walked. She didn't threaten me, she didn't say anything to make me feel uneasy, but there was something about the gestalt of the situation that told me to drop it and move along.

The perpetual assembly continued, almost every day. One day I mentioned that to one of my mentors. I asked him what all the students were doing in the auditorium? Didn't they have a class to go to?

My mentor pulled me aside, looked up and down the hallway to ensure that nobody was standing near us, and whispered quietly, "Neil, those students are there because the teachers don't want them in class. They disrupt the class, and there's no real way to get them to stop. So, the teachers say to students, 'If you stay in the auditorium during my class, I'll give you a D. But if you come to my class, I'll give you an F. That's why they're there."

He paused and looked at me, reading my reaction as the weight of his words sunk in. He said, "It's babysitting, Neil."

When my mentor told me this, it was clear by his tone of voice that he was not proud, or even happy, to tell me the truth, but he respected me enough to do so, and for that I thank him.

I'm not revealing this to tattle on him or to make it seem like I'm better than him; if I were, I would have told you his name and his school and would have written a list of ways to eliminate this day-long babysitting ritual. I'm revealing this so people will discuss it and try to come up with ways to reduce it. Or, maybe I'm naïve; maybe it can't be stopped. I know I don't have a clear answer for it, and maybe nobody else does, either.

All educators should ask what it does to a sixteen-year-old's self-esteem to be told that he is truly not wanted; to be told that he is not worth being educated; to be told that the teacher doesn't care enough about him to do anything possible to help him become an educated person. I'm not blaming the teachers because some of the students I came across in this school were truly antieducational; they fiercely, tirelessly, and effectively kept attempts at education at bay.

So seamless and well constructed is their armor against the patience and kindness of an educator that even those with decades of experience and a long lifetime of wisdom are unable to break through. Some students curse and threaten their teachers, disrupt classes literally at every possible opportunity, refuse to do any schoolwork, and miss school frequently. The slightest thing—a headache, a late night, feeling tired—is a good excuse to cut school.

I would love to have the time to learn more about the relationship between these two phenomena: a teacher that tells a student by exclusion from the classroom that he or she is an uneducatable nuisance who is nothing more than the dregs of an already prejudiced subset of society, and a chronically truant, hostile student who hates school, hates the teachers, and hates the whole place.

35

MY MENTORS

During my student teaching experience, I worked with three separate teachers, each of whom acted as a "mentor" teacher. Mentor teachers are experienced teachers who have agreed to work with a local university and act as a mentor to a student of the university's teacher training program. In exchange for the work that's involved in mentoring a student teacher, the mentor teacher is given credits by the university to allow him or her to take free courses. It seems to me that being a mentor teacher is a combination of difficulty and ease, although I don't know for sure because I've never been a mentor teacher. I imagine that it's difficult to allow your classroom to be taken over by somebody whom you don't know and who might, frankly, be a poor teacher. Every year, students are rejected from teacher training programs solely as a result of their student teaching experience.

It's probably difficult to sit down with poorly performing student teachers and give them the encouragement and feedback they need without crushing their spirit. On the other hand, there's a certain amount of ease that goes along with being a mentor teacher; after all, someone else is basically doing your job for a significant percentage of the day for fourteen weeks or so, but you're still getting paid your full salary.

I have a feeling, though, that the difficulties of being a mentor teacher outweigh the convenience of having somebody else do your job, and this was evidenced by the difficulty my professor had when trying to obtain a student teaching position for me. Even though the semester began during the third week of August, I didn't have a student teaching placement until the first of October.

This delay puzzled me a great deal: why wouldn't every teacher in the city of Chicago jump at the opportunity to have somebody else do most of their job for fourteen weeks, while being paid the same salary, and be able to take graduate courses for free at a local university? I guess it must be more difficult for the mentor teachers than I thought.

On October 1, I learned of the Chicago public school at which I would be doing my student teaching. For fifteen weeks, I would be a teacher there, essentially. I would be there all day, every day (except Thursdays, which was a half-day), teaching about half the time and observing my mentor teacher and other teachers about half the time. I don't want to tell you the name of the school and the name of my mentor teachers because I don't want to hurt them; some of the things that I'm going to tell you about them, and about the school in general, might be seen as uncomplimentary, and it will serve no purpose for me to identify these people by name.

During my fourteen weeks at the school, my mentors treated me in a friendly, professional manner and made me feel welcome and competent. However, their practice of pedagogy left much to be desired.

Some people might say to me, "Who the hell are you to judge these people? You only have one year of experience under your belt, and at the time that you were student teaching, you didn't have any teaching experience whatsoever. Who the hell are you to come into this environment and observe the teaching practices of seasoned professionals with a challenging student population and pass judgment on them? You're not even observing a normal classroom environment! You're observing what's taking place in a classroom where you are a recent invader, which is distracting to a population of students with learning disabilities, emotional disturbances, and cognitive impairments. These students require a stable, safe classroom environment as one of the prerequisites to an effective education. How unsettling it is to the students that after months, and possibly years, of working closely with a particular teacher, all of a sudden some new person is inserted in between them and their beloved teacher, and this new person looks different, talks different, uses different teaching practices, sets different classroom expectations, puts into place new rules, teaches different material, and grades differently than their regular teacher. You come in there for a few short weeks, see things that you don't like, and pass judgment on something about which you don't even know the first thing. How dare you."

Yes. You're right.

I don't dare; I don't dare to pass judgment on you, whether you're one of the specific mentor teachers I'm talking about, you're a teacher that fits the description of my mentors, or you're someone else who'd like to pull me aside and tell me a piece of your mind.

Fortunately, I'm forty-two years old and learned in my thirties that I don't know everything, I don't know half of everything, and in fact I know very little. In my teens I thought I knew everything, like many teens do.

In my twenties, I was convinced that I was surrounded by idiots and that I had a better way of doing things, a better way of writing programs, a better way of managing an IT staff, a better way of inventing electrical products, a better way of running a graphic design agency, a better way of maintaining a long-term relationship, and a better way to make chocolate chip cookies.

I learned in my thirties, in reference to the above, in order: They're not idiots at all, I don't, other people have written better programs, making employees happy is very tough stuff, few people who make purchasing decisions care about the efficiency of lighting fixtures, it's difficult to get people to give you money to do things they think that they can do themselves but they can't, sometimes it's impossible to make somebody happy even though you tried as hard as you could, and stick with the Toll House recipe because it's better than your recipe.

So, I'm not judging the people whom I'm going to discuss.

I don't have a set of rubber stamps that say "good teacher," "bad teacher," "effective teacher," "ineffective teacher," and so on, but I am going to tell you what happened in the classroom and tell you my opinion about what I saw that I liked and that I didn't like.

I said in the previous paragraph that I learned that I don't know everything; however, that is not to say that I don't know anything. So far, over the first year of teaching a challenging population of teenagers, I've held it together. I've been observed on four occasions by experienced administrators and have received positive evaluations. My students have, over and over again, risen to the challenges I've placed before them. They usually treat me with respect and affection (the teenage version of this, which can include arguments, being asked inappropriate questions, and being told shockingly true stories). There's always the occasional temper tantrum over a rule, including a generous helping of language not appropriate for, shall we say, dinner with Father O'Flaherty, but the temper tantrum is followed by a friendly hello and compliance with the rule the next day.

By the end of the year, among many, many other things, I had students writing ten-page research papers, composing their own websites, being able to speak intelligently about the true meaning of the fine print in advertising and credit card offers, and understanding and being able to write clearly about the surprisingly numerous differences in character and plot between the classic horror film "Frankenstein" and the original text written by Mary Wollstonecraft Shelley.

They've read novels in their entirety and put forth trenchant statements about plot and conflict that never entered my mind. Of course, there are better days and worse days; good luck trying to finish off that lesson plan the Friday before spring break or the day after the Sox win the World Series, and good luck trying to get Lorraine to act right the morning after she got into a fistfight with her father.

36

MENTOR #1:
CANDY MAN

Vince shares the same characteristic as all of my mentors at this particular school: he does not invoke academic rigor inside the classroom.

When I observed Vince doing a lesson, he was reading "My Bloody Life," an extremely popular book with urban teens because of its graphic description of life inside a gang.

The lesson consisted of Vince standing in the front of the classroom and reading out loud from the book. There were no lesson plans, there were no copies of the book for the students to use if they wanted to follow along, there were no assessments to check to see whether the students understood what they were reading, there was no discussion about vocabulary building, there was no invocation of any research-based learning strategy, there was no homework, there were no writing assignments, and there were few requirements on the students' part to engage in any higher order thinking.

However, the students were highly engaged, they took a great personal interest in the book because the issue of gang involvement touches most of them deeply, they were eager to come to class, they sat and listened quietly, and they engaged in highly personal and poignant stories about how they can relate the reading to their own personal life. The lesson does align with a few of the Illinois learning standards for the English language arts, such as:

1. 1.b.5.a. Relate reading to prior knowledge and experience and make connections to related information.
2. 1.c.4.a. Use questions and predictions to guide reading.
3. 2.b.5.b. Apply knowledge gained from literature as a means of understanding contemporary and historical economic, social, and political issues and perspectives.

Yes, I understand why they were reading that book. I understand that they were highly engaged and motivated to read, I understand that they found it interesting and it stimulated honest dialogue between the students, and I understand that it increased the likelihood that they were going to come to school at all.

Yes. Good. Wonderful. Laudable.

But, what have the students learned that will help them when they graduate from high school? The result of these "Bloody Life" readings is the increased knowledge of the life of a Puerto Rican teenager and his involvement in and exit from the Latin Kings. If the course was more rigorous, this text, admittedly a high interest work of literature, could have been used as the starting point for a variety of lessons which would truly improve the literacy of the students in the classroom.

There are many different activities that Vince could have required of his students, which would have been interesting and which would have forced them to engage in higher order thinking and develop their minds.

He could have asked his students to write, each day, a summary of what they heard and also write out a prediction about what would happen in tomorrow's reading. However, he didn't.

He could have asked his students to create a short sketch where characters engaged in dialogue that extended and gave greater depth to a scene depicted in the book. This would have hit many more learning standards and would have been fun for the students to do. However, he didn't.

He could have asked students to take the role of police officers and ask his students to pretend they had to fill out a police report of a scene depicted in the book. This would have required them to create a coherent summary and restatement of the scene. Such an exercise requires far higher intellectual skills than merely listening to a story and would have improved the students' literacy skills. However, he didn't.

He could have obtained copies of the book somehow for the students to read as he spoke aloud. This simple step would have greatly extended the impact of the reading because such a multimodal delivery of literature reaches students with both auditory and visual preferred learning styles. However, he didn't.

He could have asked the students to take turns reading aloud from the book. Such a basic practice might seem unsophisticated, but research shows that students do not get enough time to simply read during the day. Students are inundated with so many literacy activities that there is almost no time allotted during the day for them to be able to simply read aloud or read to themselves. Such a simple act would also have greatly improved the literacy of the students. However, he didn't.

He could have asked the students to compose a poem or create a poster that represented a character or a scene from the book and give a short speech that explains the contents of their work and the justification for including it. Such an activity allows students with different expressive styles to become enthusiastic over the assignment, invokes higher order thinking processes, is aligned to many more learning standards than simply reading aloud, and would also have been a high interest activity for the students. However, he didn't.

My goodness, he could even have been less imaginative and simply created a traditional exam that asked the students to remember and locate facts in the book, even though such an activity is only marginally effective at improving reading comprehension. However, he didn't.

There are plenty of other ways to utilize the high interest level of this book to help motivate students to engage in activities that will improve their ability to read, write, analyze, and think. But, Vince didn't do any of them, and he viewed my efforts to do them with a detached amusement. Oh, he supported my efforts to invoke my newfangled university education in his classroom but never made me feel as though the things I wanted to try in his classroom were the things he would do upon my leaving. He knew he had a better way of motivating students to come to school. Vince's approach was to forget about improving self-esteem and forget about giving his students the skills they need to fight back when they're given a parking ticket that they don't deserve.

No, his way was better—he would manipulate their blood sugar levels.

Snickers bars. Mike N' Ikes. Kit Kats. Laffy Taffys. Sprees. M&M's. Bit-O-Honeys. Bonkers. REESE'S Peanut Butter Cups. Sugar. Cocoa butter. High fructose corn syrup. Soy lecithin. I'm the most popular teacher around. Chocolate. Motivation. Peanuts. Partially hydrogenated soybean oil. Operant conditioning. Milk. Milk fat. Milk solids. Skim milk. Almonds. Coconut. Smarties. Starburst. Strawberry. Cherry. Lemon. Lemonheads. Orange. Lime. Potassium sorbate. Adrenaline. Reinforcers. Insulin. Heart rate. Euphoria. No lesson plans. Energy. Mood elevation. Happiness. Tootsie Rolls. Caramel Creams. Dilated pupils. Jawbreakers. Bubble Gum. Sour Balls. I'll read a book today and go home at 3:00. No, not these, I don't like these. Butterfingers. Blow Pops. Milky Ways. Three Musketeers. The red ones, I want the, no, not that one, the other red ones. Frankie got two—it's not fair. He already got one, and I didn't even get one. I did not; she's lying—this is the only one I got. That's bogus—I saw you put it in your pocket.

This was Vince's Way. The rising and falling of glucose levels, the secretion of insulin, the easing of hunger pangs. This is how he motivated his students. Every Friday was candy day, and every day that wasn't Friday was a day without candy, and tomorrow is candy day, right? Oh wait, today's Wednesday.

The money is worth it to him. The money he pays for bags and bags of bulk candy bars —shiny, sparkling, satchels of scrumptious, sumptuous sugar—red, orange, yellow, green, blue, silver, gold, checkered, striped, swirled, extruded, blended, whipped, layered, coated, stuffed, filled, molded, quiet bliss, a break from the ho-hum, a roomful of undulating tongues hidden behind a sea of silent smiles.

Not an idle pancreas in the vicinity.

I have to give it to him; it's an effective reinforcer. It trumps straight As, self-respect, and—wait for it—achieving a difficult educational goal.

When a student starts to misbehave, all Vince has to do is ask The Question: "You do want candy on Friday, don't you?" The Question is made more effective by a pause and a solemn facial expression prior to its articulation. They freeze in their tracks, ladies and gentlemen. No plea to uphold morals, no threat of slaving in a dead-end job when you're forty because you didn't graduate is as effective as The Question in getting a bunch of fifteen- and sixteen-year-olds to get with the program. The threat of NGCOF, or Not Getting Candy On Friday, is as serious to these students as is the threat of congestive heart failure to a roomful of nursing home residents.

Of course, difficulties arise when the offensive behavior happens on a Tuesday, and it's time for NGCOF on Friday.

Teens, by definition, push limits. It's written in their contract to investigate What Happens If I Do This. And, as a teacher with, I admit, competent behavior management skills, Vince has to mete out consequences for misbehavior. The most dreaded is NGCOF. The difficulty, however, comes from the fact that by the time Friday rolls around, neither the students nor Vince can remember which students are marked for NGCOF.

So, everybody gets candy.

One time, a student who was particularly difficult on a Wednesday was marked for NGCOF and, on Friday, both Vince and I remembered which student. It was Gerardo. He didn't really deserve to get any candy as he went over the top and needed to have a consequence. Easy enough to say to a sixteen-year-old, "You're not getting any candy today because of what you did on Wednesday," but, as they say, the devil is in the details. The student had allies in the Candy Distribution System and used these allies to get a fistful of goodies without the teacher's knowledge. This can happen because the odds of handing out accurately metered quantities of candies to a bunch of finicky children are low, low, low indeed.

This one doesn't like peanuts; that one wants Starburst but can't stand the orange kind. This one can't eat gum because she has braces. This one has a thing for Kit Kats. This one can't eat chocolate because it makes him break out. Mike is really hungry this morning; he didn't have any breakfast, so can he have two? Carlos wants to give one of these little red heart things to his girlfriend because it's her birthday. Frankie was absent last Friday (don't you remember?) and says that it's not fair—he should get two because he's been good for over a month.

Keep seated? That's a laugh. They form a semicircle around the desk, their legs quivering with excitement. You forget who you started with. Suzanne insists that she hasn't gotten any candy yet and smiles, revealing chocolate stuck between her teeth. She's a great kid, always cooperates, you give her another Kit Kat. After all, the whole bag only cost about eight bucks. But what of NGCOF? What of Gerardo, who told the teacher on Wednesday to go do something that might not be physically possible? He's munching and happy, an empty candy wrapper on his desk. Someone gave him candy, but who? Well, what does it matter? He's been better since Wednesday, and look how happy he is. After all, he's just a kid. And, after all, a student with a mouthful of caramel nougat doesn't challenge the teaching assignment and doesn't say unkind things to less desirable peers.

If there are any pro-behaviorism professionals out there reading this, I'm sure that by now you have bitter tears of sadness streaming down your cheeks.

The behavioral modification broke down. You can't administer a consequence on Friday for an infraction done on Wednesday with this student population. One of the most basic concepts you'll learn in Behaviorism 101 is that consequences have to be administered very shortly after the behavior whose frequency you're trying to modify.

When Gerardo told you to attempt the physically impossible act, something had to be done at that moment: a hallway conference, a rebuke from the teacher, exclusion from the classroom, feedback as to the inappropriateness of the comment, and/or a combination of all of these, and possibly other follow-up consequences to help reduce the likelihood of such inappropriate behavior being exhibited again.

Telling a student that you're not going to get candy on Friday as a result of an inappropriate behavior performed on Wednesday creates a classically bad situation of the student thinking to himself that there is no longer any motivation to behave for the rest of the week. This "I have nothing to lose" mindset is a predictable and understandable reaction to being told of an extremely delayed consequence to a misbehavior. What happens if, as a result of the sugar high from the beginning of class on Friday, a student misbehaves towards the end of Friday's "Bloody Life" reading? The result is a delay of seven days for the consequence of NGCOF, which is unacceptably long. And, as we have seen, for practical purposes, there is no such thing as NGCOF; everybody gets candy because of the nerve-racking hullabaloo that occurs when the sugar sack is first ripped open.

So why does Vince do it?

Why does he dispense literally pounds and pounds of candy to his students all day on Friday? Is it because it makes him popular? Probably.

He boasted to me on several occasions that he was nominated for, and won, several awards over the years that recognize extremely popular teachers. These awards are obtained by having enough of your students vote for you as a good teacher.

Of course!

When you're fifteen years old, you don't understand the importance of education throughout the course of your life. You can't talk to a fifteen-year-old about what it's like to not have enough money when you're thirty. To these students, nearly all of whom live near the poverty line and have never held a job, the idea of making nearly $1,000 a month by working at the big-box store is indistinguishable from being a billionaire. They don't know anything about mortgage payments, utility bills, credit card bills, the cost of diapers, and $2,300 for the dentist or you're never going to get any sleep. They are still kids, and kids like candy.

When you're eating candy, you don't need to worry about getting a job, about the fact that your father has just been laid off, or that they turned off the heat to your neighbor's house last weekend and you're next. They don't understand that education is the key to getting the promotion, getting the good job, and getting enough money to actually make your rent and your grocery bills and your utility bills and have at least a little bit of money left over for bus fare and a new pair of shoes.

They don't understand that the employees who actually read the manual and learn how to operate the machine correctly are the ones that are going to get the promotion.

They don't understand that the employees that communicate effectively in writing are going to impress their supervisors and influence their decision when it comes time to pick a new regional manager.

They don't understand that being able to understand the fine print of a payday loan store agreement could result in their not signing it and avoiding the payment of hundreds of dollars in usurious interest rates.

That's why we, as teachers, have to find ways to inculcate a love of learning and a positive self-image into their extremely impressionable minds. We have to give them a difficult task which requires them to read, think, analyze, and write, and look them in the eyes and tell them that they can absolutely, positively do this. We have to show them that their brains are just as good as anybody else's, that a learning disability can be compensated for, and that their strengths can be developed so they rise head and shoulders above other peers who look in the mirror and don't believe.

Candy won't do these things.

Sure, it'll make you popular because the image of your face falls on their retinas as their glucose levels spike, and an association is made. But the lollipop isn't going to help little Adriana when she's twenty-seven and been wrongly referred to a collection agency. The fact is that Vince has been shaped by behavioral principles that are just as powerful on teachers as they are on students. Vince hands out candy, the kids settle down, they're happy, he's happy, everybody's happy, and there are few incidents of misbehavior on Thursday afternoons and Fridays. Simple operant conditioning—Vince hands out the candy, nice things happen, and the likelihood is increased that Vince will hand out candy next Friday.

We all have the responsibility as education professionals to understand the cognitive development of children. Vince should understand that he has a much more important obligation to his students than merely to satisfy hunger, and I don't think that he does.

Again, as I said before, I'm not going to judge his character and say that he's a good person or a bad person. He's a very nice guy and does have a brain in his head. He was kind and patient with me almost the whole time that I was there. He cares deeply about his students and is constantly helping them work out personal problems. If he was outside the school and someone came up to one of his students in a threatening way, I'm 99 percent sure that he would jump over there in half a second and make sure, at his own personal risk, that nothing happened to his student. I was only in this Chicago public school for a few months. Maybe I don't know what it's like to teach there year after year; maybe Vince was equally interested in the skilled classroom execution of research-based pedagogical principles when he began, and some other powerful forces slowly shaped his behavior into becoming primarily a candy-dispensing orator.

This may have nothing to do with Vince—it may have to do with the nature of the machine of which he is a part.

Vince never made me feel as though the sorts of lessons I was trying out would be the types that he would attempt in the classroom. On one instance, he was emphatically against my trying out a lesson that seemed to me to be a good idea, which was highly recommended by my professors in graduate school and was well aligned with several Illinois language arts learning standards. I was truly puzzled at his expression of displeasure at my describing the lesson. I'm going to tell you now what I did, why I did it, and why it made life unpleasant for me during my student teaching for some days thereafter.

This lesson had to do with improving literacy skills. One of the most important things that good readers do is analyze the parts of unknown words to try to understand their meaning. This involves doing a contextual analysis to try to glean some meaning of what an unknown word means by looking at the words near the unknown word. Here's an example:

Your apartment is so unkempt, the cockroaches wear slippers.

If you didn't know what the word "unkempt" meant, you can begin to figure it out by looking at the rest of the sentence; "unkempt" must mean either that your apartment is very dirty or that your apartment is very cold. However, we're talking about cockroaches here, and it would be funnier if the cockroaches were wearing slippers because your apartment was disgusting, so "unkempt" must mean messy or dirty.

It's a simple procedure, but a lot of students with reading disabilities simply don't do it, and from my experience, most of the time they don't do it because they didn't know that they could do it. So, my idea was to create a lesson using the projector and a PowerPoint presentation that was filled with examples of how to do a contextual analysis of unknown words. The students would also be given a companion worksheet that would allow them to practice doing it on their own with some more examples. The lesson involved some direct instruction, reading from a projector, reading from a sheet, and coming up with answers to relatively challenging exercises.

All in all, this was a good lesson because it presented a sound, research-based reading comprehension strategy, was presented with a multimodal approach, was aligned with learning standards, and gave students plenty of time to engage in supervised practice. I'm not saying it was the best lesson in the world, I'm not saying that I'm anything special—all I wanted to do was try out something that I was taught as being effective by my reading and literacy professor at grad school. I typed up the lesson plan and gave it to Vince. I was waiting for enthusiastic confirmation.

Time for a big surprise. His lips pursed. His eyebrows furrowed.

He looked at me as if the lesson plan said that I was going to come into the classroom tomorrow with a bottle of fuchsia nail polish and ask the five toughest male students to take their shoes and socks off because I was going to paint their toenails with this positively glam shade so that they could get away with wearing pink glitter sandals, which I was also going to provide.

"Why would you want to do this lesson?" was his response. The skin around his lips continued to compress itself in a disapproving series of creases. I said that it was something I wanted to try out that I learned in school. He said to me that there was absolutely no connection between this lesson and my students' lives. He said that the students would not have the slightest interest in this lesson because they wouldn't be able to relate to it. He said that there was no content within the lesson that they could identify with, and without the students being able to identify with something in a lesson, it's doomed to failure.

I thought to myself, "What?" The things he was saying went against what I was learning in graduate school.

He noted that I wanted to use a projector to put up part of the lesson as a PowerPoint presentation. He asked me why I wanted to use a projector. I said that I wanted to present the lesson in a slightly different format to try to mix things up in the classroom and because I was hopeful that the electronics would help hold the students' interest. Plus, I said, I wanted to use colors to help the students distinguish the unknown words from the other words.

The response to this was a long disapproving look at the lesson plan, and "Well, you can try it out if you want to" coupled with a skeptical tone of voice.

Here was a veteran teacher who had been in the trenches for nine years with a challenging student population. He looked at my lesson plan and was highly critical of its content. This upset me quite a bit for two reasons. First, I thought that there was a major and perhaps uncorrectable flaw in the way that I was actually executing my bookish university education. Thus far in graduate school I had a 4.0 grade point average; could this mean that I was fine as long as writing papers and memorizing facts were concerned but that I was pathetically and laughably misguided in the way that I executed the theory and facts that I had learned? My lesson plan was not merely met with ambivalence; Vince was wholly against it and seemed to object strongly to the fundamental approach of the whole thing.

Second, perhaps more disturbing, was my interpretation of his strong disapproval as an indictment of the very education I was receiving in graduate school up until this point. I had heard whisperings from other teachers that a common complaint by long-term teachers is a dearth of lengthy real world experience in the classroom among an unacceptably high percentage of university professors. Indeed, some of my professors had taught for a long time, but some had only taught in the public school classroom for a few years before continuing on to their doctoral studies and their ultimate careers as college professors.

Could it be that the research-based principles that are so strongly promulgated by my professors and by other education professionals in general fall flat on their faces when implemented in a classroom full of clever, streetwise minority students with learning disabilities and behavior disorders?

I was so disoriented by Vince's reaction that I sought the advice of another veteran teacher I had gotten to know during my time at the high school. He said something that sounded much more sensible to me at the time: give it a shot.

He said, "Neil, nobody really knows how a lesson is going to go unless you give it a shot. I respect Vince and what he has to say, but nobody has a crystal ball. The lesson sounds okay to me, based on what you said, so try it out. If it doesn't work out, and you lose the kids' interest, you still learned something. You're not going to do any harm; you're not going to hurt the kids by giving them a presentation about how to figure out what words mean, for crying out loud." He looked at me and smiled and then continued grading papers. I thanked him and decided I was going to go ahead with it. I had two English classes the next day, and I would present the lesson during both of them.

I set the projector up, and I was much more nervous than I thought I would be; part of this was caused by Vince harrumphing into the classroom with a weak "Good morning." He wasn't doing a very good job of trying to conceal his disapproval of this lesson, but I learned that a good student teacher soldiers on in the face of adversity. Everything was set up, and the students started showing up. One student saw the projector and excitedly said, "Are we going to see a movie?!" I said no, we're going to learn about how to figure out what words mean. He looked disappointed and sat in his seat. I got started with the lesson, and I'll do you the very great favor of not detailing everything that I did; you get the general idea of what was going on—some direct instruction, PowerPoint slides, the worksheet, questions from the students, and so on.

Both Vince and I were very surprised by the reaction of the students.

They cared.

They were paying attention.

They were volunteering information and raising their hands to answer questions.

They came up with their own examples on the worksheets, and their examples were relevant and their solutions accurate.

The expression on Vince's face was a mixture of irritation and surprise. The expression on my face was a combination of relief, happiness, and apprehension. I was relieved that I wasn't fundamentally misguided and that my professors were teaching me the right thing the right way. I was happy to see my students were interested in improving their literacy skills. But, and this is a big "but," I was apprehensive about the future of my formerly good relationship with Vince. The students were so interested and so engaged in this lesson that if I were Vince, I would have wanted to dig a deep hole right there in the classroom and bury myself in it—I would have been so embarrassed.

The lesson took nearly the entire period. When the bell rang, the students filtered out, leaving Vince and me in the empty classroom during the time normally arranged for us to talk about the lesson and give me advice on how to improve it. It was a truly uncomfortable moment, and I was nervous about his reaction for a reason that you might not realize.

Vince, being my main mentor teacher, is largely responsible for my grade in the student teaching internship. Although my professor is responsible for entering the grade, Vince's evaluation of me at the end of the internship is a big part of the grade. Also, recommendation letters from mentor teachers are an important part of the job application process when applying for teaching jobs.

If this experience had put me on Vince's blacklist, not only would the remaining several months of the internship be highly uncomfortable but the lack of a recommendation letter would be a hindrance to my obtaining gainful employment next August.

It was time to go into ego-saving mode and prevent anything showing on my face that would indicate any hint of "AHA! I told you so!" I tried to look as innocent and surprised as possible. I looked at him without saying anything. He said quietly, "Well, that went well. They were certainly engaged."

No smiles, no eye contact, and no supportive tone of voice. I said to him that I was very glad that it did because I was nervous that it would not have; more ego-saving talk because what I was saying was only partially true. I had a feeling that the lesson would go well. I knew my students wanted to learn, I knew that they were, deep down, embarrassed about their lack of literacy skills. Their hunger for education showed me that my intuition was on the mark. He said, "Yeah, it just goes to show, sometimes even an old teacher like me can learn some new things." He smiled weakly at me. I said, "Well, we'll see how it goes this afternoon." Little did I know that this comment was much more than just small talk.

Tenth period showed up, and I had all my materials ready. The same projector, the same handouts, and the same deal as before. Everything was the same. The students were about the same age as third period, they were approximately the same ethnic and gender makeup, in the same room, in the same school, on the same day, with the same weather, experiencing the same relative humidity, and influenced by the same planet alignment.

You get one guess as to how it went, and if you guess "well," you guessed wrong.

The students were talkative, it was hard to get them focused on the lesson, they were coming up with frivolous answers to my questions, and they were reluctant to complete the worksheet. The lesson went okay; it wasn't a disaster, but it just didn't go nearly as well as third period. We got through the lesson, but it took quite a bit more work from me and some support from Vince to do it. I expected him to be smug about this, but I believe that he was just as puzzled as I was as to the difference in the behavior of the two classes to exactly the same lesson.

But, a class of students takes on its own collective personality, and this group personality differs from one day to the next, from one minute to the next, from one hour to the next. Third period is in a great mood today, and tomorrow it's a room full of sourpusses. The same exact lesson, presented to two different groups of highly similar students, can go very differently for reasons yet unknown to mortal humans.

But, a good teacher doesn't have a problem with making students do something that benefits their ability to understand what they read. Even though some students might fight you, they will still pay attention for the most part, and they will still turn in work that generally shows improvement. They'll complain sometimes, but their literacy will improve as a result of the lesson.

Fortunately, Vince did not harbor any resentment toward me as a result of my showing him a couple of new ideas. I think that the less-than-optimal way that the tenth period lesson went took some sting out of the ego wound he suffered during the shockingly smooth and academic third-period lesson. But, I kept the new ideas out of the classroom for a while because I wanted to ensure that my relationship with him was preserved. I wish he had been more receptive to introducing new ideas into his classroom; I would have learned more if I was able to try a wider variety of teaching techniques without worrying about incurring his wrath and ruining my grade.

37

MENTOR #2: A STUDENT'S OLDEST FRIEND

Although I worked predominately with Vince, mentor number one, I also worked with Gene, mentor number two. Gene was friendly to me and seemed eager to take me under his wing and show me the ropes. I was going to observe his history class for a few weeks and then take over the teaching.

I was surprised and a little bit upset at what I saw in his classroom. When I came into the classroom, the students were not actually working on anything for quite a while because Gene was not teaching them anything. He was engaged in a side conversation with a few students about what happened at a party over the weekend, and the conversation that was taking place between them had a strange characteristic to it that I couldn't identify. Eventually, we began talking about World War I but in a relatively superficial way.

There were textbooks, but they weren't being used.

Gene was talking to the students about a couple of characters involved in the war, was writing a few things on the board, and was asking some of the students a few questions. This continued for a little while, but the classroom then lost its structure, for lack of a better term. A few of the students walked to the back of the room and began having a conversation that most definitely was not about the causes of World War I.

Gene made no effort to stop this conversation, and after a few minutes, the lesson degraded further; another group conversation started in the front of the room, and Gene was part of this front conversation. This conversation, too, had a strange characteristic to it that made me somewhat uneasy, just like the first conversation that took place at the beginning of the period. What was it that was different about these conversations?

Gene's lesson, like Vince's lesson, lacked a lot of the characteristics that you would expect in a classroom.

There was no review of the previous day's work; there was no requirement for the students to actually do any work; there was very little opportunity for Gene to be able to assess the extent to which the students were learning anything; there were no textbooks in use, few notes being taken, few meaningful conversations about the subject matter, and no analysis of the war's causes; no photographs, no film, no posters, and no artifacts; no introductions and no summaries; no opportunities for the students to share with each other their opinions of the war; and no lesson plan for this class, the previous class, or any class in the future.

It wasn't a lesson, it was a brief contextless conversation about a topic of which the students knew almost nothing and about which they cared even less. However, the students did get the opportunity to talk about who almost got arrested over the weekend and the probability of upcoming fights between particular students and the factors that would increase or decrease the likelihood of these fights.

Part of what was somewhat unsettling about Gene was his appearance. He was wearing black boots, jeans, a black belt with a silver buckle, a black Metallica T-shirt, a flannel shirt over the T-shirt, a silver ring, and a large platinum necklace.

Before I go any further, I want to tell you that I'm not a fancy dresser. I'm not a fashion snob. I don't have a subscription to GQ. Expensive clothing doesn't impress me. (In fact, many of the wealthy people I've met in my life dress very casually.) I'm not overly concerned with the clothing that I wear. On the weekends I wear T-shirts, jeans, and sweatshirts. I've never spent more than $30 for a dress shirt. Last fall I was thrilled to pick up three pairs of shorts at Sears for $10 each.

But let me tell you, ladies and gentlemen, I wanted to grab Gene and ask him what the hell was he doing showing up at school dressed like he was getting ready to go to a Metallica concert. He didn't always dress down that much, in his defense. Sometimes he wore a nice sweater. It was interesting to me that just when I noticed that something about the way he dressed was inappropriate, he volunteered information that revealed why he dressed the way he did and told me many things about himself that finally helped me pinpoint what it was about the nature of his conversations that was faintly unsettling to me.

His explanation of why he dressed the way he did started with a criticism of the way I dressed. Each day, I wore khakis or black dress pants and a dress shirt, but no tie. He told me that I ought to dress down a little bit to help make myself more accessible to the students.

He pointed to his screaming, shouting, honking, ring-a-dinging, jingle-jangling, bling-blinging, drink-in-one-hand-hot-chick-in-the-other, how-you-doin'-baby, sit-down-right-here-next-to-your-man-Gene platinum necklace.

This necklace is so big, it practically needs to be plugged in. He said that the reason he's wearing a rare metallic chain around his neck is because it would be an object his students would admire and would therefore make them like him more and would therefore make them more likely to cooperate in the classroom.

Oh . . . kay.

Gene, a man whose skin is as white as the whitest white Caucasian white man you ever saw sitting indoors drinking milk and eating marshmallows during a snowstorm, told me that I talk too formally, that I sound entirely too high class and . . . white. He said that I shouldn't speak so intelligently because I'm going to intimidate and put off the students.

At that moment I had the famous AHA! experience you learn about in Psych 101.

That was what it was—sitting before me was a man with a lumi-nescent, pale ivory epidermis who spoke like a brotha who grew up in the baddest projects in the roughest 'hood on the wrong side of the tracks on the south side of town. The disparity between his speech and his appearance was beyond amusing—it was stunning, it was riveting, and it was an object of fascination.

Sample Gene sentence to his student: "You ain't never gonna git your homies to go along wid dat." I listened to him saying these words as I watched the light from the fluorescent tubes reflecting off of his smooth, vanilla-hued pate. The students were listening to him, I have to admit.

But wouldn't they still have listened to him if he had said, "Your friends are never going to agree with that"?

This isn't about race, folks. There were all races in his classroom: Puerto Rican, Mexican, light and dark skinned African-American, Caucasian, mixed race, and everything. It's actually a beautiful thing; the school is situated on the border among Polish, Mexican, and Puerto Rican communities, and there is a beautiful diversity to the students at the school. As you walk down the hallway, you hear English, then Polish, then Spanish, then Polish, than Spanish, then English, and so on. Hearing this language diversity made me wish that I had paid more attention in Spanish class almost twenty-five years ago.

This chapter is getting close to the whole issue of whether stan-dard English is something that should be spoken by everyone. Per-sonally, I think that it's more important to let students express them-selves freely without constantly interrupting them and saying, "It's not, 'you ain't never,' it's 'you aren't ever.'"

This sort of thing is what gives a lot of old-school English teach-ers a bad name. If a kid comes up to you and excitedly starts telling you something important that happened to him yesterday and uses the word "ain't," for God's sake don't correct him, just let him speak, listen to him, and celebrate the fact that he respects you enough to be comfortable enough to share something personal with you.

On the other hand, casual conversation is one thing, but formal written communication is another. It's true that in most cases we need to invoke our best writing skills when trying to accomplish an important task, achieve a lofty goal, or right a wrong that has affected us. Because of this, it's very useful and desirable for students who normally use nonstandard English in conversation to know how to use standard English when applying for a job, speaking to your girlfriend's father for the first time, filling out a college application, and so on.

Standards are useful; they allow people from different generations, different cultural backgrounds, and different races to communicate effectively with each other. If a kid from the inner city of Chicago tells a friend who just moved in from Florida that her car is tight, and the recently transported Floridian has no clue what a tight car is, the problem will be solved within a few seconds when the Chicagoan sees the confusion on the Floridian's face and explains just exactly what it means to have a tight car. Hint: it's a good thing. However, if the Chicagoan is trying to get into college and writes on the application that her current supervisor is tight, the woman evaluating the application, who was born in Portugal, might throw the application in the "NO" pile because she heard that "tight" means "cheap," and she has been irritated by the decision the applicant made to insult her former supervisor on a highly formal college application.

I hope you see that I'm not saying standard English is better than any other language, dialect, or slang. Slang is good; it makes a language more efficient. It's a lot easier to say to your buddy, "Bullshit!" than to say, "I feel close enough to you to be able to tell you that I very much doubt the truth of your last statement."

So please, now that I have shown you that I don't put price tags on language styles, let's get back to my original point, which is that I found it very strange that Gene was significantly changing the way that he spoke, depending on his audience. When he was speaking to me in the faculty lounge, he was an eloquent and amusing conversational partner. When he walked into his classroom, he sounded like a very different person.

I believe that he made this change in his speaking style for two reasons: 1) he wanted to be liked rather than to be respected, and 2) he felt that it was highly unlikely that his largely minority students would warm up to a white man. Did he feel that his students were so prejudiced at their young age that it would be impossible for them to see past the color of his skin, and so he had to talk "like them" in order to help compensate for his shameful whiteness?

Did he feel that his students had been so consistently mistreated by white people that they would automatically shut down their minds when they heard the words "I'm not going" instead of "I ain't going"?

Let's say that this was the case for argument's sake. Let's say that his students were in fact extremely prejudiced against white people because the only white people they knew were cops who had treated them unfairly or lawyers who worked together to send their brother to prison. Don't you think that if this prejudice and mistrust was the case, it's even more important to present yourself as—gasp!—a white man who is going to accept his students for who they are, who will treat them with kindness and compassion and patience, and who will do what he can to help them out?

But I digress.

Let's get back to the whole issue of academic rigor in the classroom.

The issue is that there was no academic rigor in Gene's classroom. One day, I showed up to observe the class, and Gene came in a few minutes later. He walked to the back of the room, turned on the television, and turned to the class.

He said, "Guys, we're going to do two things today. Jack Shit."

The class then divided itself into two groups. The first group sat around and watched television. The second group sat near me and Gene and discussed boyfriends, girlfriends, previous fights, upcoming fights, and who was in and who was not in a gang.

A week earlier, Gene had told me in the faculty lounge that the important thing about teaching a lesson was to engage their higher order thinking. He said, "The content of the course is bullshit. The point of the whole thing is to use the content as a reason to get them to think and to evaluate and to improve the decision-making process." I saw that one of the ways that he helped his students improve their decision-making abilities was to have them walk into a classroom and have to decide whether to watch an inane show on television or to listen to students glorify the gang life by virtue of talking about it with their undivided attention, with the teacher as conversation facilitator, for a very long time.

I was there for the final exam. Do you know what the exam was?

You wouldn't guess right even if I gave you a thousand years to try.

The final exam of American history class—the final assessment, which allows the educator to truly get a clear picture of what "big ideas" the students are likely to leave the course with. It's an assessment of the cumulative effect of eighty or ninety lessons: the final exam. I'm going to tell you what the final exam was in Gene's class. The entire final exam of Gene's history class is reproduced in the next paragraph.

Name a weapon.

The previous paragraph is a reproduction of the entire final exam of Gene's history class. It is a paragraph that contains a total of three words. Or, eleven letters and a period. The consonants "r," "s," "t," even "d," all of whom are immensely popular and are usually in such demand this time of year, are sitting quietly along the wall on rusty metal folding chairs, wringing their hands, wondering what went wrong. They call their vowel friends "i" and "u" for some type of explanation and are shocked to find them home washing their hair and with no plans either, believe it or not, on Finals Day.

You can practically hear the cranial neurons firing by the billions. Say "gun" and you got yourself an A. Say "knife," "bomb," "arrow," "rocket launcher," "howitzer," "snowball," "spitball," it's all the same, it doesn't matter, take your A-plus home and show Uncle Louie.

I'm sorry because I said that I wasn't going to be judgmental, but my frustration and irritation is manifesting itself with satire. I wanted to stand up when he said the "Jack Shit" comment and say to him, "Man, what are you DOING?" If this is what you're doing when you're being observed by a student teacher, what goes on in this room when it's just you and the kids?" What in the world is this man thinking about?

Just as unsettling—no, outrageous and ridiculous—as his comments was the reaction of his students. They were perfectly fine with watching television and, disturbingly, didn't seem surprised by his announcement. This made me wonder how many times this had happened in the past.

Gene's students seemed pleased at not having to work in his class, but I believe that, deep down, they were not at all pleased. Gene forgot one thing: a classroom lesson teaches, above all, your value judgment of your students. Of course, a lesson teaches about vertex angles or the use of flashback in "Occurrence at Owl Creek Bridge," but, just as importantly, it teaches the students your opinion of their worth and their capabilities.

When you look a student in the eyes and say to him that today's lesson will involve reading a short, boring story and learning two vocabulary words, you communicate to him two things: one, you do not feel he is worth preparing a more interesting lesson plan, and two, you do not believe that he is capable of understanding more difficult concepts or doing more difficult work. With a boring, easy lesson plan, you teach the students that they are unworthy of your effort and incapable of appreciating it.

Don't fall into the trap of being rewarded with good behavior in exchange for lowering your standards.

The students may talk about how cool you are, they may vote to give you a Most Popular Teacher award, but you will have done nothing to educate them or help them as people. Your students, no matter how much they protest, desperately want to be educated, to be given lofty goals, and then given the help they need to reach them.

How do I know this? On the second day of my job, I asked my students to write down on a 3x5 card what they want out of English class. They initially asked, "What you mean, what do we want?" I clarified and told them to write down what skills they wanted to improve or write down something they don't do well right now but wish they did. Fifteen pens started writing on fifteen cards. They all turned them in, anonymously.

Almost all of them contained a similar message: they were dissatisfied with their writing, their spelling, and their reading comprehension, and they wanted to improve it.

One student wrote, "I want to understand what I read."

Another one wrote: "I hate that I can't write well."

The most amusing one was this: "I want to have better English etiquette."

And of course, the obligatory "I want to get an A!!!"

Let's look at that last comment in a little bit more detail. At first glance, it seems superficial, and many educators might roll their eyes to the ceiling and toss the card aside, assuming the student was saying it merely to get a laugh and for absolutely no other purpose. But wait a minute. Why did the student say that he wanted to get an A? Why didn't he say that he wanted to pass the class? Why didn't he say that he wanted to stay out of trouble? If he wanted to get a laugh, why didn't he say something like, "I want to learn how to be a millionaire," or "I want to be the class clown"? He said that he wanted to get an A because he values school and has a respect and desire for education.

I'll be honest with you, you're not always going to get an enthusiastic response when you ask your students to do work which is indeed challenging. An example of such a lesson is where the students listen to me read Edgar Allan Poe's "The Raven" as they read along, and they rewrite it, stanza by stanza, to explain it so that a ten-year-old child could understand it. During these difficult lessons, you must provide a lot of scaffolding or give your students just enough help so they can figure it out on their own. My students don't know what the word "obeisance" means. They don't know what dying embers are. They never really entertained the concept that a large black bird can beguile you to smile.

The only assumption in their heads is that Leonore was an extremely hot chick.

But, I pull them through it, line by line. I explain what "mien" means. And you know what? They get it. It takes a lot of effort, both on their part and on mine, but most of them—not all of them—actually find the poem to be intriguing. No, wait: "cool." As I said, not everybody appreciates it.

One of my students walked into the classroom on the second day of the lesson, saw a gigantic picture of a raven projected on the screen, scrunched up his face, and cried out, "Oh, no! Not this bird AGAIN!"

The only thing I could think to do was to remind him that this was one of the most famous poems ever written. The look on his face in response to my statement was unforgettable; it was a fascinating combination of disgust, irritation, incredulity, boredom, impatience, and condescension. The most seasoned actors in the world could not represent these emotions as well as the student did. Yet, as I've said before, there is more to my disdainful student than meets the eye.

When the lesson began, he got to work. He didn't complain, he didn't make a disruption, he just got to work. He listened to me as I tried to explain that having purple curtains does not automatically indicate homosexuality, and that a bust of Pallas does not mean that a bodacious female was walking around wearing nothing but a smile.

They weren't enthusiastic, there weren't smiles on their faces, but they were listening and they were writing. Nearly all of them were trying hard to understand what the poem was about and then trying equally hard to describe it to a ten-year-old child. This lesson represents a double challenge to my students because it requires nearly grade-level reading comprehension and good expressive language ability, both of which are areas of difficulty for my students.

Don't let your students' being intimidated by the difficulty of the lesson stop you; you need to give them something challenging in order to see what their limits are.

This procedure of increasing the level of difficulty from time to time allows the educator to discover the limits of what the students can do; this is a common method used not only in education but also in sports and physical conditioning.

If you want to see how much weight a student can lift, you can't just load ten pounds on the bar. The student will lift it, and you will have learned almost nothing about the limits of his strength. You have to put more and more weight on until he can't lift it. You record the last amount that he lifted successfully, and you have discovered the limits of his strength, commonly known as his "one rep max."

A necessary component to this method is eventually putting more weight on the bar than he can lift; if the student understands what you're doing and understands that an unliftable weight is a necessary component of discovering his limits, he will not be upset by his failure to lift that weight.

The same is true in the classroom if—and I stress the word if—you are sure to tell the students what you're doing. You have to tell them that they're about to try something difficult and that not everybody is going to be able to do all of it well, but everybody is going to be able to do some of it. Try using the weightlifting analogy; your students will understand it intuitively and transfer that understanding to what's going on in the classroom.

In this situation, where you present challenging materials to your students, you have to do three things well in order for it to be a successful lesson.

First, you have to have a good understanding of what it is that you're teaching. You cannot have just read the poem, or novel, or whatever else for that matter, and have merely a superficial understanding of its content. Make sure you have read it thoroughly, understand it thoroughly, and have researched what other people have to say about it.

Second, you have to keep a sharp eye on your students, read their body language, and provide scaffolding where needed. Don't assume that they understand that a "chamber" really means a "room." Explain everything. Write explanations on the board. Use props. Use humor. Ask students to restate lines in their own words. Ensure that most of them understand most of what's going on before you move on to the next stanza.

Third, you have to provide encouragement to your students. Tell them it's going to be difficult. Tell them it's going to be slow going at times. Tell them that it's okay if they don't understand everything, but that they have to try as hard as they can to do so. Some of them will find the lesson to be an almost insurmountable obstacle and might become disillusioned. This disillusionment might manifest itself as disruptive behavior or refusal to do the assignment. But, if you explain it well, give encouragement, and help the students when needed, I've found that they will approach the lesson diligently and try their hardest to do a good job.

When I finished this lesson, I read their writing, and most of them wrote explanations that were largely accurate.

I then stood in front of them and told them what they had just done. I told them that they had just successfully completed a difficult activity that would challenge students in Honors classes (a high academic level class offered at my high school). I told them that they were now capable of discussing one of the greatest poems ever written, and they had an understanding of it that was deeper than most of the other students in high school. When I finished saying these true statements, the classroom was silent.

The students were looking at me and looking at each other. A few were smiling. It was a beautiful moment, and I actually shut up and let it linger for a while.

At that moment, I wondered if Gene ever experienced the satisfaction and happiness I felt? I thought about his "Jack Shit" lesson, and realized that he probably hasn't in a long time. Maybe one day he'll turn off the television in the classroom and do what he needs to do to experience it. I'm sure it feels better than wearing a platinum necklace.

38

APOLOGIA

If you are reading this and are angry with me for revealing to the general public what went on inside these classrooms, I would like to ask you a question: why aren't any of these students' parents asking their kids' teachers why their kids aren't achieving at a higher level?

Maybe my perspective is naïve; perhaps the parents know what's going on and are satisfied with it. In fact, maybe everybody but me knows what's going on, realizes that it is immutable and inevitable, and has come to inner peace with it.

The challenges facing teachers of tough inner-city children are daunting, and the blame for the above-described classroom situations does not fall exclusively on the teacher's shoulders.

George Bush says that no child shall be left behind; but how do you teach a student who misses class a few days a week because he's too drunk to come to school?

How do you get a student to concentrate on the lesson when that student learned, twenty-four hours earlier, that she is pregnant?

How do you control the behavior of a child who lives with only his mother, and his mother tells you, and I quote, "I can't keep an eye on him twenty-four hours a day, he is a teenager; teenagers do these things."

The environment surrounding an insulated upper-middle-class school is different from the environment surrounding a school that sits on the border between two gang territories. Real gangs, not the Jets and the Sharks, but groups of people whose cultural norms include violence and murder as a means for increasing one's social status, and where education means learning how to spot undercover detectives on a sting. I observed these students for seven months and taught them for four; this short experience will result in most veteran teachers laughing derisively at my lack of experience and saying that I have no right to judge them unless I've been in their shoes for years.

To that statement, I say you're only partially right. I am not judging you, and I admit that my experience is brief. However, my relatively brief experience does not give anyone the justification to utterly disregard my statements. I observed what happened in that school and participated in the teaching for seven months; during that time, I was a keen observer and discussed and reflected upon what I saw with my peers and my professors.

I may not have the whole picture, but I do have part of it, and I'm saying to you that I think there's a lot of room for improvement.

Again, I am not judging the teachers. Most of the teachers were dedicated professionals who had a genuine affection for all of their students and who worked very hard to do what they could for their students, both in and out of the classroom. One of my mentors had a student whose teeth were rotting in several places, but the student was poor and did not have the money to go to the dentist. My mentor found a free clinic, which took a significant amount of his time out of school, and arranged for the student to visit the clinic to get the problems with his teeth fixed.

In the faculty lunchroom, teachers regularly discuss students, brainstorming ways to reach them, to encourage them to come to school, and to encourage them to try harder. In the lunchroom, I saw a teacher give a student a very difficult time about missing class. The teacher was harsh—almost strident—and wouldn't tolerate any excuses from the student, who shifted his weight around and squirmed nervously during this episode.

The teacher made it clear what his expectations were about attendance and work performance, and the student quietly nodded his head and promised that he would do better. It was clear to me that the teacher had a real concern for the student and that he didn't arrange the meeting to blow off steam or to give the student a hard time just for the sake of it; it was clear by subtle indicators in the teacher's tone of voice, word choice, and body language that he cared very much for the student and that it was important to him that the student come to class and learn something.

Somehow it's the system that breaks the teacher. Gene once said to me, "I was like you when I started. I was enthusiastic, and I tried to do my best, but believe me, you get a lot more respect and a lot more done in the classroom if you behave more like them and have realistic expectations for what they can do."

I bristled inside when I heard this; I wanted to say to him, "So a realistic expectation for your history students is to watch television for forty-eight minutes?"

Maybe I'm more like Gene than I think; maybe the system will break me, too, and make me hold popularity as more important than academic rigor. But it hasn't yet, and I teach tough kids just like they do.

When you teach, many of your students will come from economically disadvantaged homes. For some of these students, work during evenings and weekends is a requirement for survival, not a way to buy the latest rims for their Beemer. For some of these students, Dad is in prison and Mom is living with a man who resents their existence. Some of them will know much more about the intricacies of gang life than you do. Most have already drank alcohol, and some have tried, and regularly use, illegal drugs. They know that they're not going to Northwestern and that it's unlikely that they will earn a high salary.

Yet, you should push them. Tell them that they must do an eight-page research paper. Tell them that they must learn how to create a website and fill it with information that they've researched. Tell them that they must write a long essay analyzing the changing nature of the relationship between Tuco and Blondie in "The Good, the Bad, and The Ugly." They will respond. They will do it. They may complain for a little while, but they will know that you will be there for them to help them, and you should give them no choice other than to believe in themselves.

So far, it's worked, and it will probably continue to. The look of satisfaction on your students' faces when they hand you their research paper and say "I'm done"—well, that makes it all worth it.

39

THE DIFFERENCE
BETWEEN
MEN AND WOMEN

They say that men's brains and women's brains are wired differently, and a fascinating experience I went through while I was student teaching supports that theory.

I was observing another mentor teacher, one that I have not mentioned yet, in her science classroom. She let me help out when I could, doing things like answering student questions, handing out books and paper, and so on. Things were going along as usual when she asked a student to please put away her CD player. The student disregarded the teacher's request. My mentor teacher asked her a second time to please put away the CD player. The student again disregarded the request. I walked over to the student to quietly remind her of the school policy of no CD players in the classroom. I stopped next to her and began saying in a calm voice, "Come on, Julie (not her real name), you know . . ."

That was all I was able to get out before Julie started yelling out, "GET AWAY FROM ME! LEAVE ME ALONE! MRS. LOPEZ, TELL HIM TO LEAVE ME ALONE! GET AWAY FROM ME! WHY YOU WALKING UP NEXT TO ME LIKE THAT! MRS. LOPEZ! GET HIM AWAY FROM ME!"

I was stunned by the suddenness and the intensity of her shouting. I stood there, dumbfounded.

My first instinct was to stand my ground, mostly because of what I was taught in graduate school about operant conditioning. If I were to walk away, I would instantly reward her outrageously inappropriate behavior. I wanted to be sure that she understood from the very beginning that screaming nearly at the top of her lungs would not result in the withdrawal of an unpleasant stimulus, that is, my walking away and leaving her alone to listen to her CD player in the middle of science class.

Another reason for my standing my ground was testosterone. There was no way that a disobedient, disrespectful fifteen-year-old, of all people, was going to intimidate me into backing down from what I knew to be the right course of action. I understand that this mindset is what starts wars, but it partially took control of me in the heat of the moment.

The student continued to shout at me, completely interrupting the lesson. After about ten seconds, I started to rethink the wisdom of my standing my ground. I looked over to Mrs. Lopez, who gave me a subtle nonverbal indication to back down, which I did. I moved back to my usual place in the front of the room and sat down. The student stopped shouting and, interestingly, took her earbuds out of her ears but did not put away the CD player. The students recovered from this distraction so quickly that it made me realize that this was not the first time that this young lady had had an emotional meltdown—or was it a performance?

For the rest of the period, I thought about what I did.

Although I was 90 percent sure that my initial instinct to stand my ground was wise, I couldn't help but notice that my walking away from her did result in her taking the earbuds out of her ears. I couldn't wait to speak to Mrs. Lopez after class to talk about her opinion of what had happened. When I did, the really interesting part of this episode began.

Mrs. Lopez was not happy. "If you knew that you were pushing a student's button, why would you deliberately do that?" she said to me, somewhat exasperated. "You saw that by standing next to her, that made her go off. You saw that doing so clearly pushed one of her buttons. These students have emotional difficulties, Neil. Why would you aggravate one of those emotional difficulties by doing something that you see is clearly irritating her?"

My face was getting warmer as I felt more and more embarrassed. She wasn't done with me.

"You're not in a battle with a student. This isn't a contest to see who wins. Why did you feel as though you were in a contest that you had to win? Why didn't you back down when you saw that you were upsetting her to that degree?"

I weakly told her about my understanding of operant conditioning and my belief that if I had backed down in response to her screaming, it would have rewarded the screaming. She replied, "And so you'll stand there? For how long? Five minutes? Ten minutes? In the meantime, her screaming is making it impossible to teach the lesson. Why would you do that?" I had no answer. She said, "Neil, I was going to talk to her about the CD player after class, and approaching her in that way would've probably been more effective and wouldn't have disrupted the lesson."

This experience upset me because, like many other experiences while I was student teaching, it made me begin to question some of the fundamental things that I learned in my psychology classes. It was driven into my head over and over again that a behavior that is followed by a reward will increase the likelihood of that behavior.

As I walked down the hallway after I left Mrs. Lopez, I really began to question my competency, the importance of psychology, what I had been taught in school, almost everything about psychology and education. Had I been sold some snake oil in my introductory psychology classes? Was classical and operant conditioning not the foundation of behaviorism? Many upsetting thoughts started running through my mind, but the most intriguing one was a question which I thought was impossible to answer: how do you tell the difference between a child who is truly having an emotional breakdown and one who is merely a skilled actor?

What do you do with a student who is an emotional hypochondriac?

By backing off every time a student gets upset, we teach that student and every other student within earshot how easy it is to manipulate the teacher into leaving you alone so you can finish doing what you're doing, regardless of whether or not it's permissible. I wanted to talk to some other people about this, so I spoke to the program coordinator of the special education department, a man with many years of teaching and administrative experience. I told him about what happened and his unexpected answer simultaneously made me feel better and made me feel even more confused—but it was a fascinated rather than a disillusioning confusion.

"I would've done the same thing you did," he said.

He continued, "You can't let yourself be pushed around by a student. She can't be made to feel that all she has to do is start shouting to get whatever she wants. That was very bad advice that Mrs. Lopez gave you. You can't just back down! If you do that, you'll totally lose control of the classroom—the students will see how easy it is to get you to leave them alone and that's the end of it. What should've happened is that if she continued to scream, you should've called security to remove her from the classroom and more serious consequences should have been given. We can't have students screaming at the top of their lungs as soon as a teacher asks them to put away their CD player!" His voice started getting a little bit louder as he said these words. "Oh, how horrible, I can't listen to my CD in the middle of a science lesson, oh boo-hoo," he said, sarcastically.

Now I was really confused, so I did what any marginally competent researcher would do—I collected more data. I spoke to a male English teacher with over twenty years experience at that school, and I spoke to the female chairperson of the special education department about this situation. Interestingly, the woman strongly supported the "back down and deal with it later" approach, and the man strongly supported the "stand your ground and don't let her get away with it" approach.

This was another lesson that they don't teach you in graduate school—that the gender of a teacher can be a significant factor in how he or she handles a behavior problem. This is illustrated at the school where I currently teach. It has one male and one female assistant principal.

Each assistant principal is responsible for dealing with student discipline problems, along with a number of other responsibilities. Their goal is to reduce student behavior problems and make the school as safe as possible. One of them is a strict male who goes very much by the book but will make accommodations when he sees contrition and maturity from a student. Based on comments I hear from my students, he is generally disliked. Yet, his stern approach toward the students results in a clear understanding that improper actions will have definite negative consequences.

The other assistant principal is a more patient, nurturing, and accommodating female who is liked more by the students with whom I have contact. She also follows the book and is just as concerned with improving student behavior and maintaining school security as the first assistant principal, but she has a softer approach when the student in trouble is sitting on the other side of her desk. Each assistant principal takes approximately half of the student load; one gets juniors, and one gets seniors.

I bring my two colleagues up at this point because I have a great respect for them and the different ways that they handle the same sorts of student situations.

I would say that they are both equally effective, based on my informal review of the times that I've written up students over the past year. It seems to me that the strict male and the kind female approach, if you'll pardon the sexist overtones of that last phrase, seem to work equally well.

When I say that those approaches work well, I don't mean that students who have seen them once spend the rest of the year raising money for the homeless, picking up gum wrappers off of the floor, and guiding other wayward students down the path to morality by the light of the glowing halo over their heads. The assistant principals often see the same students over and over again. Each of their unique approaches sometimes works and sometimes doesn't. But what seems to me to be the right thing to do is to watch your colleagues, observe what they do, observe the effect it has on the students, and select the parts that feel right for you and put them into practice.

If you're not a strict person, don't let anybody tell you that the strict way is the only way. If you feel that it's more effective to be harsh with a student, or if you feel that the hard-nosed approach would get results based on your knowledge of a student's personality, then go ahead and do it, but only if it feels right to you. Be yourself in the classroom—that's the only advice that I can give with which I believe few educators would disagree.

But, if you hear from colleague after colleague that you're doing something wrong, listen to what they have to say and take constructive criticism.

Achieving the right balance between letting your own personality come through and changing what you do in the way you teach based on student and colleague feedback is a difficult thing to achieve; your wisdom and your intuition are always the right things to listen to when attempting to achieve that balance.

The point of this whole chapter? The answer is, "it depends"; it depends on you. What did you get out of it? The point for me is that there is no such thing as one right way of dealing with a student; do the best you can while being yourself and learn from any mistakes you make. Don't let anyone tell you that there is only one way to deal with a difficult situation.

40

"WHY ARE YOU TEACHING US THIS SHIT?"

I have a student in my class named Muñoz. One day, before the bell rang, I walked up to him and said, "Hey, guess what? I heard some guy yesterday at school saying really awful things about you. He said you were an idiot." Muñoz looked at me and started getting visibly angry. He said, "What?" I said, "Yeah, he said you are an idiot and that you couldn't learn anything and that you are too stupid to understand anything." His eyes were as wide as saucers as he said, "Who said that? You mean he goes to this school? Who said that?" I said, "This guy—I have his picture." I handed the paper to him that he opened up as fast as he could. When he looked at it, his expression and body language instantly changed. He looked at me and said, "Ha, ha, ha."

I had given him a picture of himself.

This was all in response to something that happened in the classroom the previous day.

Everything I said to Muñoz was true. He had said that he was too stupid to learn anything and that he was an idiot who didn't deserve an education. Of course, he didn't use those words, but what he said to me communicated essentially the same concept: don't teach me because I'm too stupid to be able to learn.

It's a pervasive problem. I've found that my students will insult themselves and minimize their capabilities more viciously and more completely than any other student would dare. They say to me that they can't learn, that they can't spell, that they can't read, that they can't understand what they read, that they don't remember what they read, that they can't write, they can't express themselves, they can't do it, they have never been able to do it, and they never will be able to do it, so what's the point?

Rot, blather, and drivel, all of it.

Yet this thinking is deeply entrenched inside of many of my students' heads. They believe they can't, and so they don't try. Sometimes, they vigorously question why we're doing what we're doing in the classroom. It's the classic question, "Why do we need to know this?" One day, while I was student teaching, Muñoz took this questioning to a new level. The vigor with which he challenged me spoke volumes about his self-image.

We were reading Shirley Jackson's "The Lottery," one of the most deliciously sickening short stories in American literature. The story was originally published in the *New Yorker*, and it created such a furor that many people called the magazine to cancel the subscription.

We were reading it together, with me narrating out loud as the students followed along. Part of the macabre allure of the story is its initial disarming ordinariness and how this ordinariness hypnotizes you into a false sense of security, leaving you complacent and vulnerable. At just the right moment, out of the blue, Jackson violently bashes in your vulnerable head from behind and walks away quietly, leaving you to your confusion, anger, and emotional pain. It's a masterpiece of literature. To appreciate it, you must be patient; you must assume that there is a point to its existence; you must have confidence in the author; you must pay careful attention to what's happening; and you must, above all, believe that you will be able to understand the story.

Muñoz, like several other students in the room, did not possess or was not able to put into execution, the above skills. He wanted there to be a point to it, and he wanted that point to be obvious within the first few paragraphs. He wanted the story to be directly relevant to something in his life; he wanted it to dazzle him, to shock him, to intrigue him almost immediately.

In graduate school they teach you that you're supposed to create interest in reading by triggering previous knowledge in the students, asking them to talk about concepts relevant in their own life that are similar to those in the book, and in general to get them pumped up to want to read the story. I know these things, and I try to do them.

But this story doesn't lend itself to such a prereading exercise. The story is so bizarre and so unexpected that it needs to be mostly a secret when you start reading it; you can get into a detailed discussion afterwards, but you don't want to spoil the surprise ending. (A similar type of story would be "The Diamond Necklace" by Guy de Maupassant. It's the last sentence that gets you.) As I said before, you need to trust the teacher, trust the author, turn on your visual imagery strategy, and start reading the story together. In the middle of the story, most of the students were actually engaged because I did do a little bit of a prereading exercise when I told them that the story was very famous, that they'll never forget it, and so on. But in the middle of the story, Muñoz decided that he had had enough, and that it was time for him to express himself.

"WHY ARE YOU TEACHING US THIS SHIT?" he suddenly exclaimed.

There was a look of true disgust and dislike on his face as he stared me in the eyes. "Why are you having us read this story? Look at us! Are you forgetting what kind of class this is? This ain't no college-level class! Why are you teaching us this shit?" He threw the story on his desk and continued. "None of us are going to remember any of this shit. None of us can remember any of it. I guarantee you that when you finish reading this story, none of us will understand what it's about, and if you talk to us tomorrow or the next day, not one of us is going to remember anything about it. This story is boring. Who gives a shit about a bunch of people standing around talking a bunch of bullshit about some lottery? Who cares? Why don't we read "My Bloody Life"? Why don't you read things that we can relate to? If you would read "My Bloody Life," it would actually be interesting and we could relate to it—not this shit you're reading to us."

Now remember, at the time, I had just begun student teaching. I was unsteady on my feet and easily intimidated, and here comes Hurricane Muñoz with an admittedly eloquent and persuasive argument against the lesson. I was upset for three reasons.

First, he was interrupting my lesson.

Second, I disagreed with what he said that implied that there was no intellectual difference between the students in the room and a box of hammers.

Third, I worried that his politically influential words had destroyed the fragile state of attention I had cultivated. They say you're not supposed to argue with a student in the classroom, and the chief reason is the student will usually win. This is because the student may say anything he likes but you may not. Plus, teenagers employ sophistry in their arguments, and teenagers are easily swayed by sophistry.

(A classic sophism is when a student says something to an adult that's vicious and untrue, and such invective causes the adult's face to flush red with anger. The teenager then says the classic, infamous, maddening line, "You're angry because you know it's true," or, equal in infamy, the line "You see? You get mad because you don't want to hear the truth." Doesn't that drive you absolutely up the wall? After its utterance, most of the teenagers in the vicinity nod their heads up and down in agreement. This happened to me once in the classroom, and it was so irritating that I at once did a little demonstration. I drew an imaginary man on the board. I told my students his name was Nathan. I walked up to Nathan and said, "So, Nathan, I hear your mother's a crack whore." This resulted in incredulous whooping from my students. I said to my students, "Now, Nathan's mother is most certainly not a crack whore, but somebody has just asked him this question. What do you think Nathan's reaction is going to be?" My students said, almost in unison, that he was going to be extremely pissed off. I said, yes, he was. I told him that he was mad not because the statements were true, which they were not, but because the statements were an insult to his mother, and therefore, to him. I said to them, "Now you can take this expression 'You're angry because you know it's true' and forget it." I told them that just because somebody gets mad when you say something, it doesn't mean that it's true. This seemed to be an effective demonstration, but who knows for sure?)

Back to Muñoz. Circular reasoning is, of course, part of sophistry, and such reasoning is the core of Muñoz's argument.

We're stupid because we're in Special Education, and we're in Special Education because we're stupid.

We shouldn't read anything advanced because this is a special education class, so we won't be able to understand it. We know we won't be able to understand it because we're here, aren't we?

So what the hell are you doing? Johnny here does poorly on reading tests? How do we know? He's in Special Ed. Why is he in Special Ed? SCHMUCK! Because he does poorly on reading tests, of course! This was the core of Muñoz's argument, but if he wanted to get into it with me, I was more than happy to get into it with him. In retrospect, it wasn't the wisest thing to do, and it did interrupt the lesson, but I was a student teacher, and so I could get away with this by claiming ignorance.

I shot back, "What are you saying? That you're too stupid to understand this story? The whole story is only about ten pages long and it doesn't use any big words, and it's one of the most famous stories ever written, so what's the problem? Are you saying you're too stupid to understand a simple ten-page story?"

He said, "No, man, no, that's not it. My point is that it's boring. Nobody in this class gives a shit about this story."

I said, "Hold on, hold on. Don't talk for anybody else. Speak for yourself. This guy next to you didn't tell you to speak for him; you're not his lawyer, so don't speak for him. (At this point, the student next to him said, "It IS boring." Thank you very much, little buddy.) I continued: "Speak for yourself. The only book you ever talk about is "My Bloody Life." Haven't you ever read any other book? The only thing you want to read about is how a guy got into a gang? Don't you have any other interests? Don't you want to read anything else?'"

His voice dropped in volume, yet he continued. "That's not the point, man. You teach us all these vocabulary words and flashback and all this other stupid shit, and nobody here is going to remember any of this stuff within one day. Victor, are you going to remember any of this tomorrow? SEE! He said no. So what's the point?"

"What you're saying is not true. Muñoz, what you're saying is not true. You're saying that you're not going to remember anything, but that's not true. You may forget most of it, but you're not going to forget all of it. Listen to me! You are wrong. You are wrong. You do remember stuff. Why do you keep saying that you don't remember anything? Why do you keep saying that you're so stupid that you can't remember one thing and that you can't understand anything else besides a book about how to get into a gang?"

His voice continued to lower in volume. "I'm not interested in this stupid story. I don't give a shit about a bunch of these dumbass people standing around talking about some stupid bullshit lottery. What does that have to do with my life? Nobody in this room gives a shit about this story. Oh my God, there's no point in talking to you; you're not even listening to what I'm saying."

At that point, Muñoz walked out of the room in exasperation.

I hoped then, as I hope now, that he walked out because I showed him cracks in the foundation of his argument and not because he felt as though I wasn't listening to him.

This is a common statement by people, especially teenagers: "You're not listening to me!" I think that people say this in frustration when they realize that they cannot get the person with which they're arguing to see things from their own point of view. Rather than either admit the flaws in their own argument or agree that it is possible that the other person clearly understands your point of view but disagrees with it, they accuse their conversational partner of not listening, a universally loathed characteristic which gets boatloads of sympathetic agreement from all of their teenage peers.

All too often, their peers join in the adult hating party rather than examine the wisdom and the foundation of their flawed argument, such as the one that states that they are too stupid to understand anything.

After Muñoz walked out, I turned to my mentor, who was looking at me with an amused smile on his face. I realized at that moment that he was enjoying every moment of this; he was relishing the startlingly effective graduate education I was receiving here in room 108.

Interestingly, the classroom was silent. Muñoz had received little support from his peers during his speech, likely because the issues that were raised during it made them think, or at least I hope that's the reason for their remaining quiet.

As they say in show business, the show must go on, so I told the students that we would continue reading from where we left off. We completed the story, and many of the students enjoyed it. Some of them asked what the point of the story was, which triggered a very interesting discussion about why people write, why people create art, why people write songs, or why people express themselves. It was a fascinating discussion where they brought up some interesting points about the reasons for artistic expression. One student shared with the whole class for the first time that he was secretly writing rap songs, and we discussed why he was doing it.

This student was positively elated when I told him about the existence of something called a rhyming dictionary. This is what I call the "hidden education" in a good classroom: the hundreds of beneficial lessons you teach that are beyond the lesson plans.

Your students may not be able to write a persuasive essay on the instances of foreshadowing in "The Lottery," but if you take advantage of a "teachable moment" like this, you can be sure that to a small extent, it's made your students understand how awesome it is to stand in a library or a music store and be struck by how much beauty and pain is expressed in the CDs and the books surrounding them. The result of this is your making them want to read just a little bit more to understand that there doesn't have to be a point to eat an ice cream cone other than the fact that it tastes good.

Muñoz came back into the room just before the end of the lesson. We were all engaged, so he sat down quietly, sulking. As the bell rang, just as he was walking out, I said to him, "Don't diss yourself, Munoz." He ignored me.

CHAPTER 40

Soon, my student teaching was over. On the last day, I got choked up when I said good-bye to the kids. I hope that, years later, they are all doing well and that they'll remember a little bit about our time together.

41

DON'T WISH
FOR QUIET

B ack to my first year of teaching . . .
Sometimes teachers wish for a classroom full of quiet, well-behaved students. They say, "Oh, why can't they all just do what I ask them to do and sit quietly?" Some teachers might want that but I don't because I enjoy classroom discussion, and if the topic of the discussion is somewhat controversial, then all the better.

Don't get the idea that my classroom contains a bunch of over-stuffed sofas and coffee tables lying around, and all we do is sit around and talk about the latest celebrity news gossip. It's a classroom, and the students do a lot of work in it. But, a good classroom is not composed solely of seatwork.

Sometimes you have to stop the lesson and expand on an idea with a discussion; many times, a group discussion is part of a lesson plan to give the students something tangible to write about. These moments are when talkative, sometimes-disruptive students become welcome members of the classroom. They open their mouths, and they say what they think.

Sometimes they say things that aren't true, and sometimes they say things that are controversial, but you'll find that their statements are almost always what they really believe to be true. The students with the big mouths are the ones that encourage the other students to say what *they* think. They foster discussion; they vocalize the process by which they take what they read and try to make sense out of it in relation to their own limited life experiences.

Can you imagine what it would be like to start a good class discussion with a bunch of extremely well-behaved, shy, quiet students?

Here's why some students actually might like your class even though they like to complain about it. Don't back away from controversial subjects in the classroom. Fortunately, the novels, short stories, and poetry you will read will cover difficult subjects that your students are either dealing with right now or will likely have to deal with when they get out of high school and become their own adults.

Talk about drug addiction, mental illness, euthanasia, parental abandonment, death of friends and family members, murder, infidelity, violent crime, marriage, divorce, relationships, war, genocide, racism, love, art, beauty, truth, and honesty.

Why should you allow these discussions in the classroom? Kids need to have something to write about. You can't just ask them to write essays about what they did on their summer vacation or what they want to be when they grow up. In many ways, they are grown up. Many of them are working—hard—at menial jobs to support their families. Many have nonexistent mothers and fathers. Many have been in serious trouble with the law and have brothers, sisters, and other family members who are in prison.

When we discuss real issues in the classroom, it gives them material to write about and passion to write. Many of the essays and stories that my students write are poignant narratives of the emotional turbulence that is their lives; the passion motivating their writing helps them understand the importance of improving their vocabulary, of making a clear point, of choosing the right words, of smacking the reader across the face with the iron pipe of reality.

Plus, on a personal note, I believe that these young adults need to have a safe place to explore their thinking and bounce ideas off of each other. True, they're talking about drug abuse, but they're in a safe environment with Mrs. Grimaldi, the paraeducator (who is an intelligent, highly moral person), and me.

She and I closely supervise them, listen to them, and help them understand the things they say that make sense, the things they say that are the result of flawed thinking, and the ways they can increase their understanding of the world around them. If the discussion strays from the topic, we get it back on track. If a statement is made that's untrue, such as the time an immature student said that he heard that you drive just as well drunk as you do sober, Mrs. Grimaldi and I immediately objected and illustrated, with convincing language, the ridiculousness of that comment.

The students listened to us closely at that moment; thank goodness that such an outrageous comment was made in my classroom, where I could show them how untrue it was than at a party somewhere where the other kids might wonder to themselves, "Wow, is that true?"

Aside from helping the students to establish good thinking habits, Mrs. Grimaldi and I are careful to leave most of our personal opinions about religion, politics, and so on, out of the classroom.

The students don't know my political beliefs; they don't know how I feel about abortion or euthanasia or sterilizing people with mental retardation or spaying and neutering dogs and cats.

Once, while we were discussing George W. Bush and the Iraq war, a student said, "Well, Mr. Goldman, what do *you* think of Bush?" I said, "It doesn't matter what I think; what do you think of him?" This irritated the student, and she said, "Mr. Goldman, believe it or not, some of us actually look up to you and see you as an authority figure. I know it's hard for you to understand given the way some of us behave, but it's true. So what's the harm in asking you what you really think? There's nothing wrong with asking you what you think!"

I said, "Here's the reason why I'm not going to tell you. Let's say that you were for Bush and I was against Bush. Then, you take a test, and you don't score very highly on part of the test. You might say, well it's because he doesn't agree with my political views, and that's not true at all. When I grade your exams, I try to be as fair as I possibly can and leave any personal opinions aside.

"Plus, there's another reason why I'm not going to tell you what I think: I want you to form your own darned opinion. I want you to actually read the paper, read magazines, and listen to what people are saying. Think! Evaluate what you read! Does it make sense? Does it seem true? Don't adopt other people's opinions as your own. Form your own opinion; read, listen, and form your own opinion about what's going on, and the important thing is that you have formed your opinion based on things that you've read, not because you heard somebody say so.

"So, when somebody challenges you and says, why do you think that—that's really stupid, you'll be able to say well actually I read in *Time* magazine or at BBC.com, such and such and so-and-so and that's why I feel the way I do, not because my English teacher told me that he likes vanilla ice cream, so I like vanilla ice cream, too."

The students benefit tremendously from these discussions; during the time that this is happening, you can guarantee that nearly all the students are almost completely engaged. And then, soon after, when they write, they write with passion; when they watch a film, they've truly connected their background knowledge to it and the level of detail that they can later recall is surprisingly high; when they read the next chapter in the novel, they are *reading* it, not gliding their gaze across the paper; they are participating in the learning process and thinking about the real meaning of the words in front of them.

Plus, is English class 100 percent learning about the visual imagery in "The Raven"? I don't think so.

Of course, it's important to teach your students the language arts curriculum, and you must, but there is a little bit more to it than that. Students need to learn about life. They need to have the opportunity to be exposed to the real world around them and to be able to develop their abilities to analyze it, draw valid conclusions about it, and develop an intelligent, logical, and healthy action plan on what to do about it.

This requires occasionally diverging from the lesson plan, taking advantage of teachable moments, bringing in the very latest news, and letting my students have a little bit of time to digest it.

You'll learn, too.

How many times will your students point out a conflict in a novel that you never noticed? You'll be shocked at how much you'll learn about what it's like to be Mexican, or African-American, or a woman, in today's world. You'll be amazed at how many times your students will make you burst out laughing. You won't believe how many things you'll learn about what it's like to be seventeen, and in learning these things, gain a greater understanding of why your students act the way they do.

Every day, you'll learn. Every day, you will be taught by your students. And you can be sure that every day, they'll learn just a little bit during the fifty-three minutes you have with them.

Next year, sixty or seventy students will walk into my classroom for the first time and almost immediately show the sense of humor, affection, and inquisitiveness that is so delightfully rich within their personalities. I'll hear new perspectives, shocking new twists on shocking old questions, and stories that will help me remember what it was like when I was their age.

I am very much looking forward to it.

ABOUT THE AUTHOR

Neil M. Goldman spent fifteen years in a corporate cubicle as a substance abuse counselor, computer programmer, web designer, and information technology director before making a life-altering career change to become a special education teacher. He received a Bachelor of Arts degree in Psychology from Temple University in Philadelphia, a Master of Arts in Psychological Services from the University of Pennsylvania, and a Master of Science in Special Education from the University of Illinois at Chicago.